NATIONALISM

NATIONALISM

A CRITICAL INTRODUCTION

Philip Spencer and Howard Wollman

SAGE Publications
London • Thousand Oaks • New Delhi

SAGE Publications Ltd
6 Bonhill Street
London EC2A 4PU

SAGE Publications Inc
2455 Teller Road
Thousand Oaks, California 91320

SAGE Publications India Pvt Ltd
32, M-Block Market
Greater Kailash – I
New Delhi 110 048

British Library Cataloguing in Publication data

A catalogue record for this book is available from the British Library

ISBN 0 7619 4720 5
ISBN 0 7619 4721 3 (pbk)

Library of Congress Control Number: 2001 132952

Typeset by Keystroke, Jacaranda Lodge, Wolverhampton
Printed in Great Britain by Biddles Ltd, *www.biddles.co.uk*

Contents

Acknowledgements

This book has emerged from a collaboration of some six years of thinking, reading, writing and teaching about nationalism, and more than 40 years of friendship, discussion and (sometimes) of argument. We would like to thank all of our colleagues and friends who have helped us with this book and sustained us over a long period of gestation. In particular thanks to Mike Hawkins for his patience and care in reading several drafts, and to Joe Bailey, Brian Brivati, Terry Sullivan and Paul Auerbach for their helpful comments on various chapters. We would also like to thank the support we have had from our institutions, particularly the time (and some funds) made available from the Faculty of Human Sciences at Kingston University, and the Faculty of Arts and Social Sciences and the School of Psychology and Sociology at Napier University, and its then Head, Norman Bonney. Our editor at Sage, Lucy Robinson, has been consistently cheerful and helpful and, through this, has substantially lightened the load in the final stages of our endeavour. We would like to thank her and her colleague Vanessa Harwood for their help.

Finally, the conventional thanks to our families is in this case richly deserved. Thanks to Rosa and Reuben for engaging in some illuminating discussions with their father. Adam and Anna perhaps found their father more distracted at times than he would have wished and for rather longer than he had anticipated. Above all, we are much indebted (respectively) to Jane and Ginnie, who have been tirelessly encouraging throughout, and without whose support we could not have completed this project.

This book is dedicated with affection to our parents. Albert Wollman has taken an enthusiastic and proud interest in progress throughout. Sadly, Adele Wollman, Trudy Green and Cyril Spencer died in earlier stages of our joint work and we only wish they could have been here to see it come to fruition.

PERMISSIONS

Some chapters of the book draw on material previously published in journal articles or book chapters elsewhere. We are grateful to Ashgate Publishing Limited for permission to use material from 'Nationalism, Politics and Democracy in the Development of Post-communist Societies', in C. Williams and T. Sfikas (eds) *Ethnicity and Nationalism in East-Central Europe and the Balkans*, Ashgate, 2000; Taylor and Francis for material from '"Good" and "Bad" Nationalisms: A Critique of Dualism', *Journal of Political Ideologies*, 3(3), 255–74, 1998; and Palgrave Press for material in 'Civic Nationalism, Civic Nations and the Problem of Migration', in S. Ghatak and A. Showstack Sassoon (eds) *Migration and Mobility – the European Context*, Palgrave, 2001.

Patriotism has an inherent flaw. By preferring one segment of humanity over the rest, the citizen transgresses the fundamental principle of morality, that of universality; without saying so openly, he acknowledges that men are not equal ... true morality, true justice, true virtue presuppose universality, and thus equal rights (Tzvetan Todorov, 1993, p. 183)

At one meeting at which no Pole was present, Brauner [a participant at the first All Slav Congress in Vienna] told an anecdote of how peasants in the district of Sacz in West Galicia, when asked whether they were Poles, replied 'We are quiet folk.' 'Then are you Germans?' 'We are decent folk.' (in Lewis Namier, 1944, p. 107)

Introduction

We began to think seriously about nationalism, perhaps like many others, when faced with the catastrophic consequences of what appeared to be a sudden explosion of nationalism in the former Yugoslavia in the early 1990s. How, we wondered, did some people, who had been living side by side in cities, towns and villages, end up driving out their neighbours from their homes, killing and raping them in the brutal process that came to be called 'ethnic cleansing'? For those of us brought up in the shadow of the Holocaust, the atrocities being perpetrated in Yugoslavia produced both a terrible sense of impotence and an insistent need to think critically about what sorts of beliefs drove people to act in these ways. What exactly is claimed for the nation and its identity in situations like these, what is it that seems to matter so much, and what role do nationalists play in the mobilization of such powerful and destructive forces?

In trying to think critically about nationalism in this case, we began to think more generally about nationalism as an ideology, about what is involved in arguments about the 'nation' and, especially, about national identity. We had expected, it has to be said, to find a literature that was highly critical of nationalism. Instead we felt increasingly that much of the literature in its claims to 'take nationalism seriously' had become oddly uncritical. The relatively small number of writers who were critical of nationalism were often specifically attacked on the grounds that a critical stance would somehow get in the way of a real understanding of the phenomenon. On the other hand, in many areas of study impinging directly on nationalism, in writings on such matters as ethnicity, racism, identity and cosmopolitanism, there seemed to be a growing literature, from a variety of disciplines, that was implicitly or explicitly critical of treating the nation or national identity as a fixed, necessary and wholly positive feature of human society.

Our analysis of nationalism has been influenced by these writings, which we use to illuminate, contextualize and problematize the nation, and it differs from what we see as the dominant voices in nationalist studies. It is not just, as Hobsbawm has argued, that 'no serious historian of nations and nationalism can be a committed political nationalist' (1992, p. 12). It is, more generally, that a profound scepticism about nationalist claims is indispensable for a clear understanding of nationalism and national identity. In developing a sceptical viewpoint, more particularly, it became clear to us that there were certain features inherent in all forms of nationalism. This is not to suggest that there are not different kinds of nationalism, or that different nationalist movements cannot have distinctive aims, policies or philosophies. However, what is common to nationalist claims is in our view as, if not more, important than what differentiates them. We have come to accept the arguments of those who suggest that fundamental to all forms of nationalism are processes of categorization that create and reproduce as enemies, strangers and others those who do not fit inside the nation, just as they also seek to provide a sense of 'deep horizontal comradeship' for those who are included inside the nation (Anderson, 1991, p. 7). The divisive consequences of this have implications – in the short or long term – for issues of democracy, human rights, citizenship and sometimes even the survival of minorities within nations.

In identifying the common elements, as indeed in discussing anything to do with the nation, there is the fundamental difficulty of definitions. As Kamenka once noted in this connection, 'definitions, if they are useful, come at the end of an enquiry and not at the beginning' (1976, p. 3). Certainly, as anyone remotely familiar with the vast literature on this subject knows, the central focus of nationalist attention and energy, the *nation*, is a slippery and elusive object. For Louis Snyder indeed, the compiler of an extensive encyclopaedia of nationalism, 'the term nation is fundamentally ambiguous' (1990, p. 3). The criteria for deciding on what constitutes a nation are highly contested, involving complex issues relating to identity, culture, language, history, myth and memory, and disputed claims to territory (we discuss these in Chapter 3). In the modern period especially, claims to territory have often led to a confusion between the terms *nation* and *state*. Although there is certainly a close relationship between them, as a number of writers have shown (see Chapter 2), they are not quite the same thing. One (the state) has to do with sovereignty, with power and authority over a given area and population; the other (the nation) has to do with relationships between people, with how people see themselves as connected over both time and space, as sharing some kind of collective identity. There are, too, both multinational states and stateless nations.

The conflation of the terms *nation* and *state*, which may seem simple common sense to many people, is in part a tribute to the power and efficacy of nationalism as a political movement, committed to a certain view of the world. This, at the risk of simplifying and anticipating key themes of the book, we may define in the following terms: *nationalism* is an ideology which imagines the community in a particular way (as national), asserts the primacy of this collective identity over others, and seeks political power in its name, ideally (if not exclusively or everywhere) in the form of a state for the nation (or a nation-state). In our view nationalism is also of crucial import in the genesis and reproduction of *national identity*, a less directly political and more fluid concept than that of nationalism itself. National identity involves a process of identifying oneself and others as a member of a nation, although there may be profound differences in the salience which each attaches to the national as opposed to other identifications. Group membership with some form of collective identity is seen by most writers as an inherent part of human social organization. This book explores how it is that 'possessing' a *national* identity has come to be seen as almost natural, and examines critically the necessity of membership of a nation to viable political and social organization.

Plan of the book

In Chapter 1 we examine the nineteenth-century roots of theorizing about nationalism, discerning in political and social thought ideas that provided an ambivalent legacy – accommodating to nationalism, on the one hand, but, on the other, providing certain critical insights and resources. Chapter 2 illustrates the ways in which much contemporary theorizing, basing itself in many ways on these nineteenth-century frames of reference, has tended (although there are exceptions) to take national identity and the nation too much for granted as an inherent part of human society. In the much discussed debate between primordialists and modernists on the origins of the nation and nationalism, for example, it is clear that both sides for the most part share a view that nations are here to stay, that there is no alternative to the nation-state.

If it seems so 'natural' that nations are here to stay, how does this come about? How is national identity invoked, constructed and reproduced by nationalism? At the core of our argument in Chapter 3 is an insistence on the politically charged nature of cultural processes that have usually been treated as neutral. National identities have, we argue, been shaped and formed much more on the basis of nationalist imaginings than by any inherent or fixed features of a reified culture. These nationalist imaginings are often depicted, explicitly or implicitly, as falling into two categories. There are the 'good' forms of nationalism, that are hailed as desirable or necessary by many writers, and then there are the 'bad' forms, that are more easily criticized. In Chapter 4 we examine critically these sorts of distinctions, stressing what they have in common and the dangers of slippage from one type to another. From another angle, we attempt to disentangle the different elements in what are compound concepts and to show that what is good in 'good' nationalism depends much more on the other element in the compound (for example, its civic or liberal character), than on anything specifically to do with the nation.

Those who advocate 'good' forms of nationalism as a solution to problems of identity and belonging in late modernity often argue for the existence of a strong and positive relationship between nationalism and democracy. In Chapter 5 we return to the most commonly suggested birthplace of this relationship – the French Revolution – and unravel a more complex picture, one that brings into question any idea of the inherently democratic nature of nationalism. Indeed, through a range of case studies, both historical and contemporary, we argue that nationalism and democracy involve diverging logics, with the former pointing towards exclusionary practices and the latter having a potential for much greater inclusiveness.

In Chapters 6 and 7 we examine various ways in which contemporary political and social forces might take us beyond nationalism. In Chapter 6 this is through an examination of the impact of globalization on nationalism and identity. We discuss the arguments that globalization is producing more fluid identities which move us away from reified concepts of ethnicity and nationality. However, there is also evidence of new fundamentalist reactions which re-emphasize national differences and move in a markedly exclusionary direction. Finally, we apply the analysis developed in Chapters 4 and 5 to the nationalist movements in Scotland, Quebec and Catalonia and query the claim that we are seeing here the emergence of a modern nationalism, free of the prejudices of the past and able to build on the new identities and structures of a more globalized world.

In Chapter 7 we take this further, arguing that neither new supranational structures like the European Union, nor institutional and constitutional arrangements can take us convincingly into a non-national future. We discuss the arguments for and possibilities of various forms of internationalism, transnationalism and cosmopolitanism, and the development of a democratic politics where identities, citizenship and human rights do not depend on the nation-state or affiliation to a nation. The challenge, it seems to us, is to build on those existing initiatives which strengthen such a politics, and to look to a future beyond the nation-state, nationalism and national identity.

1

Ambivalent Legacies: Nationalism, Political Ideology and Social Theory

INTRODUCTION

If we want to think critically about nationalism, we cannot do so in a vacuum. For better or for worse, our thinking has been shaped to a greater or lesser extent by the major political ideologies and social theories of the modern era, all of which have had something to say about nationalism, whether explicitly or implicitly. In this chapter, we look in particular at the way in which liberals, Marxists and conservatives wrestled with the problems posed by nationalism, before going on to consider the complex and at times contradictory views of Durkheim and Weber. In each case we can identify how they both opened the way to the possibility of thinking critically about nationalism, but also how they also accommodated to it in certain respects, thus bequeathing a somewhat ambivalent legacy to subsequent theorists.

Liberalism and the idea of self-determination

Many writers begin their discussion of nationalism by identifying a particular period in which liberalism and nationalism were closely entwined
(Hobsbawm, 1992; Kohn, 1965; Woolf, 1996). This is usually held to be
from the time of either the English or French Revolutions up until 1848, at
which point their paths are seen to diverge. Why were liberals so enthusiastic
initially about nationalism and what impact has this had on the way we
can think about nationalism?

Before we begin to answer this question, it may be worth noting that
early liberal enthusiasm for nationalism, perhaps like most enthusiasms,
was not always clearly articulated or argued. Rather there was, as Hobsbawm
(1992) has remarked, 'a surprising degree of intellectual vagueness . . . due
not so much to a failure to think the problem of the nation through, as to
the assumption that it did not require to be spelled out, since it was already
obvious' (p. 24). This is, on the face of it, somewhat surprising. If the core
liberal value is the freedom of the individual, then it might seem problematic
for liberals to wax enthusiastic about a doctrine which prioritizes a
collectivity. Yet this apparent contradiction may be swiftly dispelled when
we realize that for many liberals the same principle could be applied to
both. This is the principle of self-determination. In order to understand how
this came to be, we need briefly to consider the work and legacy of Kant.

Although Kant himself was not a nationalist, and is often seen to be
a quintessentially cosmopolitan Enlightenment thinker (Kohn, 1965, p. 35),
he did in a crucial way lay the foundations for the rapprochement of liberalism
and nationalism. As a liberal he was committed, as Berlin put it, to 'the
timeless, unchanging rights of the individual, whoever he may be, whatever
his time, whatever his place, his society, his personal attributes, provided
he is a man [sic], the possessor of reason' (1996, p. 233). Yet there is a
crucial sense in which, as both Berlin and Kedourie (1993) have suggested,
Kant's insistence on autonomy and will opened the way in social and political
theory for a central perspective on nationalism, the idea that *nations* should
have the right to self-determination. In arguing that morality required the
exercise of free will, that one could not be truly human without determining
one's own goals and future for oneself, Kant opened the way for others to
think about nations along the same lines. For Kant's successors, although not
all of them were liberals, it was but a short step to endow nations with the
same qualities and potential as individuals, to assert that nations too had
wills, had to become self-conscious and aware of their potential and pursue
the project of self-realization. As Fichte for instance put it, 'nations are
individualities with particular talents and the possibilities of exploiting those
talents' (in Calhoun, 1997, p. 45).[1] There was then a profound imperative,
an implicit challenge laid down to each putative nation, to rouse itself, to
emancipate itself from whatever shackles, internal or external, were deemed

or felt to be holding it back. This link with individualism, via the notion of self-determination, gave nationalism then, as Kedourie (1993) argues, a great source of vitality and dynamism (p. 23).

For liberals, it was this connection which made it possible to see nationalism in so positive a light. In the minds of thinkers such as Mazzini, in many ways the archetypal liberal nationalist of the first half of the nineteenth century, the connection between individual and national freedom was more or less self-evident. The struggle for national self-determination was a struggle against oppression, against domination, against a social and political system which prevented both nations and individuals from being free, from being able to fulfil their potential. As Alter (1989) explains, Mazzini and his fellow thinkers were committed to 'the right of every nation, and with it the right of *each* and *every* member of a nation, to autonomous development, for in their minds, individual freedom and national indepen- dence [were] closely connected' (p. 29; emphasis in the original).

Assumptions of this sort may have helped to push liberals into seeing nationalism in a positive light in relation to democracy too, at least once liberals had made up their mind to support it. In his 'Considerations on Representative Government', John Stuart Mill extended the idea of self- determination by arguing that

> where the sentiment of nationality exists in any force, there is a prima facie case for uniting all the members of the same nationality under the same government, and a government to themselves apart . . . This is merely saying that the question of government ought to be decided by the governed. (1996, p. 41)

Indeed, Mill went further, claiming that 'free institutions are next to impossible in a country made up of different nationalities' (p. 41).

Not all liberals, however, agreed. Lord Acton famously challenged this liberal enthusiasm, seeing nationality as 'a confutation of democracy'. For Acton (1996), 'the combination of different nations in one State is as necessary a condition of civilised life as the combination of men in society' (p. 37; p. 31). Acton was seriously concerned that without such diversity, there would be no effective barriers against centralized and potentially absolutist state power and looked to the presence of different nationalities within the same state to defend freedoms. At the same time, however, it is noticeable that even Acton accepted that national identifications were of primary significance, that the diversity he sought was (multi) national in character. Like Mill, moreover, he made certain assumptions which, as we shall see later, tend to vitiate efforts to develop a 'good' version of nationalism (see Chapter 4). For both men, it turned out that not all nationalities were of equal value. For Mill, it was clearly preferable to belong to some nations rather than others.

Nobody can suppose that it is not more beneficial to a Breton or a Basque . . . to be brought into the current of the ideas and feelings of a highly civilised and cultivated people – to be a member of the French nationality . . . than to sulk on his own rocks, the half-savage relic of past times, revolving in his own little mental orbit, without participation or interest in the general movement of the world. (1996, p. 44)

Some of Acton's formulations are even more problematic. He defended his proposal for multi-national states for instance partly on the grounds that 'inferior races are raised by living in political union with races intellectually superior' (Acton, 1996, p. 31).

It is unlikely that contemporary liberals would express such opinions but the appeal of nationalism not just to supporters such as Mill but to critics such as Acton tells us something of the pressure it exerted from the outset on liberal thought. It was only gradually and perhaps with some reluctance that liberals came to see dangers in nationalism. The impact of the First World War did much to shift opinion here, as many liberals were horrified at the way states deployed nationalism to mobilize the masses for war. Liberals then came to play a prominent role in international campaigns between the wars for peace and disarmament (Heater, 1996). Nationalism came to be seen by many liberals (such as Popper and Hayek) as a collectivist ideology threatening the freedoms, rights and security of the individual (Vincent, 1997).

In more recent years, however, there has been a distinct resurgence of liberal interest in and optimism about nationalism. A number of writers have sought to reassert the essential compatibility of liberalism with nationalism (MacCormick, 1982; Tamir, 1993). Although we deal in more detail with these arguments later in this book (see Chapter 4), it is worth noting here that there is a recurring tendency to assume the necessity of nations.[2] To the extent that this has been the case, it may help to account for what, at the risk of considerable simplification, we could summarize as the overall ambivalence that liberalism has exhibited towards nationalism. Whilst some liberals have seen nationalism as a threat to individual freedoms, rights and security, this has been balanced if not outweighed by others with an initial enthusiasm and a later and more optimistic acceptance of its benefits.

Marx and Marxism: a contradictory legacy?

Is the same true of Marxism? At the very moment indeed when liberalism and nationalism were most closely linked, in 1848 (see Chapter 5), a very different and markedly more critical attitude to nationalism was being promulgated. In the Communist Manifesto and elsewhere, Marx and Engels laid down what seemed to be an unambiguously critical approach to the national question. They began from the premise that the central division in society was not horizontal but vertical, not between nations but between classes (Connor, 1984). Nationality was an irrelevance or an illusion: 'The working men have no country' (Marx and Engels, 1976, p. 502).

> The nationality of the worker is neither French, nor English, nor German, it is labour, free slavery, self-huckstering. His government is neither French, nor English, nor German, it is capital. His native air is neither French, nor German, nor English, it is factory air. The land belonging to him is neither French, nor English, nor German, it lies a few feet below the ground. (Marx, 1975, p. 280)

Workers had no reason to identify themselves in national terms, with their fellow-nationals as such. Rather their interests were universal, cutting across increasingly irrelevant national boundaries.

> The proletarians of all countries have one and the same interest, one and the same enemy, and one and the same struggle. The great mass of the proletarians are, by their nature, free from national prejudice and their whole disposition and movement is essentially humanitarian, anti-nationalist. (Engels, 1976, p. 6)

As capitalism spread out across the world, revolutionizing production, sweeping away traditions, prejudices and hitherto fixed social relations, it undermined the salience of national divisions, both material and intellectual. 'National one-sidedness and narrow mindedness [has] become more and more impossible . . . national differences are daily more and more vanishing' (Marx and Engels, 1976, p. 503). Although Marx and Engels generally eschewed utopian thinking, it is possible to see the outlines here of a genuinely cosmopolitan vision of a future world city, a universal *gemeinschaft* in which there is no room for separate and divisive nation-states (Löwy, 1998).

These arguments have been the target of much criticism down the years, taken as evidence that Marx and Engels had no understanding of the significance of nationalism, and wilfully underestimated its appeal. Even many later Marxists have seen nationalism as Marxism's 'great historical failure' (Nairn, 1977, p. 329), accepting that 'essentially, Marxism has no theory of nationalism' (Munck, 1986, p. 2), whilst for non-Marxists such as Giddens, Marxism is held to have little to contribute to our understanding in this area (Giddens, 1985). There is though something rather odd about these criticisms. After all, Marx and Engels were writing at precisely the time when nationalism was, if not at its height, certainly becoming increasingly influential (Connor, 1984, p. 6; James, 1996, p. 52). In fact, neither Marx nor Engels was immune to the political pressures surrounding them, and at various times they were led to soften or modify this position.[3] They did so in two main ways. One was to adopt a somewhat determinist position, in which there was a distinction between two different kinds of nation – one so-called 'historic' and the other supposedly 'non-historic'. The other was more pragmatic, an attempt to integrate or graft nationalist struggles on to the communist project. Both of these adaptations or modifications were to have considerable impact on subsequent thinking about nationalism, both Marxist and non-Marxist.

The distinction between historic and non-historic nations was taken directly from Hegel. The latter category referred to 'these relics of a nation mercilessly trampled under foot in the course of history, *as Hegel says*' (Engels, 1977, p. 234; emphasis added). Thus what they called 'large and well-defined historical nations' could be contrasted with 'the ruins of peoples which are still found here and there and which are no longer capable of a national existence, are absorbed by the larger nations and either become part of them or maintain themselves as ethnographic monuments without political significance' (Engels, 1980, p. 254). In one sense this was part of their more general materialist inversion of Hegelian thought. Insofar as they were part of the overall development of capitalism, certain nation-states had played a progressive historical role, unifying people and territory and helping to break down more local barriers and divisions. One could therefore distinguish between nationalisms which promoted these objectives (in the case of 'historic' nations) and those which sought to hold back progress so conceived (the 'non-historic' cases). It has not been difficult for critics to seize upon the particular examples Marx and Engels adduced here as evidence of racism and/or Eurocentrism (Blaut, 1987; Munck, 1986; Nimni, 1991; Rosdolsky, 1986). Yet there is a sense in which this kind of criticism is to some extent beside the point not just because, as Breuilly (1996) has pointed out, 'the distinction between "historic" and "non-historic" nations was part of the political "common sense" of 19th century Europe' (p. 172). The terms in which they identified the historic character of such nations were more than purely economic, encompassing, building on and (crucially) also assuming a given and unproblematized cultural identity. The 'nation', historic or other-wise, was in some sense taken as a given. In making this kind of distinction, neither Marx nor Engels questioned the very category of the nation itself.

In later years, this particular distinction was, as it happens, largely jettisoned by both men. In its place came a different kind of adaptation to nationalism, motivated by more pragmatic considerations. In particular it was the causes of Polish and Irish independence that led them to modify their opposition to nationalism. In the first case, Marx believed that Polish independence would weaken Tsarist Russia, the reactionary gendarme of Europe. In the second, similarly, he came to believe that Irish independence would weaken the position of Britain, the world's most advanced capitalist power. In the process, particularly in coining in relation to English rule in Ireland the dictum that 'any nation that oppresses another forges its own chains' (cited in Munck, 1986, p. 15), Marx opened the way, as we shall see, to a powerful line of argument in which a distinction could be drawn (not only by Marxists) between the nationalism of the oppressor and that of the oppressed (see below).[4]

The Marxist legacy was therefore quite complex. For alongside the first resolutely internationalist position outlined above, there were at least two others in which different kinds of nationalism seemed to have been identified, one progressive, the other reactionary. Broadly speaking and at the risk of some simplification, the next generation of Marxists was to try to pursue each of these different positions to its logical conclusion. In the process the differences between them became more acute, leading not just to internal conflict within the Marxist political movement but to rather different lines of interpretation and explanation of nationalism itself.

Rosa Luxemburg and internationalism

Rosa Luxemburg, writing at the turn of the century, based herself firmly on Marx's forceful internationalism. She was insistent that there was no longer anything progressive about nationalism. At this (late) stage of capitalist development, nationalism could only play a reactionary role. Whilst she did not deny that people could identify themselves in national terms, she was resolutely opposed to the politicization of such identities. Insofar as they led to claims for independent state power, they were impossible to sort out and bound to involve the oppression of others – the Poles by the Russians, for example, or the Ruthenians, the White Russians or the Lithuanians by the Poles, and the Jews by all (Shelton, 1987). Socialists had to challenge the concept of the nation as

> a category of bourgeois ideology . . . [since] in a class society, 'the nation' as a homogeneous socio-political entity does not exist . . . There literally is not one social arena – from the coarsest material relationships to the most subtle moral one – in which the possessing classes and the class-conscious proletariat hold the same attitude, and in which they appear as a consolidated 'national' identity. (Luxemburg, 1976, pp. 135–6)

In invoking such a unity, nationalism operated to divide workers on national lines, mobilizing national identity against class identity. The First World War was, for Luxemburg, an extreme example of what could happen when, caught up in a nationalist hysteria, French and German workers turned on each other. Only a radical internationalism offered the possibility of putting an end to the ensuing barbarism (Luxemburg, 1970).

Luxemburg's arguments have, like Marx's earlier ones, been subjected to considerable criticism. Most writers have argued that she too showed a signal failure to understand the force and appeal of nationalism. She is said to have been naive, idealistic and utopian to imagine that loyalty to the nation could be overridden. This seems somewhat deterministic, underestimating the potential volatility of national identification,[5] the significance of political mobilization and ignoring cases where other loyalties have taken precedence. It has also been argued that Luxemburg was blind to the necessity for oppressed nations to assert their right to self-determination. (We discuss this issue in Chapter 5.) Relatedly, it has been argued that internationalism is a fraud, a cover for support for existing or powerful nations, although Luxemburg's own opposition to the First World War was grounded in her rejection of the nationalism of *all* the contending imperialist states, German and French, British and Russian. (We discuss this criticism of internationalism in Chapter 7.)

Whilst some later writers have, implicitly or explicitly, drawn on Luxemburgist themes (Hobsbawm, for instance – see Chapter 2), many others have integrated criticisms such as these into their conception of nationalism. In any case, Luxemburg's ideas were opposed from the outset by other Marxists. Two of these are worth considering, as in their different ways they too have had considerable influence on later thinking about nationalism.

Otto Bauer and the significance of national 'culture'

For the Austro-Marxist Otto Bauer, so far from Marxism being hostile to nationalism, it was only through socialism that workers could become fully fledged members of their nation, as they both needed and wished to be. Arguing against what he saw as irrational, mystical, ahistorical or idealist conceptions of the nation, Bauer proposed a supposedly more materialist account, tracing the development of national identity over time, as he attempted to show how what he called 'communities of destiny' had evolved. Looping back to the Hegelian strand in Marx's thought, he identified three main periods of development. In the first stage, clan society, the nation was bound by common blood, linked by an inherited and ancestral culture. In the second, in class-differentiated feudal and bourgeois societies, the nation was held together by the cultural unity of the ruling class. Finally, in the socialist stage, the nation would be united on the basis of common education, shared experience of labour, and the (unquestioned) desire to enter into and enjoy the fruits of national culture, hitherto denied to the majority by class exploitation and exclusion. This historical account has the undoubted advantage of being free from the racist or Eurocentric assumption of a distinction between historic and non-historic nations. On the other hand, there is a danger of assuming some of what needs to be explained. Bauer's focus is primarily on culture, which is seen as essentially national. What he calls 'national apperceptions' structure the way in which we must comprehend, for instance, works of art, literature or music. 'It is precisely the difference of cultural community that divides the nations' (Bauer, 1996, p. 54). Where Marx specifically argued that 'the intellectual creations of individual nations become common property . . . and from the numerous national and local literatures there arises a world literature' (Marx and Engels, 1976, p. 488), Bauer insisted on the barriers that national culture set up. 'Foreign elements never work on individuals with the same force as the original national culture . . . the individual who is culturally the child of many nations is generally little loved, an object of suspicion . . . and the cultural amalgam of two nations appears accordingly as a foreigner.' Indeed Bauer (1996) goes so far as to say that 'antipathy to cultural half-breeds [*sic*] is understandable' even if 'we should not let it lead us astray' (p. 55). At times, the sense of national specificity that Bauer articulates is asserted in quite sentimental terms. 'If I think of my nation, I remember my homeland, my parents' house, my first childhood games, my old schoolmaster, the girl whose kiss once thrilled me and from all these ideas a feeling of pleasure flows into the idea of the nation I belong to' (p. 63). It is not wholly clear why such disparate feelings, however, should merge and flow so easily and naturally into national(ist) channels. The assumption, however, that cultural identity is clear, discrete and provides a fundamental basis for national identity, has proved very influential. Whilst Bauer was by no means the only thinker to promulgate such views, his prominence as a Marxist has led him to be hailed as a pioneer by a number of later or neo-Marxists struggling to make sense of nationalism, particularly in recent years (Jenkins, 1990; Löwy, 1998; Munck, 1986; Nimni, 1991).

Lenin and the right of (oppressed) nations to self-determination

The third strand in Marx's thought on nationalism was developed by Lenin and has been equally significant. Drawing out the fuller implications of Marx's position on the Irish question, Lenin drew a sharp distinction between oppressor and oppressed nations (Munck, 1986, p. 74). Marxists, he argued, could understand and sympathize with the latter, whilst maintaining a critical attitude to the former. Many have argued, however, that this distinction, if not incoherent, was essentially pragmatic, as was Marx's in the first place, driven by strategic considerations in relation to the struggle against the Tsarism empire, or even incoherent (Hobsbawm). It is true that Lenin did not trouble himself greatly to define nations, or to explain how national identity, even if suppressed, comes into existence in the first place. This task he left to Stalin, whose cumbersome effort to define the nation as 'a historically evolved, stable community of language, territory, economic life and psycho-logical make-up manifested in a community of culture', as well as drawing significantly on Bauer, was motivated in the first instance by fairly narrow internal party political considerations (Munck, 1986, p. 77). Beyond this, it was used to fashion a supposed solution to the national question in the Tsarist Empire and, it was claimed, a basis for the subsequent institutional structure of the Soviet Union in this respect. In reality, these arrangements were not only quite arbitrary in many respects but also, in the long term, did little to defuse the appeal of nationalism, ultimately helping to facilitate the break-up of the Union on highly divisive national lines (Spencer and Wollman, 1999).

It has, however, been argued that the full significance of Lenin's distinction only becomes clear when taken in conjunction with his theory of imperialism (Blaut, 1987). In the latter, Lenin (1970) argued that capitalism had, as he put it, 'singled out a handful of exceptionally rich and powerful states' to divide up the world for the purposes of plunder and the extortion of superprofits (p. 9). In this context, some have argued, the struggle for self-determination is a core part of the struggle of oppressed nations against (oppressive) imperialism, which are claiming the legitimate right of self-determination. However, there are some difficulties with this line of argument. The theory of imperialism is in the first instance a critique of the conduct of (imperialist) nation-states as agents of capital at this 'highest stage of capitalist development'. There is no discussion of nationalism as such, and few and only passing references to national oppression. Perhaps more seriously, Lenin made the potentially contradictory or rather optimistic assumptions that, once nations had been granted and asserted the right to self-determination, they would not necessarily wish to exercise it. Using the analogy of the right to divorce, which has to exist but need not be exercised, Lenin seems to have believed that, at least under socialism, nations would voluntarily federate. There was, it has to be said, very little evidence at the time to back up this optimistic perspective, as Luxemburg 1970b noted. More generally, as Michael Löwy has more recently argued, although this form of 'Marxism proposes a capital distinction between the nationalism of the oppressor and of the oppressed . . . [this] is made difficult by a well-known characteristic of modern nationalisms: each oppressed nation, as soon as liberated (even before), considers its most urgent task to exercise an analogous oppression over its own national minorities (1993, p. 137).

None of this seems to have prevented later Marxists from seeking to build on Lenin's problematic legacy. Throughout the twentieth century Marxists of various kinds from Gramsci to Mao, and from Cabral to Guevara have attempted to develop a perspective in which nationalism can be made compatible with Marxism. Faced with the apparent prevalence and salience of national identifications, Marx's successors tried various ways of accommodating to nationalism, of seeking to turn it into a positive asset, a vehicle which the rising proletariat could deploy or harness in the struggle for socialism. Whilst some have claimed that this has been the secret to whatever successes the socialist cause has enjoyed,[6] others have urged socialists to go down this path for fear of the consequences of nationalism falling into what they see as the 'wrong hands', allowing nationalism to be appropriated by the political right (Schwarzmantel, 1991).

Conservatives and nationalism

There are some good grounds for this fear. By the latter part of the nineteenth century, there was accumulating evidence that nationalism was an ideology which conservatives could turn to their advantage (see Chapter 5). This was the period when nationalism is held by many to have 'mutated' (to borrow Hobsbawm's term) from its supposedly original popular democratic, liberal phenomenon into something altogether more congenial, more useful to ruling elites, monarchies and empires (Anderson, 1991, p. 86). It is certainly the case that the latter viewed the nationalism they associated with the French Revolution with undisguised horror, seeing it as a new, destabilizing force, subversive of existing institutions, beliefs and values. The conservative reaction, most eloquently articulated by Edmund Burke, attacked nationalist claims as inventions, as the imagination of overheated intellectuals or fanatics, driven by grievances, obsessions and fantasies.

However, it was not long before conservative ideology too began to come to terms with nationalism, to find ways of accommodating to it. The association of nationalism with subversion, with radicalism, became less necessary or compelling, whilst the potential or actual consonance of nationalist themes and conservative ones became more apparent. The fundamental reason for this is that the association of the French Revolution with nationalism, which seemed so obvious, was (as we shall argue in Chapter 5) in many ways deceptive. As far as conservatives are concerned, what they fundamentally objected to in the French Revolution was much less its nationalism than the principles of equality (especially), liberty (insofar as it was linked to equality) and fraternity (until or unless this could be re-articulated in nationalist terms).

In fact, so far from nationalism being the primary target, the conservative critique of and reaction to the French Revolution was often couched precisely in national terms. Burke's arguments, for instance, were in many ways formulated as an assertion of British difference, even superiority. As Thody (1993) puts it, Burke seems to have 'implicitly wondered throughout the Reflections on the Revolution in France, why on earth the French could not be more like the English, and urged his fellow countrymen to be very wary of anything coming from Abroad' (p. 47). The German conservative reaction too, as expressed by writers such as Novalis, Muller and Fichte (albeit also driven by a particular sense of humiliation at the hands of Napoleon), was informed by a parallel sense that Germany was different and superior (O'Sullivan, 1976, p. 76). Even in France itself, conservative hostility to the revolution, articulated by people like Barrès and Maurras, was grounded in part in a sense that the revolution was in some sense alien, unnatural, antithetical to the deeper values of French blood and soil (Sternhell, 1991).

A central conservative critique of the Revolution was that it tried to break with the past, with tradition. Yet this past was often conceived of in national terms. Through it, each nation had organically developed its own unique character, distinct from all others. For Herder, a key component of this character was language which he believed, as Minogue (1967) explains, 'expressed a nation's soul or spirit . . . a kind of coded history of the sufferings and joys of the nation' (p. 60). It was essential too in Herder's view to the maintenance of the 'bond of social classes' (cited in Minogue, 1967, p. 60). This too was not difficult to view in national terms, and increasingly conservatives came to think about the cohesion and unity of society in this way. This is particularly evident in nineteenth century France where writers, from Bonald and de Maistre at the beginning to Maurras and Barrès at the end, promoted a narrow, even extreme ideal of national unity (O'Sullivan, 1976, pp. 35–6). It was also true in Germany. Fichte took up where Herder left off in arguing that 'those who speak the same language are linked together . . . they belong together, they are by nature one indivisible' (cited in O'Sullivan, 1976, p. 71). For all of these thinkers, internal diversity was to be avoided as were internal conflicts (particularly of a class kind), which might threaten to disrupt social cohesion or tear the nation apart. Of course this was more difficult in cases where the existing state was multi-national, as in the case of the Austrian Empire. Yet what is noticeable here is the relative paucity of conservative thinking devoted to justifications of such states. It turned out to be easier to favour one nationality over others than to forge links across or between nations. In the case of Tsarism, stability and unity could be promoted by a vague and woolly Slavophilia but was rather more effectively and self-confidently pursued through policies of Russification, what Anderson (1991) describes as 'stretching the short, tight skin of the nation over the gigantic body of the empire' (p. 86).

Such policies were the work of states of course, and indeed the state was assigned a particular role in the nationalist thinking of conservatives. In the work of the historian Heinrich von Treitschke for instance, the national state was of overarching significance. Individuals are and must be subordinated to its demands, to its pursuit of power ('*Staat ist Macht*'). Sooner or later this has to lead to war between nations, which Treitschke appears to regard as in some way not only inevitable but essential:

> Over and over again has it been proved that it is only in war a people becomes in very deed a people. It is only in the common performance of heroic deeds for the sake of the fatherland that a nation becomes truly and spiritually united. . . . War is a sharp medicine for national disunion and waning patriotism. (cited in Guibernau, 1996, p. 8)

Here national identity is both forged by and necessary to the state, which ensures the nation's unity and commands its subjects' loyalty. Other nations are, ultimately, always and necessarily a threat. It seems to have become peculiarly difficult for most conservative thinkers, certainly as the nineteenth century wore on, to tolerate or conceive of the idea of a cosmopolitan world, beyond or without nations. Increasingly for conservatives, human beings came to be thought about as in some fundamental sense inescapably and essentially national. To see them otherwise was to render them hopelessly abstract, almost disembodied. As de Maistre put it 'there is no such thing as *man* in the world. In the course of my life I have seen Frenchmen, Italians, Russians etc. . . . But as for man, I declare that I have never met him in my life; if he exists he is unknown to me' (cited in Berlin, 1991, p. 100).

At its extreme, for some conservatives such as Fichte the nation came to be viewed as part of the enduring, irreducible reality of the world, a kind of primary datum, underpinning and antecedent to society (O'Sullivan, 1976, p. 71). Whilst this may be thought to stand in some contradiction to other conservative emphases on history, so central for instance to Burke's justifications of present arrangements, beliefs and values, what is interesting is the shared focus on the nation, which can thus be justified from quite different angles.

Broadly speaking then, conservatism turned out to be compatible with nationalism, able to integrate basic nationalist ideas into its own ideological framework. This is not to deny that there have been conservative thinkers who have been critical of nationalism. Both Kedourie (1993) and Minogue (1967) for instance in relatively recent times have been among its most lucid and penetrating critics. What it suggests, however, is that once its novelty had worn off, once the potentially different logics of nationalism and democracy had become clearer (see Chapter 5), conservative thought could accommodate nationalism without major difficulty.

More generally, it seems that none of the three great political ideologies of the modern era have mounted a sustained opposition or resistance to nationalism. Although there are important aspects of these ways of thinking which can help us think critically about nationalism, they are balanced by other more accommodating tendencies. This is true too, we shall now suggest, for two of the major social theorists of the twentieth century, Emile Durkheim and Max Weber, who have been equally if not more influential in shaping the ways in which later theorists have thought about nationalism.

Classical social theory and nationalism

Here we encounter something of a paradox. At the very time when nationalism was becoming a hegemonic doctrine among European states, neither thinker seemed, at first sight at any rate, to have much to say on the subject. Perhaps the very hegemony of nationalism as an ideology, as we have noted already, made it so taken for granted a background to the society of their day, so unremarkable a part of daily political life, that systematic analysis was not a priority. Yet both Weber and Durkheim did comment on nationalism and the nation and contribute to our understanding of it, although arguably what they had to say directly on the subject was rather less important in many respects than the elements of their more general theorizing – of religion, ethnicity, social solidarity, culture, social closure, modernization – that have influenced generations of later scholars in a number of different ways and made it possible to throw a more critical light on the subject (Smith, 1983).[7]

Durkheim

Durkheim wrote relatively little directly on nationalism. However, he did express himself on the issue at a number of points in his career, in debates, in his teaching and in writing, particularly during the First World War. These contributions were not always consistent: his definition of nationality for instance changed over time, as Llobera (1994b) has pointed out, incorporating latterly a significant ethnic element, when he had earlier applied the term to 'human groups that are united by a community of civilization without being united by a political bond' (in Giddens, 1986, p. 206).

Durkheim was of course a child of the French Third Republic, working in a particular political context in which different forms of nationalism were apparently in conflict, notably at the time of the Dreyfus case. On the one hand there was a reactionary, traditionalist, anti-liberal and anti-republican form, articulated by (amongst others) Barrès and Maurras . On the other hand, it is often argued, there was a very different form of civic, republican nationalism, with whose fundamental principles Durkheim should be associated. In fact, as we shall argue in Chapter 4, the distinction between these two forms is not clear-cut. Nevertheless, Durkheim clearly thought that he was a firm defender of republican values and that the form of nationalism he espoused was progressive, focusing on the central importance of patriotism. According to Durkheim, where the nationality and the state were one and the same (where political bonds and cultural unity are found together), a nation existed. Within such a state, certain beliefs or values played a key role in sustaining social cohesion. These were central to patriotism, essential because 'man is a moral being only because he lives within established societies' and 'patriotism is precisely the ideas and feelings as a whole which bind the individual to a certain state' (in Giddens, 1986, p. 202). In turn this state could, by imposing obligations on its citizens, give the moral authority and discipline that the individual needs to develop. Such a state (or *patrie*) was autonomous, with clearly demarcated borders, identified by Durkheim as the 'limit of the collective personality' (in Llobera, 1994b, p. 151). Without the *patrie* indeed, he argued, civilization itself was at risk (Llobera, 1994b, p. 149).

At the same time, Durkheim believed there was no necessary contradiction between such particular attachments and other, broader, more universal commitments and loyalties. There was only an apparent clash between the national ideal of patriotism and what he calls the 'human ideal' of 'world patriotism' (in Giddens, 1986, p. 201). Although universal beliefs are at the apex of a moral hierarchy, there is no contradiction between loyalties to the nation and to humanity as a whole.[8] The ideals of the nation-state could be those of humanity as a whole; there need be no discrepancy between 'national and human morals', so that 'civic duties would be only a particular form of the general obligations of humanity' (in Giddens, 1986, pp. 203–4). Indeed it is only through the nation-state that universal ideals, 'the ideals of mankind', can be achieved (Durkheim, 1973, p. 78). Durkheim defends then a 'patriotism' which is 'interior' rather than 'exterior' directed (that is against another group). If this is the case, then there will still be national pride: 'but societies can have their pride, not in being the greatest or the wealthiest, but in being the most just, the best organized and in possessing the best moral constitution' (in Giddens, 1986, p. 204).

This advocacy of patriotism as a route to achieving the 'objectives of mankind in general' (Durkheim, 1973, p. 76) was, however, easily translatable into defence of the French nation and hostility to the German nation in the First World War. For French nationalism could be seen by Durkheim as precisely an example of the interior directed type, whilst German nationalism could be seen as exemplifying the exterior directed type hostile to its neighbours. In the war indeed Durkheim had no doubts that Germany was to blame for everything. 'Germany's culpability is obvious. Everything confirms it, nothing can attenuate it,' whilst 'France's attitude has always been irreproachably correct' (in Giddens, 1986, p. 30). He saw the spirit of Treitschke's conservatism and expansionism as the essence of German nationalism, a clear-cut case of social pathology: 'the outrageousness of its ambitions alone would suffice to demonstrate their pathological nature' (p. 232).

Durkheim's arguments were, of course, an intervention into a debate that had major implications for theories of nationalism. For Durkheim was not only defending the French *patrie* against its German enemy but also French patriotism against internationalism. In targeting Treitschke, Durkheim was criticizing German nationalism for raising the state above international law, morality and civil society (Llobera, 1994a). He was silent, however, on the question of French responsibility for the war, projecting all the aggression on to the German side. In this context, Durkheim's arguments could be used to delegitimate opposition to the war, to foster the patriotic attachments necessary for the war to go on.[9]

Yet at another level, Durkheim's work can be drawn upon to help us think more critically about some of the ways in which such patriotism is so fostered. For his central concerns with social solidarity and the changing basis of social cohesion do have important ramifications for the student of nationalism. Perceiving the inadequacy of 'organic solidarity', with its complex division of labour, in guaranteeing social cohesion, he was led to seek other ways in which a moral order in society could be provided. One of these was through education which, as he put it, 'assures a sufficiently common body of ideas and feelings amongst citizens without which any society is impossible' (in Guibernau, 1996, p. 25). The French Third Republic, famously, designed and implemented a national, secular system of education in part precisely to generate and reinforce attachments to the nation. This national education system provided a kind of cultural cement to enforce the idea of a civic nationalism which was central to the developing French model of the nation (see Chapter 4.)

A more interesting and influential contribution to the understanding of nationalism lies, however, in his analysis of religion, particularly in the distinction he drew between the 'sacred' and 'profane', and in his analysis of the social functions of both religious rituals and beliefs (Durkheim, 1976). Durkheim provides a powerful description of the intensity with which such rituals can transport individuals away from their everyday lives, whilst pointing to the ways in which religions express the social totality and help to bind and integrate people to society. He laid particular stress upon the important role of religions in transmitting a cosmology, in giving accounts of how the world was formed, of why we are here, of the meaning of life. The link with nationalism here was one that Durkheim himself noted, as he pointed to the similarities between traditional religious celebrations and a 'reunion of citizens commemorating the promulgation of a new moral or legal system or some great event in national life' (Durkheim, 1976, p. 387). As an illustration of this he pointed specifically to the way during the French Revolutionary period that 'Reason', 'Liberty' and the 'Fatherland' were made the objects of veneration and became 'transformed by public opinion into sacred things' (Durkheim, 1976, p. 214). A number of writers have, subsequently, sought to apply such Durkheimian ideas to nationalism, particularly that of a civic religion (Bellah, 1970). The flag, the Constitution, the Monarchy can be seen here as elements of this religion with attendant rites and ceremonials whilst the nation itself, its monuments, its institutions, its symbols, and its sacrifices may all be held sacred (Bellah, 1970; Shils and Young, 1953).

There is of course a difficulty or danger here, common to Durkheim's work more generally, that it has a tendency to ignore conflict and struggle, and to overemphasize social integration. The promulgation of such state or national religions is problematic, whilst promulgation is not the same as popular or universal appropriation or endorsement. As was evident in the

First World War, there is resistance to the religion of the nation, which cannot be adequately registered without a more political understanding of the ways in which this religion is both fostered and challenged. Similarly, there is a danger that too great a focus on the mechanisms that are used to hold the nation together can give a misleading impression of the extent to which it is in fact united. It can lead to a blindness to the existence of minorities who may not share wholly or in part in its 'civilization'. The legacy that Durkheim then bequeathed to later thinking about nationalism is therefore ambivalent, both opening up useful lines of critique but also, in the direction of his overt writings on the subject as well as in aspects of his general work, providing support for the idea of nationalism as a principle source of social cohesion.

Weber

Much the same may be said about Max Weber, like Durkheim a strong supporter of his country in time of war. Weber was indeed a German nationalist all his life, a member for a time of the Pan-German League, a liberal imperialist, hopeful that a policy of rearmament would induce the other world powers into granting Germany, a latecomer to nation-statehood, its proper share of colonies (Mommsen, 1984). This initial political affiliation to an expansive nationalism was not limited by Durkheim's humanistic concerns and doubts. His 1895 inaugural lecture, clearly intended as a political intervention into contemporary arguments and debates, was replete with a crude Social-Darwinist imagery of superior and inferior races and peoples so common to the age (Hawkins, 1997, pp. 11–12). In this address, Germans are seen as 'the more highly developed element' (Weber, 1980, p. 441); Polish peasants are part of a 'race which stands on a lower level' (Weber, 1980, p. 436). In addition, the lecture firmly supports German economic expansionism in ringing nationalist terms: 'we cannot lead our descendants to peace and contentment but only into the endless battle to maintain and expand our national culture and people' (cited by Mommsen, 1984, p. 40).

At this time Weber was strongly against the Polonization of the eastern part of Germany. But, according to Mommsen, after 1900 he began to distance himself from some of the cruder, more emotional forms of German nationalism, much as he became increasingly sceptical of the utility of Social Darwinism more generally (Hawkins, 1997). He adopted a more pragmatic tone, supporting some cultural autonomy for the Prussian Poles, but (crucially) tailored to the interests of the dominant nationality and the German state (cited by Mommsen, 1984, p. 59).

Guibernau (1996) has argued that Weber's ideas on nationalism were influenced to a significant extent by Treitschke, whose emphasis on violence and territoriality helps as she put it to 'explain Weber's faith [*sic*] in the intrinsic relation between power and the state, Machiavellianism and the importance of great leaders' (p. 31). However pragmatic he became, opposing for instance the annexationist war aims of the German government in the First World War on essentially strategic and tactical grounds, Germany, for him, had to be a 'power state' (*Machtstaat*), to be a major player on the world scene, to assume its responsibility to defend its own and Central European culture generally against the Russian (and later American) threat (Lassman and Speirs, 1994, p. xv).

Weber's central concern with the fate of the German nation implied that, within his influential definition of the modern state, as 'a human community that (successfully) claims the monopoly of the legitimate use of physical force within a given territory' (Weber, 1948, p. 78), was an assumption that this community is a national one and that the state is fundamentally to be understood as a nation-state. It is only such a state that can call on the subjective sense of its citizens of belonging to a community leading them (as in 1914) to sacrifice themselves willingly for its sake. In such 'a *community of political destiny*', as he put it,

> the individual is expected ultimately to face death in the group interest. This gives to the political community its particular pathos and raises its *enduring* emotional foundations, [giving rise to] groups with joint memories which often have a *deeper impact* than the ties of merely cultural, linguistic or ethnic community. It is this community of memories which constitutes the ultimately decisive element of national consciousness. (Weber, 1978, p. 903; emphasis added)

There is, however, a prior question, which is how such memories came to be shared or assumed in the first place. There is nothing automatic about the creation of such subjective feelings of loyalties. Rather, the state itself played a key role in creating these assumptions and this sense of sharing, as Weber elsewhere recognized. For at other times and in other respects, Weber was alert to the problematic nature of the nation-state, of the category of nation and of national identity. First of all, he recognized clearly that the nation was not coterminous with the state, and was sceptical of any objective definition of the nation. Common language, for instance, was not a necessity for a nation. Equally, although 'the *idea* of the "nation" is apt to include the notions of common descent and of an essential but *frequently indefinite* homogeneity' (Weber, 1978, p. 923; emphasis added), this too was not necessary. Secondly, he recognized the key role of intellectuals in 'propagating' the national idea, and recognized that this is linked to certain sorts of power interests (pp. 925–6). Thirdly, he was aware of the role of coercion in 'enforcing' sacrifice. 'The political community is one of those communities whose action includes . . . coercion through jeopardy of life and freedom of movement applying to outsiders as well as to the members themselves' (p. 903). (Such coercion, as we have noted was a common enough feature of sacrifice in wartime.) Above all, perhaps, he recognized and at times emphasized the role of political factors in mobilizing and sustaining national identifications.

Similar considerations apply to Weber's more general account of ethnicity, argued by some to lie at the core of nationality (Smith, 1986). Whilst again this is dealt with only briefly in his writings it has had an influence out of proportion to its length of treatment. Weber defines an ethnic group in the following way:

> We shall call 'ethnic groups' those human groups that entertain a subjective belief in their common descent because of similarities of physical type or customs or both, or because of memories of colonization and migration; this belief must be important for group formation; conversely, it does not matter whether or not an objective blood relationship exists. Ethnic membership differs from the kinship group precisely by being a *presumed* identity, not a group with concrete social action, like the latter. In our sense, ethnic membership does not constitute a group; it only facilitates group formation of any kind, particularly in the political sphere. On the other hand it is primarily the political community, no matter how artificially organized, that inspires the belief in common ethnicity. (1978, p. 389; emphasis added)

This account has a number of interesting features. As Richard Jenkins (1997) points out, Weber suggests 'that the belief in common ancestry is likely to be a consequence of collective political action rather than its cause; people come to see themselves as belonging together – coming from a common background – as a consequence of acting together' (p. 10). Weber stresses that the key factor in the formation of ethnicity is a belief in common descent, not common descent itself, and that it is the political community which often induces and organizes such a belief.

From another angle, Weber's emphasis on the significance of status groups may also throw some light on the inherently political character of such identifications. For whilst language, religion and other cultural traits can lead to a belief in common ethnicity, this belief can then become the basis for precisely the social closure which is central to the existence and maintenance of status groups. This would involve the application of principles (and policies) of inclusion and exclusion which, as we shall argue later, is pivotal to the operation of nationalism.

CONCLUSION

Weber's writings therefore, like those of Durkheim or Marx and his followers, or more generally much of conservative and liberal ideology, contain contradictory elements, some of which may be used to sustain nationalism, whilst others may help to provide the basis of a more critical approach. What is interesting is that for the most part it is the former which seems to dominate the tone or more explicit formulations, whilst the critical elements generally seem more buried, more implicit, less openly articulated.[10] This may help to explain then why twentieth-century social theorists too have been (as we shall suggest in Chapter 2) inclined at times to adopt an uncritical approach when trying to explain nationalism's apparently unchallengeable hold upon people's loyalties, its seemingly unstoppable dynamic.

FURTHER READING

Detailed considerations of the main theorists discussed here are to be found in the works themselves referred to in the text. For more critical discussion of Marx, Weber and Durkheim see James' extensive and sometimes challenging discussion in *Nation Formation* (1996) and also that in Guibernau (1996). Erica Benner (1995) provides a detailed and thoughtful consideration of Marx and Engels in this context, whilst some of the differences between Marxists are captured in Nimni (1991) and Munck (1986). Llobera (1994b) focuses directly on Durkheim's views on the national question. For two classic and contrasting liberal perspectives, see the essays by Lord Acton and J.S. Mill, selections from which may be found in Balakrishnan (1996) and in Woolf (1996) respectively.

NOTES

1 For a further discussion of this and other connections between individualism and nationalism see Calhoun (1997, pp. 44–6).
2 Andrew Vincent, who has argued compellingly against this revived liberal nationalism, has noted how such assumptions underpin, for example, even the opposed liberal economic theories of Adam Smith and Friedrich List (Vincent, 1997).
3 Erica Benner, however, sees Marx and Engels as having a more coherent and consistent position than we have suggested here. She argues that they had a more subtle approach from the outset, distinguishing between different kinds of nationalism, some progressive, others dangerous (Benner, 1995).
4 Not everyone agrees about this. Connor for instance argues that Marx and Engels were merely displaying an opportunistic flexibility here and that otherwise

and elsewhere 'they were most niggardly in proffering support for national movements' (Connor, 1984, p. 13).

5 During the First World War, to take the case in point, there is significant evidence, especially as the war carried on, and once the initial euphoria had worn off, of mounting opposition to nationalism in both France and Germany (Schorske, 1972; Wohl, 1966).

6 As Munck (1986) puts it 'nationalism responds to deeply-rooted popular aspirations for socio-economic, political and cultural liberation. When these do not take a socialist form this is largely because of Marxism's failure to understand nationalism and articulate its progressive elements' (p. 166).

7 In singling out here the work of Durkheim and Weber we are not of course claiming that these are the only social theorists of the period who have influenced modern theoretical writing on nationalism. However, in terms of their extensive influence on the writers we discuss in Chapter 2 such as Gellner, Smith, Giddens and Mann, and on certain key issues such as ethnicity in the case of Weber or the tradition of republican patriotism in the case of Durkheim, they stand out from other writers in relation to the main themes of this book.

8 In an interesting aside about the idea of a united states of Europe, Durkheim anticipates later criticisms, including ours, of the negative side of a European identity or a European superstate, pointing out that it does not provide a solution to the problem of nationalism:

> a confederation of European states, for instance, is advanced, but vainly as a half-way course to achieving societies on a bigger scale than those we know today. This greater federation, again, would be like an individual state, having its own identity and its own interests and features. It would not be humanity. (in Giddens, 1986, p. 203)

9 On the internationalist opposition to the war in France, see Gras (1972). Hawkins (1999), however, has pointed out that Durkheim was prepared to court personal unpopularity and attack from the right as unpatriotic over issues of rights even during the war.

10 The importance of Weber in providing the intellectual basis for ideas of modernity and modernization lies beyond our scope here. But it is clear that there is a large intellectual debt owed to Weber by those who explain the development of nations and nationalism by linking it to the rise of industrialism or modernization, Gellner being a key example here.

2

Contemporary Approaches to Nationalism

INTRODUCTION

In this chapter we aim to give a critical overview of selected contemporary theories of nationalism. In many ways these draw on the theoretical traditions discussed in the previous chapter, sometimes explicitly, sometimes implicitly. As with the legacy of nineteenth-century thought, however, in the contemporary literature, critical insights into nationalism are combined with a tendency to assume, if not the universality of nationalism, then at least its ubiquity and the impossibility or undesirability of transcending it. Although there are many issues at stake in contemporary theoretical debate, we concentrate in this chapter (although not exclusively) on debates about the origins and nature of the nation and of nationalism.

Primordialism versus modernity

Perhaps the most significant axis of debate in the literature on nationalism has been that concerning the modernity or otherwise of the nation. It has become conventional to distinguish between primordialists and modernists in accounts of the origins of the nation and the national idea. This simple division has become complicated by the debates of the past few years, which have seen the emergence of more nuanced positions, and by the difficulty in pinning down some writers to a specific stance. We need to distinguish between a range or continuum of positions from pure primordialism to modernism and even postmodernism.

Primordialism and perennialism

Primordialism suggests that nationalism has deep roots in human associational life.[1] Biology, psychology and culture may all be summoned in support of the idea that nations are an ancient, necessary and perhaps natural part of social organization, an organic presence whose origins go back to the mists (or myths?) of time. Many nationalists offer a model of their own nationhood which implicitly or explicitly subscribes to this view, and it could be argued that such views are influential in the 'common sense' (in Gramsci's terms) basis of nationalist ideologies (Gramsci, 1971). A typical (but interesting in the context of subsequent history) example of this approach can be seen in Franjo Tudjman's monograph on *Nationalism in Contemporary Europe*:[2]

> Nations . . . grow up in a natural manner, in the objective and complex historical process, as a result of the development of all those material and spiritual forces which in a given area shape the national being of individual nations on the basis of blood, linguistic and cultural kinship, and the common vital interests and links of fate between the ethnic community and the common homeland and the common historical traditions and aims. . . . Nations are the irreplaceable cells of the human community or of the whole of mankind's being. This fact cannot be disputed in any way. (1981, pp. 288–9)

A step along our continuum from primordialism is that which asserts either the continuous or continually recurring nature of nationalism throughout human history. No longer claiming that nations are natural, perennialists claim to find major continuities in ancient and modern concepts of the nation across different historical periods and in very different places (Smith, 1998).

Ethno-symbolism

Few modern scholars provide such an unambiguous position in the perennialist and certainly not the primordialist camp. For example, Anthony Smith, whom many see as tending towards a rejection of the idea of the modernity of nations, distinguishes his own position as one midway between primordialism and modernism, and in recent work has tended to classify himself as working from within a paradigm he names 'ethno-symbolism' or 'historical ethnosymbolism' (Smith, 1998; 1999). However, whilst apparently rejecting primordialism, he is nevertheless a vigorous opponent of what he calls the 'modernist fallacy', for its own mythic character, and its failure 'to grasp the continuing relevance and power of pre-modern ethnic ties and sentiments in providing a firm base for the nation-to-be' (A. Smith, 1995b, p. 40). He claims that modern nationalism did not appear *ex nihilo*, but has clearly premodern antecedents. For him, the rise of nations is predicated on the prior existence of ethnic groups, and nations are formed around 'ethnic cores', developed from premodern 'ethnie' whose members possess a collective proper name, share a myth of common ancestry, possess one or more differentiating elements of a common culture, share historical memories, associate themselves with a specific 'homeland', and have a sense of solidarity for significant sections of the population (Smith, 1991, p. 21). It makes no difference whether these beliefs are themselves rational or irrational; they exist and are effective.

To deny the continuities between primordial ethnic identity and modern national identity is, for Smith, to fly in the face of reality. This is not to say that nations are not in some sense constructions or rather reconstructions, but rather that there is no question of mere or arbitrary invention. 'The "inventions" of modern nationalists must resonate with large numbers of the designated "co-nationals", otherwise the project will fail' (Smith, 1998, p. 198). 'Creating nations is a recurrent activity, which has to be renewed periodically' (Smith, 1986, p. 206). Such inventions as there are in the making of nations are 'novel recombinations of existing elements and motifs' (Smith, 1986, p. 178). In all this, nationalism is an important force, but,

> For ethno-symbolists, what gives nationalism its power are the myths, memories, traditions and symbols of ethnic heritages and the ways in which a popular *living past* has been and can be rediscovered and reinterpreted by modern nationalist intelligentsias. (Smith, 1999, p. 9)

Smith's work is highly impressive in its range of sources and examples from across history. However, he is difficult at times to pin down in these debates. Seeming to stress the similarities of ethnie and nation, he none the less defends himself against the charge that he, like some perennialists, is guilty of 'projecting back into earlier social formations the features peculiar to nations and nationalism'; rather, he suggests he is simply concerned with '*la longue durée*' (Smith, 1998, p. 196). Whilst highly critical of the arguments of the modernists, he is aware that not all ethnie go on to become nations, and he writes of the processes involved in constructing the nation. Clear that the choices for nation-builders are highly limited by the symbols inherited from ancient ethnic communities, he writes critically about cruder versions of primordialism which suggested that nations were perennial, had always been in existence. Smith's stance has, however, tilted towards the ancient origins of modern nations and the ways in which these determined the character of the modern nation. In this sense he can be seen as articulating some key conservative themes stressing the importance of fixed identities stretching back into the past. These roots are valuable, not to be scorned. Durkheim, too is an influence: 'bound by particular identities from birth . . . ethnic and national bonds are good examples of what Durkheim would have described as the general, external and binding quality of social facts' (A. Smith, 1995b, p. 124).

This is open to the general criticism of the over-deterministic nature of Durkheim's approach, and the more specific one that it tends to reify notions of ethnicity and identity (see Chapter 3). However, there are classical liberal elements, too, in Smith's work – such as his belief in self-determination. Unlike primordialists, he also seems to have accepted that modern nationalism is associated with some distinctive changes in the modern era, and that it involves a good deal of construction by elites, states, and intellectuals. However, two major consequences flow from his overall emphasis on the continuities from ancient ethnie to modern nation. The first is that of a tendency towards reductionist explanations of contemporary nationalism in terms of pre-existing cultural loyalties. Thus, ignoring political factors and institutional continuities, Smith writes that 'the continuing power of myths, symbols and memories of ethnic chosenness, golden ages and historic homelands has been largely responsible for the mass appeal of ethnic nationalism in the aftermath of the Cold War and the demise of the Soviet empire' (1999, p. 19).[3] Secondly, and a notable feature of Smith's later work, there is a shift from his being the analyst of nationalism to being its advocate. Thus he writes that 'despite the capacity of nationalisms to generate widespread terror and destruction, the nation and nationalism provide the only realistic socio-cultural framework for a modern world order' (A. Smith 1995b, p. 159), or 'to date we cannot discern a serious rival to the nation for the affection and loyalties of most human beings' (1998, p. 195).

Nationalism before modernity

Although this is not ultimately his own conclusion, Adrian Hastings (1997) shares Smith's dissatisfaction with the arguments of the modernists. Like

Susan Reynolds, Hastings puts the origins of the modern nation much earlier than the late eighteenth century, a characteristic starting point for many modernists. For Reynolds, the medieval idea of a kingdom already involved a sense of collective identity and a notion of a people inhabiting the kingdom. 'In 900 the idea of a people as a community of custom, law, and descent was already well entrenched in western society . . .' (1984, p. 256). Myths of common descent were common in Western Europe (although not omnipresent) and patriotism was strong in Scotland, England and France by the end of the thirteenth century. However, Reynolds is careful to note that this may not have been identical to modern nationalism and that this identity did not necessarily override others (of religion, kin, locality) which may have been as, if not more, important. She recognizes that, at this stage,

> the whole set of ideas about the collective nature of peoples was too unsystematic to create claims to autonomy, or to authority over another people, which would otherwise not have been made. Feelings of community could neither create nor divide kingdoms on their own. To do that the ambitions and machinations of great men were also necessary. (1984, p. 302)

(In this last respect she seems to be making a similar argument to those such as Brass, discussed below, who have highlighted the actions of elites as crucial to the mobilization of nationalism.)

Hastings' (1997) argument is rather more insistent and sweeping, laying minimal emphasis on the activities of elites and much more on the way in which particular ethnic groups develop. There are, he argues, broadly three stages to this process. The first is where there are a number of relatively fluid, unstable, local ethnicities. In the second stage, this complexity and fluidity is diminished, and fewer, more clearly defined literary languages and larger state formations appear. The third stage is that opened up by the French Revolution, where the nature of government and the state's need to establish legitimacy requires an overriding sense of nationhood uniting the people. The modernists' focus on this last stage obscures the significance of the earlier stages, of ethnicity, and specifically of the spread of a written vernacular, a development in which the translation of the Bible plays a major role. When an ethnic group's language develops a wide literature of its own it can go on to develop into a nation; where it does not, it is likely to fail in such a development.

The origins of these processes are thus to be seen in the medieval period, and England is the prototype nation with a sense of national identity which can be traced as far back as Saxon times. By the time of Alfred, it is possible to discern the origins of the English nation-state, clearly established by 1066. The Norman Conquest then did not wipe out this embedded sense of nationhood. Rather the conquerors were themselves 'digested' by the conquered. Subsequent victories over the French in the Hundred Years War reinforced and extended this sense of national identity, which now became widely and horizontally shared. As a result 'the late fourteenth century ... represents the very latest point at which it is plausible to claim that the English nation-state had gelled' (Hastings, 1997, p. 51). English nationalism was then intensified by the Protestant Reformation and subsequent conflicts with Catholic Spain and France. This English Protestant nationalism was in turn integrated into (but remained the distinct and separate core of) a British Protestant nationalism constructed out of further conflict with France.[4]

Other nations then followed in the wake of the English, either by extension or reaction. In the case of the United States for instance, the Puritan settlers saw themselves as more faithful to the original than the English themselves. Here, 'English Protestant nationalism appears at its purest ... New England ... meant more fully Protestant, fully biblical, purged of all episcopalian and papist corruptions, the true Israel' (Hastings, 1997, p.74). Other nations faced more difficulties in following this English model. The French could only develop a nation-state through an 'abrasive' revolution; the Germans (reacting to the imperialism of the latter) by invoking the divisive idea of ethnic purity, designed to exclude the Jews, a model followed later by others with sometimes different exclusionary targets.

As this original English model comes to suffer such distortions, Hastings' original enthusiasm for nationalism appears to diminish somewhat. When it comes, for instance, to the case of Yugoslavia, Hastings is highly critical of the way in which Serbian nationalism was mobilized to destroy the ability of a territorially based state to tolerate diversity. He acknowledges too that there have always been alternatives to nationalism: Christianity itself contained alternative universalist streams in both its Eastern Orthodox and Catholic variants, whilst Islam has historically been far more antipathetic still to nationalism.

Despite these interesting, fruitful and even optimistic suggestions (some of which we take up ourselves in Chapter 7), the overall thrust of Hastings' argument is to assert the enduring necessity of nationalism. If there are problems, they must be met by remodelling rather than abolition.

Like Hastings, Leah Greenfeld (1992) also lays considerable stress on the emergence of nationalism in England. She too sees England as the first nation, in her case dating its nationhood back to the sixteenth century (rather too late of course for his liking). Turning the arguments of the modernists on its head, she sees nationalism not as the consequence of the emergence of modernity but as the outcome of the development of nationalism, as variously backward societies struggled to compete with an initially dominant England.

Greenfeld traces the derivation of the word and the concept from an original reference to a group of foreigners to its elitist use in medieval universities and in church circles, before it finally became attached to the population of a particular country (England). 'The original idea of the nation emerged in sixteeenth-century England, which was the first nation in the world (and the only one, with the possible exception of Holland, for about two hundred years)' (1992, p. 14). As the status of the English nobility came to depend supposedly on merit rather than descent, so the concept of nation came to be attached to the people as a whole as an elite (a development powerfully influenced by Protestantism) and the notion of a 'sovereign people' was born. Nationalism was thus from the outset closely linked, even equivalent to democracy. (We question this common identification in Chapter 5.) This original nationalism was civic, libertarian and individualistic, principles carried over (as in Hastings' model) to the United States, a new England, 'grounded in the values of reason, equality and individual liberty' (1992, p. 420). In this original form, Greenfeld goes as far as to argue, nationalism was not in principle particularist.

> A nation coextensive with humanity is in no way a contradiction in terms. The United States of the World . . . with sovereignty vested in the population, and the various segments of the latter regarded as equal, would be a nation in the strict sense of the word . . . The United States of America represents an approximation to precisely this state of affairs. (1992, pp. 7–8)

Unfortunately, this good form of nationalism did not take root elsewhere. Instead, there were a whole series of reactions, as different societies shaped and fashioned their own forms of nationalism, each of them deviating to a greater or lesser extent from what Greenfeld clearly sees as the preferred Anglo-American model. In France, in Russia and in Germany, civic individualism was replaced by forms of more or less authoritarian collectivism. In each case, new national identities were created which were the result of the importation of an idea first developed somewhere else. The reaction to the model developed in England was characterized by what Greenfeld identifies (following Nietzsche and Scheler) as a *ressentiment* on the part of particular social groups, an envy and a desire both to take possession of and to denigrate the original. In each case, it is argued, there was a sense that what was being created was inferior to the original, provoking a search for something that could be presented as unique, differentiating, *sui generis*.

There are many suggestive, even compelling aspects to this sweeping and ambitious study. The idea of *ressentiment* is useful and can, as we shall see in Chapters 5 and 6, help us understand the unfolding dynamic of nationalism as it spread across time and space. However, it is tied to a distinction between bad and good forms of nationalism which is not only heavily value-laden but involves quite extreme idealizations and highly selective omissions. Thus Greenfeld claims that the 'pursuit of the ideal nation [in] America' could be carried out where 'there was almost no social reality other than the one the settlers brought with them in their own minds' from England (1992, p. 402), rather ignoring the presence (not to mention the subsequent genocide) of those the settlers then encountered. In both Greenfeld and Hastings, there is something of a confusion here between the settlers' self-image and the actual reality of the construction of the nation-state via selective inclusions and exclusions, in which the distinction between good and bad nationalisms is altogether less clear-cut (as we argue in Chapter 4).

From another angle, the argument (central to all opponents of modernism) that a sense of common nationhood was widely shared before modernity is less than convincing. There are real difficulties in assessing the meanings attributed to any sense of nationhood and in ascribing nationalist feelings to the majority of a non-writing or non-literate public. There may have been clear ideas of the nation and of some sense of national identity at a much earlier stage of history than any that we might want to call modern. However, we need to know rather more about what proportion of the population embraced this sense of national identity. Hastings attributes importance to the spread of the vernacular bible; but this is a phenomenon which coincides with the first stirrings of capitalism at least if not modernity. At the time of Bede we can be far less sure about any widespread subscription to the idea of the nation. Reynolds herself says

> The conclusion I draw . . . is that throughout the four centuries under review, the inhabitants of the kingdoms I have discussed, *or at least the politically active amongst them*, seem to have taken it for granted that their own kingdoms comprised peoples of some sort of naturally collective character. (1984, p. 301; emphasis added)

Llobera, whose concern is similarly to assert that the concept of a nation is much older than the modernists suggest, claims a consensus among historians 'that by the end of the medieval period there was a clear sense of national identity in England', but then notes that it may have been '*shared perhaps by only five percent of the population*' (1994a, p. 39; emphasis added)!

A related problem is whether the medieval national idea is identical to the modern one, and whether what existed then was the equivalent of modern nationalism. For modernists, national consciousness in the modern age has to be seen as qualitatively different from that in the Scotland of the Declaration of Arbroath or England of Shakespeare or Wycliffe or Elizabeth or Cromwell. They argue instead that there has been a radical shift in what we now understand as nationalism, that it is only with modernity that a sense of national identity comes to pervade all classes, or emerges as the overriding identity. To understand nationalism, we have to locate it firmly in the development of modernity, in the economic, social and political processes that so transformed the world.

Modernism

Modernists then are not attached to a search for the primeval or even medieval roots of nations and nationalism. These are associated with modernity, however defined. Modernists, of course, come in a variety of theoretical guises. We can see in particular the influence of Weber and Durkheim, and of classical Marxism on many of the most influential writers in this vein.

Ernest Gellner: nationalism and modernization

Of all the recent modernist theorists of nationalism, the one most generally respected and widely quoted is the late Ernest Gellner. Over three decades, Gellner progressively elaborated a theory of nationalism and its development, focusing on the relationship between nationalism, culture and the industrialization process. He is ruthlessly unsentimental about nations, which he sees as products of nationalism itself:

> Nations as a natural, God-given way of classifying men, as an inherent
> . . . political destiny, are a myth; nationalism, which sometimes takes
> pre-existing cultures and turns them into nations, sometimes invents them,
> and often obliterates pre-existing cultures; that is reality. (1983, pp. 48–9)

For Gellner, nationalism is impossible, unnecessary, and virtually unimaginable in agrarian societies. Using a contrast between traditional and modern society, typical of Weber, Durkheim and Tönnies, Gellner (1983) provides a basically functionalist explanation of the social and economic need for cultural homogeneity, based on what he terms 'high culture', in a new industrial society. A shared, common culture is needed because of the requirements of the new industrial society with its different form of division of labour. Communication is needed on a different basis both because of the new complex division of labour but also because of the need for geographical and social mobility of the new industrial society. 'Its economy depends on mobility and communication between individuals, at a level which can only be achieved if those individuals have been socialised into a high culture . . . It can only be achieved by a fairly monolithic education system' (Gellner, 1983, p. 140).

Yet Gellner thinks that this construction is itself in some sense necessary and, following Weber and Durkheim, part of the transition to modernity (James, 1996). He explains the emergence of this new doctrine as a necessary part of the structural change from agro-literate to advanced industrial society. Culture (more specifically what he calls 'high' culture) comes to play a central role in providing the skills and identity of members of such a society. As Bauer had done before him (see Chapter 1), Gellner identifies this high culture as necessarily national, arguing indeed that it is this homogeneous culture, produced and required by the state-driven education system, which makes the nation. 'A high culture pervades the whole of society, defines it and needs to be sustained by that polity' (1983, p. 18). There is little or no space within this conception of modernization for the continuing existence of different cultures, or of interchanges between and across (fluid) cultural boundaries (see Chapters 3 and 6).

In a later addition to his theory, Gellner proceeded to distinguish between different zones in which nationalism developed, and different time periods in which nationalist ideas emerge and are disseminated. In the West, centralizing and unifying nation-states could emerge relatively unprob-lematically. Further East, more problems appeared with regard to clearly identifiable national cultures and appropriate states, rooted in developed civil societies. Nationalism had evolved through a series of stages, from the French Revolution via irredentism and the violence of ethnic cleansing to the postwar period, when it could be finally tamed. In the process, or only in some time zones, Gellner implies, does nationalism have clearly malign effects. As time moves on, as the 'East' catches up with the 'West', so these more malign effects will pass.[5] So, although the nation is constructed by nationalism, we can (and must) put up with it.

Gellner's argument, which is often praised for its elegance, may however be subject to charges of functionalism, if not teleology, in that the theory seems to explain the development of nationalism largely by reference to its positive consequences for successful modernization.[6] It can also be argued that his use of ideas of modernization and modernity is somewhat uncritical. Although he distinguishes two types of agrarian society and one type of industrial society, his account of social change is open to the criticisms made of the simplified application of Parsonian or neo-Weberian categories to the problems of development (Roxborough, 1979). The use of indus-trialism as the organizing category for modern social change (rather than capitalism) matters because, as both Mann and Breuilly have pointed out, it is very hard to see industrialism, which came late to most of Europe, as an explanation for nationalism when nationalist ideas developed earlier and began to spread in advance of industrialization.

Gellner was not particularly interested in nationalist ideas or in nation-alist thinkers 'who did not really make much difference' (1983, p. 124). Although he insisted that he was only too well aware of the spell and emotional appeal of nationalism (Gellner, 1996b, pp. 626–7), he viewed nationalist ideas with a high degree of scepticism and regarded nationalism, largely in Durkheimian mode, as a way in which society worshipped itself in a clear and unvarnished manner, less veiled than in the totemic forms of religion analysed by Durkheim (1976). His focus was primarily on the conditions that made the idea of nation seem so obvious, if not self-evident, and have made us in a sense all nationalists, whether we wished to be or not.

One consequence of this was a relative inattention to the political domain, to the politics of nationalism (which is not to say that Gellner was not alarmed by the spread of some forms of nationalism, particularly towards the end of his life). He did, it is true, identify nationalism clearly as a political principle, as one that holds that the state and the nation should be congruent. He was also very aware of the centrality of the state in the homogenization of culture, in the standardization of language and in mass education. He was aware too that the uneven diffusion of modernization generated inequalities that could stimulate nationalist political movements, driving people to seek states of their own to remedy this. Nevertheless, his underlying assumption was that such a state would have to be national, that the national identity of the modern state is in some profound sense determined by a deeper and altogether more significant process of social and economic modernization. This results in what some critics have suggested is a too abstract approach to nationalism, devoid of much in the way of historical detail (Laitin, 1998; Mouzelis, 1998). What is missing is much of a sense that the actions of political agents in possession of or seeking states of their own can have significant effects on the spread of nationalism, or the reverse.

In this respect, it may be argued that Gellner was more strongly influenced in his thinking about nationalism by the classical social theorists we discussed in Chapter 1 than he was by political ideology (although liberalism was central to some of his other work).[7] He draws clearly on a fundamental distinction between traditional and modern societies, owing much to Durkheim's distinction between mechanical and organic solidarity, and begins his own analysis of industrialism with a discussion of Weber's concept of 'rationalization', whilst also drawing on Tönnies in arguing that 'nationalism is a phenomenon of Gesellschaft using the idiom of Gemeinschaft: a mobile anonymous society simulating a closed cosy community' (Gellner, 1983, p. 74). There is a sense too in which his work may be usefully viewed as an extended response to Marxism, which he believed had made 'two famous mistakes – the expectation of continuing or even increasing misery of the proletariat, and the underestimation of nationalism' (Gellner, 1965, p. 72). In his famous 'wrong-address' analogy, he claimed that the message which Marxists were expecting history to deliver to the working class was actually going 'by some terrible postal error' to nations. The future was with nations not with class; the world would be national, not classless. Perhaps most importantly, Gellner shared what he took be Marx's socio-economic determinism. 'The socio-economic base is decisive. That much is true in Marxism, even if its more specific propositions are false' (Gellner, 1996a, p. 143).

However, although Gellner (like Marx) argued that nationalism is historically contingent and not a universal feature of or necessity for human societies, his destination is very different. Ultimately for Gellner, we can only choose the best type of nationalism; we do not appear to be able to choose to transcend it altogether. In respect of this profound pessimism he was perhaps more faithful to Weber than any other classical social theorist in positing in the nation-state a new 'iron cage' from which humanity cannot escape, even if we may expect the worst excesses of nationalism to be finally tamed.

Marxist influences

Some of the most influential writing on nationalism from within a modernist paradigm has come from writers rather more positively influenced by Marxism than Gellner. The three writers we now consider – Anderson, Nairn and Hobsbawm – have come from a Marxist intellectual background, although their trajectories have been different. Two have clearly moved from a position critical of nationalism to one which is more accommodating to it. Hobsbawm remains more resolutely critical, although he argues that nationalism was historically progressive at some periods and for some nations

Benedict Anderson

Like Gellner, Anderson stresses the way cultural changes are brought about by socio-economic change – in this case capitalism, or rather the combination of capitalism and the revolution in communication which he terms 'print-capitalism'. New ways of imagining abstract communities are made possible and these form the underpinning of the emergence of modern nationalism.

The idea of the nation as an 'imagined community' has formed much of the common sense of the analysis of nationalism over the past two decades. Cited by almost every writer who ventures onto the terrain of nationalism, it has become one of the commonest clichés of the literature, although invocation has, in some cases, been a substitute for analysis. Anderson argues famously that the nation 'is imagined because the members of even the smallest nation will never know most of their fellow members, meet them or even hear of them, yet in the mind of each lives the image of their communion' (1991, p. 6).

Something like this is, of course, as he points out, true of communities other than the nation. 'In fact, all communities larger than primordial villages of face-to-face contact (and perhaps even these) are imagined' (1991, p. 6). Imagination is, however, not the same as fabrication and Anderson criticizes Gellner for failing to see this and for implying that there can be communities which are 'true', not imagined, and which can advantageously be compared to nations. The issue for Anderson is not one of falsity/genuineness but of style. What distinguishes the nation is that 'it is an imagined political community – and imagined as both inherently limited and sovereign' (p. 6).

Anderson argues convincingly for the limited scope for each nation in the imagination, asserting that 'no nation imagines itself as coterminous with mankind' (p. 7). This may not, however, be only due to a limited messianism, as he suggests, but (as we shall argue in Chapter 3) to the necessity for the other in relation to which the particular nation can be identified or identify itself. He also ties the nation in this formulation to modernity, to the emergence of sovereignty in the modern era. This too is compelling, highlighting the connection between nationalism and the nation-state, the desire for which looms so large in the nationalist imagination.

The use of the term 'community', however, may be more problematic, given the way it is often deployed in a variety of contemporary discourses. In contemporary society 'community' may seem an unmitigated good. The invocation of community, however, can indicate a nostalgia for a Tönnies-like *gemeinschaft*, characteristic of a pre-industrial age. The positive feature of this ideal type are well known – a world dominated by face-to-face interactions, where kin and neighbours supply mutual support, where individuals are and feel integrated into society. But cosy community involves exclusion as well as inclusion; communities can be inward-looking, narrow-minded, controlling and keeping under surveillance the intimate lives of its inhabitants; consensual communities may penalize or ostracize dissenters; and outsiders may be despised or never integrated. The invocation of this nostalgic idea can then draw attention away from division and conflict. Class, religion and gender, for instance, have historically been powerful forces of division, which are not easily visible within a conception of *gemeinschaft* as an organic society with a functional fit between its constituent parts.

Anderson, interestingly, suggests that we need to think about the apparently 'natural ties' of nationalist identification in just this context. In terms of its similarity to the unchosen ties of parentage, gender and skin colour, it evokes 'the beauty of *gemeinschaft*' – a notion that seems here somewhat uncritical and romantic (Anderson, 1991, p. 143). A central feature of modernity, after all, has been the replacement of the *gemeinschaft* of community by the contractual and impersonal society of *gesellschaft* (to adopt Tönnies' phrase), itself generating the never-ending (and doomed?) attempt to rebuild or return to precisely what has been lost, to move back from *gesellschaft* to *gemeinschaft*.

The 'community' which is then 'imagined' in this way is perhaps more problematic than Anderson's use of these terms may make it appear. There are unresolved issues too in his account of how these communities were established. Anderson traces the emergence of nationalism back to the collapse of Roman Catholic hegemony in the Reformation, the associated decline of Latin and the emergence of the vernacular, fuelled by the development of 'print-capitalism'. It was now, he argues, that it became possible for people to imagine themselves as members of a 'community' alongside others whom they would or could never hope to meet, yet with whom they imagined themselves to share some fundamental identity. Anderson does then identify clearly a set of agents with a strong interest in spreading these nationalist ideas in printed form in the Americas in the late eighteenth and early nineteenth centuries and in central Europe after 1848: in the former case, primarily creoles; in the latter case, a significant role was played by dynastic regimes seeking to prevent popular revolt.

Although much of this is compelling, particularly his emphasis on the identifiable interests of putative or actual elites, the emphasis on creole functionaries and printmen as pioneers of nationalism is somewhat idiosyncratic. It seems to rest on an argument that they were subject to a near racial form of exclusion by metropolitan elites that generated a powerful *ressentiment* and the establishment of their own nations over which they could preside without challenge. Whilst this argument carries some conviction and can be used to throw light on a whole range of struggles then and since for nation-statehood, it is not exhaustive. Anderson has rather less to say, for instance, about the momentous events which separated these 'creole pioneers' from the development of conservative, 'official nationalism' by aristocratic and dynastic elites. In particular, although he refers to 'largely *spontaneous popular* nationalisms' (1991, p. 110; emphasis added), he nowhere analyses these in detail. The French Revolution, to which he refers, and which is often identified as the *locus classicus* of the democratic nationalist upsurge, is conspicuous by its absence. Yet, we would argue, it is a crucial although problematic point of reference (see Chapter 5).

For there is a difficulty in assuming that there is or has been at some model moment a spontaneous, popular nationalism, from which the essential force of nationalism derives. It is this assumption (at least in part) which makes it possible to assume some of what has to be explained, to treat a number of crucial aspects of nationalism as politically unproblematic, such as how nationalism takes a hold on the popular imagination, and (amongst other things) why people love their country to the point of self-sacrifice (see Chapter 3). Yet even a writer such as Smith, who sees nationalism as having deep roots, recognizes that 'there is, at least in the case of historically well-preserved ethnie, a *choice* of motifs and myths from which different interest groups and classes can fashion their own readings of the communal past to which they belong' (1986, p. 179; emphasis added). Anderson himself seems to recognize the problem when he writes that 'so often in the "nation-building" policies of the new states one sees both a genuine, popular nationalist enthusiasm and a systematic, even Machiavellian, instilling of nationalist ideology through the mass media, the educational system, administrative regulations, and so forth' (1991, p. 113–14). But, we might ask, if the latter (the instilling) is taking place, what reliable evidence can we have of the former (the popular nationalist enthusiasm)?

This problem is only one example of what appears to be a slide in Anderson's account from an initially critical stance to what seems in the end to be a defence of nationalism. As he develops his account of how nationalist imaginings began to proliferate across continents and centuries, the emotional character of his own imagination undergoes an important mutation. By the time we get to his eighth chapter, Anderson is pouring scorn on 'progressive, cosmopolitan intellectuals (particularly in Europe?)' who 'insist on the near-pathological character of nationalism'. Against them he tells us that 'it is useful to remind ourselves that nations inspire love, and often profoundly self-sacrificing love. The cultural products of nationalism . . . show this love very clearly in thousands [sic] of different forms and styles. On the other hand, how truly rare it is to find analogous nationalist products expressing fear and loathing' (1991, pp. 141–2). This seems a somewhat partial statement. The cultural products of extreme or racist forms of nationalism, or on a more mundane level, the banal chauvinism of some tabloid newspapers, would seem to contradict this overly benign assessment.

At the same time, Anderson's stress on self-sacrifice as an element in love of country obscures the fact that this sacrifice may well entail the killing of others in the process. As Balakrishnan (1996) has pointed out, war is largely absent from Anderson's considerations (although he does not note that war was actually Anderson's starting point). Coercion (including that which is threatened or inflicted upon those less willing to sacrifice themselves for the nation), violence, suffering are after all arguably rather more central to war than love, whatever (selected) nationalist cultural artefacts may proclaim.[8]

Notwithstanding these problems, Anderson's work has been enormously influential. It has predisposed a generation of scholars to examine the content and processes of nationalist imaginings. It has strengthened the modernist argument with a somewhat postmodernist appreciation of narrative and text as important ways in which the national story is told and national identity reproduced. At the same time, it has highlighted some of the ways in which core nationalist ideas have been taken up across the world in the modern era, articulated and pursued insistently by identifiable interests (including both imperialists and anti-imperialists) in a variety of contexts, from Latin America to Europe, from Asia to Africa.

Whether Anderson himself, however, can still be seen as a critic of nationalism may be in some doubt. In a recent article on Indonesia, he has called (laudably) for the construction of a more democratic and humane version of the nation by way of a critique of some of the crude nationalism of the past. However, he then goes on to berate the ruling classes in Indonesia for their anti-national attitudes in sending their children to schools and universities overseas. In so doing, he reinforces a view that sees nationalist politics as the only way in which democratic or progressive arguments can be advanced. (We review some of the limitations of this approach in Chapters 4 and 5.)

Tom Nairn

Tom Nairn is another much-cited writer whose earlier more critical stance on nationalism has been replaced by a passionate advocacy of it. Nairn's placing in this context as both a modernist and a neo-Marxist rests on his early work which culminated in the collection of essays published as *The Break-Up of Britain* (1977). His more recent work represents a marked shift from the positions outlined earlier, and still widely cited, and from modernism and neo-Marxism to toying with the need to explore genetics and other biological relationships in understanding nationalism. Alongside this he now seems to advocate a stronger version of nationalism (Nairn, 1997b).[9]

In his earlier work, Nairn stood clearly within a modernist framework, drawing critically on Marxist ideas to situate nationalism as in large part a response to the uneven development of a capitalist world system which reproduced core and periphery at a global level. The 'real origins' of nationalism were to be 'located not in the folk, nor in the individual's repressed passion for some sort of wholeness or identity, but in the machinery of world political economy' (Nairn, 1977, p. 335). In his famous discussion of the Janus-faced nature of nationalism[10] looking both backward into an archaic (and possibly fictitious) past and forward to a modern future, Nairn seemed to suggest that nationalism necessarily carried with it negative features alongside positive ones in mobilizing 'the people' against oppression by core metropolitan states.

> Real, uneven development has invariably generated an imperialism of the centre over the periphery; one after another, these peripheric areas have been forced into a profoundly ambivalent reaction against this dominance, seeking at once to resist it and to take over its vital forces for their own use. This could only be done by a kind of highly 'idealist' political and ideological mobilization, by a painful forced march based on their own resources: that is, employing their 'nationality as a basis. . . . This meant the conscious formation of a militant, inter-class community rendered strongly (if mythically) aware of its own separate identity vis-à-vis the outside forces of domination. (1977, pp. 340–1)

Despite his view that the analysis of nationalism represented Marxism's greatest failure, Nairn's background in Marxism gave him a complex and critical view even when he began developing sympathy with Scottish nationalism. Based on his earlier work (the Nairn–Anderson thesis), hotly debated amongst the New Left in the 1960s and 1970s, Nairn stressed the archaic and unmodernized nature of the British state, which was holding up progress in its constituent parts. It was in this context that he saw Scottish nationalism (although he remained resolutely opposed to the Scottish National Party itself) as a force that could be harnessed by socialists to break up the British state and drive forward socialist and progressive politics.

In his later work Nairn has adopted a sharper, and perhaps more simplistic position. He fulminates against internationalism, in a polemical linguistic style oddly and ironically reminiscent of the Third International Marxism which he so disdains, as the ideology of 'metropolitan or Atlantic left cliques', deluded Marxists and cosmopolitan intellectuals of one sort or another (1996, p. 272); he espouses the cause of small state nationalism (albeit on the whole along civic lines) as the progressive and democratic future for a world where socialism has become impossible. Opposing nationalism, he believes, involves implicitly supporting empires old or new and this is a position he attributes to 'the metropolitan left'. Opposition to new nationalist movements in the Soviet Union or Eastern Europe, he suggests, ignores that they are likely to be an improvement on the multi-national states that they replace, or that nationalism has provided a better history for humankind than the possibility of a 'globalized South Africa' (pre-apartheid). Nationalism is now less of a Janus, but it can have some faults. 'That political and economic nationalism is, very generally, a good thing does not mean that there are no blots, excrescences or failures on the increasingly nationalised map of the world' (1997b, p. 63). Nairn's partial accommodation to nationalism in the 1970s had thus become full espousal by the 1990s (especially as regards what one sympathetic critic refers to as a 'curiously sentimental' Scottish nationalism–Marr, 2000, p. 9) and he has done his best to consign opponents of nationalism to the dustbin of history.

Eric Hobsbawm

Whereas Nairn tends to understate the connection between nationalism and violence, the Marxist historian Eric Hobsbawm is all too aware of the scale and intensity of such violence, particularly in what he calls the 'century of extremes'. Unlike Anderson, Hobsbawm maintains a rigorously critical perspective, insisting that no true historian can be a politically committed nationalist (although historians were often among the pioneers of nationalism in the nineteenth century). His reasoning here is derived from a famous quotation from the French writer Ernest Renan, who wrote, 'forgetting, and I would say, historical error are an essential factor in the creation of a nation' (1996, p. 50). Hobsbawm's commitment to a robustly modernist perspective makes him the main object of Hastings' critique. However, this perspective derives, in part, from the clear perspective on what defines nationalism and distinguishes it from 'other and less demanding forms of national or group identification' (Hobsbawm, 1992, p. 9). He quotes Gellner's definition of nationalism as 'primarily a principle which holds that the political and national unit should be congruent' (Gellner, 1983, p. 1). In addition, he takes as strong a view on the commitment involved in nationalism as does Gellner, viewing it as providing obligations and priorities that override all others (Gellner, 1983, p. 1). Neither Hastings nor Reynolds makes this sort of claim for national identification or its equivalent in medieval Europe.

Hobsbawm argues that the nation is a wholly modern phenomenon, which 'belongs exclusively to a particular, and historically recent period' (1992, p. 9). Within this relatively narrow time-frame, nationalism has interacted with other movements and dynamics. Thus state-building, democratization, language construction, scientific racism, socialism *inter alia* have all left their mark on the twists and turns of nationalism. In the process, nationalism has changed its character as a political movement, being notably transformed in the last quarter of the nineteenth century when it acquired a strong ethnic focus. This emphasis on the historical processes involved in the construction of nationalist movements is a salutary corrective to both the universalistic arguments of the primordialists and the somewhat ahistorical and over-schematic work of a functionalist modernization theorist like Gellner. One of the further strengths of his analysis is that, sensitive to issues of class and literacy, he does not attempt to deduce the feelings of peoples from the evidence of the literate or writing minority.

Pointing out how so many of the traditions dear to nationalists are inventions (Hobsbawm and Ranger, 1983), and to the destructive effects of ethnic nationalism once unleashed, Hobsbawm, going back to some extent to Marx, tries to suggest that it may now be on the wane, that it has exhausted its progressive potential. Basing his arguments on the increasingly internationalized nature of economic and political relationships, the existence of alternative forms of identity, the distinction between *nations* and *states*, and the non-viability of small nation-states, Hobsbawm argues that 'in spite of its evident prominence, nationalism is historically less important' (1992: p. 191).[11] It is this assessment which makes him the target of so many supporters of nationalism from very different perspectives, such as Nairn and Hastings.

From the other angle, however, there are some ambiguities in parts of his argument which may be rooted in or reflect the tensions in classical Marxism that we discussed in Chapter 1. Unlike some, Hobsbawm is not afraid to draw attention to the extent of what he calls 'conscious and deliberate ideological engineering' by governments in the late nineteenth century, nor does he concede that this amounts to simple manipulation from above, noting how chauvinist and jingoist ideas were already present, particularly among the middle and lower middle classes (Hobsbawm, 1992: pp. 82–3). He is also sceptical about the extent or conviction of mass support for nationalist ideas in a number of cases. On the other hand, at an earlier period, he is perhaps too ready to accept the equation of nation, state and people that was promoted at the time of the French Revolution, and the subsequent assumption by many liberals that nationalism was linked to progress both politically and economically. Working within a Marxist framework, he implies that nationalism was at one stage a unifying force as a limited number of nation-states emerged which were economically viable, large-scale units. 'Classic nineteenth century liberal nationalism was the opposite of the current search for a definition of group identity by separatism. It aimed to extend the scale of human social, political and cultural units: to unify and expand rather than to restrict and separate' (Hobsbawm, 1996, p. 257). The form of this nationalism was initially articulated in the French Revolution, 'a revolutionary concept of the nation as constituted by the deliberate political option of its potential citizens' (p. 88). Yet he also notes that this idea was in crucial respects not nationalist at all, but state-based, relating not to any self-evident notion of the nation but to the idea of the sovereign people. Like many other writers, Hobsbawm holds to a distinction between two forms of nationalism, one inclusionary and progressive, the other exclusionary and divisive (we discuss this further in Chapter 4). Thus he writes,

> It is important to distinguish between the exclusive nationalism of states or right-wing political movements which substitutes itself for all other forms of political and social identification, and the conglomerate national/citizen, social consciousness which, in modern states, forms the soil in which all other political sentiments grow. In this sense 'nation' and 'class' were not readily separable. If we accept that class consciousness in practice had a civic-national dimension, and civic-national or ethnic consciousness had social dimensions, then it is likely that the radicalization of the working classes in the first post-war Europe may have reinforced their potential national consciousness. (1992, p. 145)

Hobsbawm's primary point of reference here is to the anti-fascist move-ments of the 1930s and 1940s in Europe, which presented themselves as the contemporary expression of the legacy of 1789 (and of 1848, and 1871). It is significant, however, that Hobsbawm himself stresses the internationalist aspect of anti-fascism here far more than its nationalism. Again, in his brief discussion of national liberation, his focus is much less on the national than on the international (conceived here in terms of a generalized anti-imperialism). What may be obscured in both cases are the longer-term consequences of yoking democratic, or even socialist, programmes to nationalist ones. As we suggest in Chapter 5, the critical link between nationalist and democratic movements, or later between nationalist and socialist movements, may need more critical scrutiny than Hobsbawm is sometimes able to give it. The logic of each may be different, and point in different directions.

This might help to make more sense of (and perhaps bolster) Hobsbawm's own conclusion that nationalism is no longer a progressive force, linking his arguments about its now divisive character to criticism of arguments (voiced equally by Woodrow Wilson and Lenin) for the right of national self-determination (Hobsbawm, 1996). If the desire to exercise this right through possession of a state for the putative nation is driven now, as he argues, by competitive considerations of fear, resentment and insecurity, this may have been implicit in nationalist politics from the outset.

Modernism and politics: Mann; Giddens; Breuilly; Brass

An explicit concern with politics has been the focus of much recent work on nationalism from within the modernist camp. Among the key contributors here have been Michael Mann, Anthony Giddens, John Breuilly and Paul Brass. Although they focus on different aspects of the political, they all emphasize the importance of the state.

For Mann and Giddens indeed, the emergence of the nation-state is a critical feature of modernity. According to Mann (1996), a qualitatively new political form emerged in Europe in the sixteenth, seventeenth and eighteenth centuries, a state whose size and relevance had expanded massively in relation to society. Its finances had swelled in order to support both an expanded and professionalized administration and (especially) standing armies and navies. These were required because states were engaged in fierce external competition with each other, a struggle for survival from which only a few could emerge victorious. As these conflicts proceeded and intensified in scope, states were driven to involve themselves in developing capitalist economies in order to draw advantages from the financial and technological resources they generated. At the same time, it was vital for these states to succeed in a prolonged process of internal pacification, in order that they could not only claim but also possess a monopoly over the means of violence within their secured territories. In Giddens' formulation, what then emerged was the 'bordered power-container' that we know as the modern nation-state, which 'exists in a complex of other nation-states, is a set of institutional forms of governance maintaining an administrative monopoly over a territory with demarcated boundaries (borders), its rule being sanctioned by law and direct control of the means of internal and external violence' (Giddens, 1985, p. 121)

There is much that is both significant and salutary in this analysis. It reminds us that competition, conflict and violence have been central to the emergence of nation-states from the outset, as they have to the issue of how and where to draw borders and boundaries between one nation-state and another. What is less clear is quite why these modern states have had to be national, or more precisely perceived as national. For the equation of state and nation here is more problematic than it may first appear. As Tilly (1994) has pointed out, at least two of the first such states (Britain and France) cannot easily be seen as nations if a homogeneous culture is used as the criterion. That these and other states come to be seen as nation-states, has a great deal to do with a view of the world as divided up now or always into nations, each of whom has or ought to have a state of its own, and thus with central elements of the ideology of nationalism.

Whilst this is not the primary focus of either Giddens or Mann, they do offer some pointers to how we might think about the link between nationalism and the nation-state. Giddens begins by saying that nationalism is a primarily psychological phenomenon, but then points out that any postulated need for identity is too vague and cannot explain the connection with states. Defining nationalism then as 'the cultural sensibility of sovereignty, the concomitant of the co-ordination of administrative power within the bounded nation-state' (1985, p. 219), he also recognizes that there is no intrinsic link between nationalism and the doctrines of sovereignty (such as that put forward by Bodin) which were taken up by the emerging nation-states. Why then did nationalism develop? According to Mann, this had to do with the pressing need of states to communicate with the subjects now located within their secured borders. Drawing to some extent on Anderson's notion of the nation as an imagined community in time and space, he argues that 'nationalism is an elaborated ideology shared by many people right across a territory' but points out that 'if ideologies are to spread, they must be organized through specific channels of communication' (Mann, 1996, pp. 150–1). His own account of how different forms of nationalism then developed is structured around the different channels of communication that emerged in different states; Britain is taken as one model, Austria and Prussia as another, and France as a mix of these two.

Communication, however, was not for its own sake but for particular purposes. In a context of violent inter-state conflict, a major priority for states was the mobilization of men for war. Giddens notes, following Barrow, that the origins of early nationalist feeling (so important to anti-modernist writers like Hastings) lie in the state's mobilization of different classes and strata to fight against a common enemy (although he does not explain how or why the enemy came to be seen as common). The greater the numbers the state could mobilize, the more successful it was likely to be. This was a major issue at the time of the French Revolution, as the French state succeeded in mobilizing unprecedented numbers in its war against its neighbours. This was a lesson not lost in its adversaries, who sought in the nineteenth century to emulate this example (see Chapter 5). The ideology which could so mobilize was nationalism, enabling the state to invoke a common identity for its subjects in opposition to an other, seen as intrinsically hostile and dangerous. But this invocation came both at a price and with certain conditions. As David Held puts it,

> the more costly and demanding the war became, the more rulers had to bargain with and win the support of their subjects . . . the more people were drawn into preparations for war and war-making, the more they became aware of their membership in a political community and of the rights and obligations such membership might confer. (1995, p. 57)

However, whilst nationalism may well have fulfilled a crucial legitimating function for the emerging modern state, drawing some masses into a compact with some elites, others were necessarily and inherently excluded from this arrangement and its advantages. What Held (like Giddens and Mann) says rather less about is that these rights and obligations were from the outset and of necessity to be denied to others, to those now identified as dangerous and threatening to the nation-state (see Chapters 4 and 5).

This nation-state was, however, now the object of intense and mounting political competition, as heterogeneous elites struggled to gain control over its expanded and expanding powers. For John Breuilly, it is this struggle for and over the state which explains why nationalism is essentially a modern political phenomenon. In his view, nationalism is 'associated with the development of specifically modern kinds of political action; and that these kinds of political action are closely connected to the development of a new kind of state' (Breuilly, 1994, p. 134). Against Smith, he insists that national identity is essentially modern, because premodern ethnic identity lacks any widespread institutional embeddedness or structures (Breuilly, 1996). Like Gellner, he is not particularly interested in nationalist ideas which, as he notes, are after all only interesting insofar as they have political effects and consequences. 'Few would study the work of intellectuals who elaborate nationalist doctrines and supporting myths if these had not been used in a politically significant way' (1996, p. 148). The strategic purposes for which they may be used can vary, and Breuilly distinguishes usefully between movements that aim to gain control of existing states (reform nationalism); movements that aim to expand the state (unification nationalism); and movements that aim to split the state (separatist nationalism). If they are to succeed, such movements require the adoption of a set of inter-related tactics which have to do with what he calls the functions of co-ordination, mobilization and legitimation.

> Co-ordination is the part ideology plays in bringing a set of diverse political interests into a single movement by providing them with a unity of values and purposes. Mobilization is the part ideology plays in bringing new groups into the political process and providing them with political objectives and justifications. Legitimation is the part ideology plays in presenting an acceptable image of a political movement to outsiders. (1992, p. 93)

This emphasis on how nationalists operate is a useful corrective to the somewhat over-general approach of other modernists, even of those who emphasize the primacy of the political. However, although Breuilly is right to point to the effectiveness of such tactics, his emphasis on its rationality rather than irrationality may lead him, at least implicitly, to downplay to some extent some of nationalism's more problematic or negative effects, notably in relation to democracy, to rights, participation and citizenship (we discuss these issues in Chapter 5). Breuilly is concerned to distinguish his account from writers such as Kedourie (see below) on the grounds that they have too crude an approach to ideology, assuming that manipulation by leaders is a key factor in accounting for nationalism (Breuilly, 1996).

If manipulation is too simplistic a way to describe elite behaviour in this context, it is nevertheless important, as Paul Brass in particular has argued, to pay close attention to how nationalist elites do actually operate and to the interests which they seek to protect and enhance. Following and perhaps going even further than Breuilly, Brass sees both nationalism and ethnicity as 'modern phenomena inseparably connected with the activities of the modern centralizing state' (1991, p. 8). Against the primordialists, he insists that

> ethnicity and nationalism are not 'givens' but are social and political construc-
> tions. They are creations of elites, who draw upon, distort, and sometimes
> fabricate materials from the cultures of groups they wish to represent in order
> to protect their well being or existence or to gain political and economic
> advantage for their groups as well as themselves. (1991, p. 8)

Drawing on examples from both India and the former Soviet Union, Brass shows that such elite activity always involves choices, of what differences to highlight and what similarities to downplay, and that benefits always accrue to some rather than others as a consequence. Elite activity is critical, he argues, because without it injustices might be accepted, or assimilation may occur. If elite activity of this kind involves choices, then the future may be more open than many theorists of nationalism have been prepared to contemplate. Nationalism may be something less than an inescapable fate or destiny, deeply rooted in the past, or the unavoidable product of a sweeping process of economic or political modernization. Rather, as Brass suggests, 'the process of ethnic identity formation and its transformation into nation-alism is reversible' (p. 16). This is because changing political and economic circumstances and the 'dynamics of external competition and internal divi-sions and contradictions' may lead elites to ally themselves with different groups or state authorities and to discard their current 'symbolic manipulation of cultural forms, values and practices' (p. 16).

None of this is to suggest that elites have a completely free hand, as Brass acknowledges:

> Political and economic elites who make use of ethnic group attributes are
> constrained by the beliefs and values which exist within the group and
> which limit the kinds of appeals which can be made. At the same time,
> the process by which elites mobilise ethnic identities simplifies those beliefs
> and values, distorts them, and selects those which are politically useful
> rather than central to the belief systems of the people in question. (1991,
> p. 16)

Modernism and nationalist ideology: Elie Kedourie

Simplification and distortion were in many ways the central objects of Elie Kedourie's lively and still relevant critique of nationalism, originally penned some four decades ago. His stance is distinct from that of almost all the other writers we have discussed in this chapter. He was entirely clear, from what we might call a minority conservative position, about the negative aspects of nationalism. He emphasized the constructed character of national identity, arguing that 'it is very often truer to say that national identity is the creation of a nationalist doctrine than that nationalist doctrine is the emanation or expression of national identity' (Kedourie, 1993, p. 141). He drew attention in particular to the grievances that fuel it and its tendency to assert that loyalty to the nation is of supreme and over-riding importance, and the common features that are exhibited by seemingly different kinds of nationalism. Kedourie's sharp and cogent critique is in many ways hard to answer, and it is interesting to see how his critics tend to sidestep his arguments, as Chatterjee (1986) has noted. Smith's response to Kedourie is particularly instructive and symptomatic, suggesting that the very severity of his critique 'makes one wonder why it has succeeded to the extent that it has' but then implying that the more critical the stance one adopts, the less one can explain (Smith, 1983, p. 12). At the same time, Kedourie's stress on nationalism as a doctrine largely confines his argument to the level of the history of ideas, paying less attention to the political effects of nationalism, perhaps because his own opposition to it is grounded in a more general antipathy to ideological (as opposed to constitutional) politics of all forms. In this respect, it is something of a throwback to an earlier, pre-nationalist conservatism.

Postmodernism and nationalism

Nationalism would not, by and large, be a charge one could level against postmodernist theorists, who seek rather to go beyond the limitations of modernism. Postmodernists see the nation-state as a central feature of modernity but focus more critically on the nationalist discourses which have accompanied and underpinned its emergence. At the heart of these discourses is, as Bhabha puts it, the 'attempt . . . to produce the idea of the nation as a continuous narrative national progress' (1990, p. 3). Drawing on Bhabha's work, Hall has identified a variety of discursive strategies which are central to the nationalist project. There is, to begin with, the story of the nation as told in history books, works of fiction, symbols, rituals, and other elements of popular culture. Through these accounts of national triumphs and disasters, individuals are helped or invited to feel themselves connected with the past and future of a national destiny. Secondly, he suggests, there is an emphasis on 'origins, continuity, tradition, timelessness' (Hall, 1992a, p. 294) so that the character of the nation may be seen as unchanged and unchanging through all its long past history. Thirdly, there is commonly an invention of tradition in an attempt to establish a historical continuity for the nation, its symbols and rituals. Fourthly, there is the existence of a foundational myth – a story which locates the origins of the nation so long ago that it is lost in the mists of time. Finally, there is the frequent attempt to ground national identity on the idea of an ethnically pure original people or 'folk'.

Powerful and effective as these strategies have been, they are, as Bhabha (inspired to some extent by Anderson here) suggests, riddled with tension and haunted by ambivalence. There are crucial recesses that nationalist discourse obscures, elements that it has to repress in its effort to construct the *'impossible* unity of the nation as a symbolic force' (1990, p. 3; emphasis added). Bhabha's concern in particular is with those on the margins, as the nation seeks to define itself in relation to what is outside or beyond its boundaries. The problem is that these boundaries can never be secure.

> The boundary is Janus-faced and the problem of outside/inside must always itself be a process of hybridity, incorporating new 'people' in relation to the body politic, generating other sites of meaning and, inevitably, in the political process, producing unmanned sites of political antagonism and unpredictable forces for political representation. (1990, p. 4)

Counter-narratives can and will then emerge from the margins to unsettle and contest both the narrative of the nation and its boundaries. It is in these counter-narratives that Bhabha and others see openings for alternative meanings and different directions to historical change, the possibility of moving beyond the framework of the nation-state. Some see this as inevitable, pointing with some justification to the nation-state's loss of control – over information, over sovereignty, over cultural certainty – in the transition from a modern to a postmodern world (Gibbins and Reimer, 1999, pp.120–3). (We discuss these issues in Chapter 6.)

Others are less sanguine but insistent on the need to break with the repressive logic of nationalism. Partha Chatterjee (1986), for instance, uses postmodernist themes to elaborate a postcolonial analysis of the trajectory of Indian nationalism where nationalist discourse was imported, taken over from the colonial rulers by the leaders of the struggle for national liberation in pursuit of an independent state over which they could rule in the name of the (discursively constructed) nation. The 'subaltern school', of which Chatterjee is a leading exponent, deconstructs nationalism here as a 'discourse of order' which suppresses the diversity of cultures in favour of rationalization and bureaucratization.

A more general critique of the way in which nationalist discourse fits into what he calls 'the State's ordering zeal' can be found in the work of Zygmunt Bauman, who may be better seen as a writer on postmodernity than a postmodernist. His focus is on the threat posed to the nation not only by its enemies (other nations) in whom it can at least recognize similarity, and on whose antagonism it arguably depends, in an inter-national world. More unsettling than these are the strangers, those who cannot be fitted into this dyadic structure, who 'by definition represent an anomaly to be rectified' (Bauman, 1997, p. 19). Strangers are those who cannot be located, ordered and controlled, who 'befog and eclipse boundary lines' (p. 25). Neither here nor there, neither friend nor enemy, they cannot be fitted into the constructed category of the nation, cannot be integrated into a pre-given, homogenizing set of ordering assumptions about who and what the nation is, has always been and must forever be. As the nation-state expands its domain, as it extends its sovereignty, it demands and commands the allegiance and loyalty of its subjects, insisting on their identification with each other and their rulers as part of one nation. The nation-state ('the idea of a nation made into the state's flesh', according to Bauman) is driven by the desire to 'superimpose one kind of allegiance over the mosaic of communitarian "particularisms" in the name of the nation's interests which overrides and puts in abeyance all other interests' (1997, p. 190). Borrowing Levi-Strauss' terminology, Bauman argues that those who resisted had to be either assimilated (the *anthropophagic* or devouring solution) or banished (the *anthropoemic* or vomiting strategy). The force of such compelling and salutary arguments, informed by a strong ethical impulse to treat others as one would oneself, is that they enable us to think more lucidly about the exclusionary logic of nationalism. They can help us in particular and more concretely to have some insight into how nation-states (even supposedly civic ones) treat migrants, refugees, asylum seekers, those who need to move across borders and boundaries (see Chapter 4).

Feminism

Although there is no necessary connection between feminist perspectives and postmodernism, both have, in practice, paid particular attention to the content of nationalist discourses. However, whilst there is a growing feminist literature on gender and nationalism (Jayawardena, 1986; Walby, 1996; West, 1997; Yuval-Davis, 1997), it is still the case that this is often a neglected area in contemporary studies, not fully integrated into the mainstream of political or sociological writing on the subject. In part this may be because there has come to be no uniform feminist view, just as there has been no unanimity over time among Marxists or liberals or conservatives, as we saw in Chapter 1.

Such differences as have emerged are nevertheless grounded in a generally shared perception that all forms of nationalism have, until recently at any rate, been gendered. This fundamental and in many ways determining feature has, it has been argued, been almost entirely missing from the theories of nationalism that we have discussed so far. Yet invocations and constructions of national identity have had major implications for women, and helped shape the nationalist project in a variety of ways. Following Anthias and Yuval-Davis (1992), we can identify the role allocated to or taken by women as, variously, biological reproducers of the nation; participants in the ideological reproduction of the nation and transmitters of its culture; signifiers of national difference and symbols of the nation; reproducers of boundaries between national groups; and participants in the nationalist struggle itself.

To begin with, we must note how nationalists have always been greatly concerned with the physical future (as well as past) of the nation, and how women as childbearers have been assigned a central role in assuring its continuity. The concern with breeding the nation's necessary subjects can manifest itself in a variety of ways, as a concern with *size* of population, whether a desire to increase the power of the nation through increasing population, as in fascist Italy, or a Malthusian worry about too great a population, as in China, or as a eugenic concern about the *quality* of the population, associated with policies of selective breeding, as in Nazi Germany (Yuval-Davis, 1997). The association of women with children also of course forms a major plank in nationalist mobilization in times of war, when men are expected to be willing to sacrifice themselves whilst women are expected to be willing to sacrifice their male loved ones (Elshtain, 1993).[12]

As well as childbearers for the nation, women play a key role as primary socializers of the nation's youth, passing on national values and culture. In Afrikaaner nationalism, for instance, as McClintock has argued, 'white men were seen to embody the political agency of the volk, while women were the (unpaid) keepers of tradition and the volk's moral and spiritual mission' (1996, p. 276). This stress on women's role in a spiritual domain may also be seen to be characteristic of the Indian nationalism discussed by Chatterjee (1986). Here, male nationalists responded to colonial criticism of some traditional practices (such as the immolation of widows) by insisting on the vital importance for the Indian nation of women remaining in or returning to the home as a spiritual, non-materialist site. A similar insistence on the supposed sanctity of the home, and the need for women to remain in or return to the private sphere, has been a central feature of the nationalism that surged up in Central and Eastern Europe in the aftermath of the collapse of communism. As Rener and Ule (1998) have suggested, this may best be understood within a modernist frame of reference, cured of its gender-blindness. As the nation-states of this region seek to modernize, they have gone 'back to the future', simultaneously constructing the image of the (modern) national community and re-delegating the private sphere to women as mothers and wives.

This crucial, if distinctive role, in the national mission may be linked to the role assigned to women in demarcating boundaries between nations.

As Yuval-Davis has argued, 'women in their "proper" behaviour, their "proper" clothing, embody the line which signifies the collectivity's boundaries' (1997, p. 46). This may help to explain why women's behaviour becomes the object of ferocious nationalist judgment at times, why intermarriage or sexual relations with outsiders attracts so much more punishment for women than men. One example would be the shaven heads or tarring and feathering of those who 'slept with the enemy' in wartime France. It is notable, however, how this intersection of power, sexuality and nationalism has become even sharper in the wake of the wholesale use of rape as an arm of ethnic cleansing and nationalist policy in the Bosnian war (Hague, 1997; Jones, 1994; Sofos, 1996).

At a more abstract level, women are frequently required to bear the burden of symbolic representation of the nation. Although much nationalist rhetoric is largely framed with a very masculine appeal (to the fraternity of the nation), the nation is often itself depicted as female – the motherland as much as if not rather more than the fatherland. The figure of Britannia, for instance, stands as a symbol of Britain whilst Marianne is often used similarly for France.

Alternatively, the nation may be constructed as masculine in opposition to a feminized other. Ronit Lentin (2000) has argued persuasively that this was the case with Israel, where Zionists re-imagined the national collectivity in opposition to a despised Jewish diaspora unable to resist the endemic anti-semitism which had culminated in the Shoah. Where the builders of the new Israel saw themselves as heroic, male and active, the survivors of the Shoah were stigmatized as feminine, cowardly, weak and passive.[13]

If feminism is thus indispensable to the development of a critical understanding of nationalism, however, not all feminists wish to go in that direction. There is undoubtedly a consensus that, until now, one of the core nationalist claims, that all are equal within the nation-state, is highly problematic to say the least. As Anne McClintock (1993) has pointed out, 'no nation in the world gives women and men the same access to the rights and resources of the nation-state' (p. 61). The question that then arises, however, is what can be done about it. It is here that we may discern some differences amongst feminists which may be seen to parallel the disagreement that occurred earlier amongst Marxists (see Chapter 1). For some feminists, the (growing) participation of women in nationalist movements, particularly in struggles for national liberation, points the way forward to a more egalitarian nationalist future, and a new kind of nationalism (West, 1997). Others have argued that it is possible, using a feminist perspective, to distinguish between a good form of 'women-emancipation' nationalism and a bad patriarchal model (Moghadam, cited in Wilford and Miller, 1998, p. 6). (We discuss efforts to distinguish between good and bad forms in Chapter 4 and the outcomes of nation liberation struggles for the emancipation of women in Chapter 5). Other feminists are more pessimistic and critical, arguing, as Kaplan for instance does (with particular reference to the European context), that 'feminism and nationalism are almost always incompatible ideological positions' (1997, p. 3). It is true that she does manage with some considerable effort to find two exceptions to this (in the case of nineteenth-century Italy and twentieth-century Finland) but the thrust of her overall argument is to suggest that feminism is much more likely to flourish as nationalism withers (a theme we take up ourselves briefly in Chapter 7).

In support of this hypothesis, it may even be argued that women are or ought to be in some way less susceptible to the appeals of nationalism, if not more open to internationalism.[14] For example, it could be argued, following one line of feminist thought, that women are (naturally) more caring or nurturing than men, more inclined to pacifism than war. The peace movements of the 1980s (such as the women's peace camp at Greenham Common) can then be taken as an example of women showing a greater degree of internationalism than men. On the other hand, it is not difficult to point to instances of rather different behaviour. During the First World War in Britain, for instance, women (prominent amongst them being the suffragette leader Christabel Pankhurst) handed out white feathers, symbols of cowardice, to men of military age not in uniform. More recently, in the Bosnian war, it was not unusual to see the women of a village blocking the main road to prevent UN relief supplies from reaching 'the enemy'.

A critical analysis of the interplay of gender and nationalism does not then in the end yield an unambiguous meaning but has rather generated a host of varied responses in both theory and practice. Just as there have been those in the Marxist camp who have asserted the primacy and potential universality of class loyalties over national ones, so too there have been feminists who have asserted the primacy and potential universality of sisterhood. But, just as there are many on the left who have criticized the supposed Eurocentrism of the former approach, so too there have been many feminists who have challenged what they see as the ethnocentrism or otherwise of Western feminism. All of this of course raises a question of real importance in thinking about nationalism today, to do with the very possibility of establishing universalistic political values that might question nationalism and the primacy of national identity. We return to these issues in Chapter 7.

CONCLUSION

Breuilly introduces a useful distinction between what he calls nationalism as doctrine (political ideology or philosophy), nationalism as sentiments (or consciousness – common-sense ideas and feelings), and nationalism as politics (in the sense of political movements) (Breuilly, 1996). In terms of meanings one and three, nationalism is clearly a modern phenomenon, not an inherent element in the human psyche or human social organization. It is a product of relatively recent history, a modern invention or construct. Only in terms of 'sentiments', of some sort of attachment to or identification with the nation, can there be much of a serious case for the neo-primordialist or perennialist case (as Hastings' and Reynolds' work has sought to demonstrate). The modernist analysis of the nation and nationalism appears to promise a more robust and critical view of nationalism than that offered by variants of primordialism, and to open up the possibility of transcending nationalism and overcoming the limitations of the nation-state. However, very few of the modernist writers in fact go down this road. Once set loose in the world, nationalism, it seems, is here to stay. Our only choice is over what concept of the nation and what form of nationalism we will have. We argue in this book that this is not the case. For, even were it established that the medieval forms of national identity were clear forerunners of modern nationalism (a possibility in terms of nationalism as 'sentiments'), this would not entail an acceptance of the inevitability of nationalism for all time. Rather, if we understand the complex processes by which nationalism, the nation-state and modernity came to be entwined, we can envisage a future where more universalistic loyalties could replace national identifications (see Chapter 7). Before embarking on any consideration of such issues, we first of all need to pursue further the implications of the modernist (and postmodernist) accounts. In the next chapter we proceed with a more detailed examination of the cultural and political underpinnings of national identity itself and of its relationship to modern nationalism.

FURTHER READING

A very detailed overview of the various positions in the debate over the modernity or otherwise of nations from one of the protagonists, but fair in its accounts of different theorists, comes from Smith (1998). Key works in this debate include Smith (1986) and (1991), Hastings (1997), Greenfeld's lengthy (1992) study, and the classic 'modernist' works of Hobsbawm (1992), Anderson (1991), Nairn (1977) and Gellner (1983). A more recent statement of Gellner's position can be found in Gellner (1996a), in the useful general collection *Mapping the Nation* edited by Balakrishnan (1996), which also includes articles by *inter alia* Nairn, Breuilly and Mann. Gellner's work is the subject of an illuminating critical collection edited by Hall (1998). Kedourie's trenchant critique of nationalism (1993) is still worth reading. One of the best accounts of feminist approaches to nationalism can be found in Yuval-Davis (1997). Postmodernism has influenced specific studies of nationalism; well-known examples are provided by Chatterjee (1986) and Bhabha (1990). Bauman's thinking from his more general analysis of postmodernism have influenced our arguments a great deal. See Bauman (1997), especially the essay 'The Making and Unmaking of Strangers'.

NOTES

1   For the intellectual roots of this argument see Shils (1957) and Geertz (1973), but note that recent attempts have been made to suggest that Geertz's arguments are more complex than critics such as Eller and Coughlan (1993) have suggested. See Cornell (1996).

2   Tudjman's career combined this 'academic' study of nationalism with that of Titoist partisan and general, followed by becoming nationalist leader of the new Croatian republic.

3   For an alternative view see Spencer and Wollman (1999).

4   Hastings accepts Linda Colley's (1992) account of the development of a British identity but argues that she has ignored the core English dimension.

5   We discuss the distinction between 'Eastern' and 'Western' forms of nationalism in Chapter 4.

6   Gellner distinguished between the accusations of teleology and functionalism, rejecting the former but accepting and vigorously defending and embracing the latter (Hall 1998; Mouzelis 1998). However, Brendan O'Leary, in a spirited defence of much of Gellner's argument, attempts a non-functionalist reworking of Gellner's theory which suggests that some nationalists consciously adopted nationalism as a movement which would further the modernization of their societies (O'Leary, 1996).

7   See, for instance, his indictment of Marxism in *Conditions of Liberty* (Gellner 1994).

8   See Jones (1994) for examples of coercion from the recent wars in the former Yugoslavia, or the punishment by firing squad for cowardice of sufferers from shell shock in the First World War *'pour encourager les autres'*.

9   For more detailed critical discussions of Nairn's ideas and trajectory see Cocks (1997) and Davidson (1999).

10 Although Seton Watson seems to have been the first to employ this notion.

11 Hobsbawm does not use the term 'globalization', favoured by many post-modernists, but his arguments traverse a similar terrain (see Chapter 6).

12 While men are then seen to be fighting for the women and children of the nation, of course, women may paradoxically no longer be confined to traditional roles, although this rarely lasts beyond the timespan of the national crisis. Ideals of femininity have often had to change during times of war in order for the national interest to be more effectively pursued. In the United States, for instance, during World War Two, Rosie the Riveter became a heroic symbolic figure on the home front.

13 Lentin's feminist critique reworks insights from otherwise gender-blind contemporary theories. Her reference here is directly to Anderson's concept of the national imagination, whilst she also draws both on Bauman's critique of nationalism in the postmodern world and on postcolonial theory (pp. 182–93).

14 As Virginia Woolf put it long ago, 'as a woman I have no country. As a woman I want no country. As a woman, my country is the whole world' (1977, p. 125). There are some striking parallels between this statement and the opposition to nationalism expressed by Rosa Luxemburg.

3

Nationalism, Culture and the Politics of the Imagined

INTRODUCTION

A central issue for theories of nationalism is the question of national identity, the extent to which people may be seen or see themselves as members of a given nation. In this chapter, we discuss some of the conceptual and empirical problems associated with the construction of a national identity. In particular, we argue that the positing of a national identity involves drawing and invoking particular kinds of distinctions, contrasts between a putative 'us' and 'them', which can raise as many problems as they solve. Such distinctions can easily be hardened, fixed into value-laden absolutes of various kinds, and lead to or require the construction of boundaries and barriers, both material and symbolic, whose intent or effect is to exclude a negatively defined 'other'. This is not an automatic, spontaneous or organic process which happens, as it were, by itself. Rather it involves the deployment of powerful agencies, messages and symbols for particular purposes and may involve conflict and contestation between existing and potential nations, between competing nationalists, and between nationalists and others.

Identity

Identity is a term that has been used with growing frequency in a variety of contexts by social scientists, cultural theorists and others over the past thirty years. Originally a term applying to individuals, there has been an increasing application of identity to groups and collectivities. Today, it has become a common term in a range of discourses, particularly with the postmodernist interest in the development of multiple and hybrid identities as a response to globalization (see Chapter 6).

The concept of a specifically political identity can be traced back to Locke, Hume and James Mill and is itself arguably rooted in the context of the emergence of the modern bureaucratic state and its need to mobilize subjects for (especially military) purposes (Ely, 1997). John Stuart Mill drew on these previous theorizations in arguing that considerations of nationality and democracy were intimately connected (see Chapter 1) (Ely). In making such a claim, it may be argued, Mill only made explicit what was already implicit, that his predecessors' conception of identity was located within a national frame of reference, that they took for granted the assumption that there is an intrinsic relationship between personal, individual identity and group national identity.[1]

In relation to nationalism at any rate, the concept of identity is fraught with political significance. To begin with, as Ree (1992) has suggested, the very notion of an identity presumes an other from whom one is different. If identity is about sameness, about identifying with those considered similar, it is also about difference, distinguishing oneself from those who are dissimilar. However, it is, as Tronvoll has argued, important here to distinguish between diversity and difference. 'Diversity in itself cannot generate identity and in order to achieve this, to transform diversity into difference, there must be opposition, a significant other is needed' (1999, p. 1055). Any notion of group identity in particular necessarily involves some kind and process of categorization, in order to distinguish between those who are in the group and those who are outside it, between those who are similar enough to be included and those who are different and are therefore to be excluded.[2] Such categorization is, as Billig (1995) has pointed out, inherently divisive because categories segment the world, dividing 'us' from 'them', 'insiders' from 'outsiders'.

In the case of national identity, this divisive categorization raises a number of important issues. There is in the first place the question of why such categories have to be national. It may be that human beings have a fundamental and deep-seated need to belong to a group, to identify themselves with one set (or sets) of people rather than another (although the evidence for a claim of this sort is beyond the scope of this book), but it is far from clear that this set has to be a national one. Modernists, as we have seen in Chapter 2, have argued persuasively that nations are a relatively recent phenomenon. Even if, as their critics suggest, their roots may be traced further back in time, only the most committed primordialist would argue that group belonging and national identity are synonymous.

Leaving this aside, there is the perhaps more immediately pressing question of who precisely is included and who excluded by particular definitions of a given national identity. In a world of nation-states in particular, it may well be the case that the way in which national identity is articulated and promoted can have serious implications for how rights are allocated and secured (see Chapter 4). The process of categorizing 'us' and 'them' needs to be thought about from both sides, from the point of view of those excluded as much as those included. As Zolberg correctly notes, 'to understand the process of inclusion, we must consider it simultaneously as a process of exclusion' (1996, p. 57).

In this context, the arguments put forward by the social anthropologist Fredrik Barth in the late 1960s in relation to ethnic identity are particularly salient. Instead of assuming that differences between ethnic groups were in some sense given, fixed, or innate, Barth (1969) concentrated on how difference was constructed, how the boundaries between ethnic groups were organized and maintained. From this perspective, identity is formed more through the construction and maintenance of boundaries rather than being assumed in advance, taken for granted as a function of already given differences between groups.

The issue then arises of how these boundaries are constructed, whether they are primarily imposed from without or chosen from within (or, as Barth suggests, constructed through social interaction), and to what extent the sense of being included, of sharing a given national identity, is self-determined or imposed by others. In his discussion of the related issue of ethnic identity, Jenkins has suggested that while we may be able to distinguish analytically between group identification (from within) and social categorization (from without), they are inextricably linked both logically and processually, the one 'routinely implicated in the other' (1997, p. 23). Perhaps more importantly, he insists on 'the absolute centrality of power relationships' to the whole process of such identification.

> Social categorization in particular is bound up with power relations and relates to the capacity of one group successfully to impose its categories of ascription upon another set of people, and to the resources that the categorized collectivity can draw upon to resist, if need be, that imposition. (1997, p. 23)

The extent to which such groups, so categorized, take on or internalize the identity thrust upon them from outside will vary but, as he notes, even denial and rebellion is 'an effect of being categorized in the first place' (p. 71).

Where there are significant inequalities attached to them, there may be apparently compelling reasons for accepting social categorizations of this kind. The mobilization of national liberation movements in the third world, for instance, often involved the bringing together of disparate groups under the (artificial) label that the colonial power had placed on them, in order to challenge inequalities and further apparently emancipatory aims. (See Chapter 5 for a fuller discussion of this issue.) More generally, the imposition from outside of categories on particular groups may, in situations of inequality and power differences, come to be worn as badges of pride. In recent decades 'gay pride' and 'black consciousness' provide other examples of this phenomenon. However, it is also important to look closely at whose interests are being furthered (or especially furthered) as these categorizations are adopted. There may, for instance, be both short-term and long-term advantages for existing or putative elites in such contexts, as Brass has argued (see Chapter 2). Such considerations may influence the strategies of political movements which were not originally nationalist in any way or to any significant extent, inclining them not only to the kind of accommodation with nationalism we noted in Chapter 1 (as in the case of the communist movement) but to a more positive and decided embrace of specific national identities.

Social categorization of course takes place in a variety of ways and at different levels. Jenkins suggests that we need to think of a continuum of formality/informality here, from primary socialization through various kinds of public interactions and relationships, to market and employment relationships, and eventually to organized politics and official classifications which may clearly categorize groups and help constitute particular identities. What this in turn suggests is that national identities may not be automatically present, that they have to be both constructed and reproduced. This may be obscured both by the discourse of nationalism and by theories of nationalism which define it only as the ideology of those movements overtly seeking to gain recognition or power or separation, as distinct from more diffuse or widespread forms of national identification. In his careful analysis of 'banal' nationalism, Billig (1995) refuses to accept such conventional dichotomies, rejecting attempts to restrict nationalism only to its 'hot' emotional forms. What this ignores in his view is the 'banal nationalism' which is flagged daily in ways that often go unrecognized or unremarked, and indeed which become so routine that they are hardly noticed at all. Although there are important ceremonial and ritual occasions where the collective, the nation, is celebrated, these are only occasional. The mundane daily rhetoric of 'we', 'us' and 'society' constantly invokes by implication the nation. Even weather forecasting in newspapers and broadcasting is implicitly national, whilst sport too is a central site of this daily flagging, often emphasizing masculinity and sharing an affinity with war, and its metaphors, with similar themes of heroism and sacrifice. Battling for honour in these areas against foreigners may be a preparation for more serious conflicts. Much of this activity moreover has something of a fetishistic character, as Anne McClintock has argued, in drawing attention to phenomena as diverse as 'flags, uniforms, airplane logos, maps, anthems, national flowers, national cuisines and architectures' and the considerable degree of visible ritual organization and management of national spectacles (1996, p. 274). Thus, as Billig suggests, national identity is not repressed into the unconscious but is daily reproduced.

Such nationalist flagging then helps to provide much of the framework for contemporary politics. Nationalism can become not so much a particular political strategy as a condition for any other specific strategies. Parties and movements have to present programmes or demands as those not (only) of a particular class or group or set of beliefs but in terms of some putative 'national' interest. Governments and oppositions do frequently go to great lengths to present their policies as rooted in some fundamental sense of what it means to be French or German or whatever.

An emphasis on such flagging should not be taken to imply that national identity is simply an effect of elite manipulation of a credulous mass; that those who identify themselves with the nation are merely objects of indoctrination. The fact that national identities are promoted in these ways does not guarantee their uniform or universal acceptance. For transmission and reception or appropriation by a given audience or population are different phenomena. There is a grave danger of assuming that given populations do accept unquestioningly the nationalist message or that national identity does in fact always dominate other identities. Too much stress can be laid on the power of socialization or too much weight given to the notion of a dominant ideology imposing itself on individuals through socializing institutions (Abercrombie et al., 1980; Wrong, 1961). In relation to the mass media in particular, a more complex model of communication would stress, amongst other things, the capacity of individuals to select which messages they wish to hear, to give different inflections to the messages transmitted, and to extract different meanings from them.

At the same time, in the case of national identity, there may be powerful factors that inhibit or undermine such a selective or critical response. For one of the consequences of this constant flagging is that national identity becomes seen as something fixed, and the processes and mechanisms through which it is constructed become occluded. National identity then becomes reified, treated as a 'thing', closed, unalterable, not open to change or modification (at least in its essentials) (Handler, 1994), even though, as Gillis argues, 'both identity and memory are political and social constructs . . . Identities and memories are not things we think *about* but things we think *with*. As such they have no existence beyond our politics, our social relations, and our histories' (1994, p. 5).

Identity from this angle may be better thought of as a process, a way of thinking about the world; indeed, it may make more sense to talk of processes of identification rather than identity (S. Hall, 1996). This could lead fruitfully, as postmodernists have suggested, to an understanding of identity as open to change, not fixed but fluid, both over time and in the present. Individuals may be able to have many cross-cutting identities at one time, identities that may overlap or conflict, may change and adapt to varying circumstances (we discuss this further in Chapter 6).

This runs counter in many ways to the nationalist promotion of national identity, unsettling its security and rootedness in time and place, the reified image which may be an important aspect of the appeal of nationalism, as a number of writers operating from within a psychoanalytical perspective have noted (Finlayson, 1998). Slavoj Zizeck, for instance, has argued that 'national identification is by definition sustained by a relationship towards the Nation qua Thing' (cited in Finlayson, p. 154). Drawing on Lacan's reworking of Freud, Zizek argues that the nation is imagined as something which gives order and structure to social life, the loss of which is continually feared, a fear which is repeatedly projected on to selected others.

The psychoanalytic concept of projection in turn has also been used by Carolyn Vogler to link sociological and psychological explanations of the appeal of nationalism. Drawing not so much on Lacan as on the work of Melanie Klein and her successors in the British object relations school, she has suggested that nationalist leaders not only evoke but also share with their followers a set of powerful feelings (of love, hate, shame, and anger for instance) which articulate with sociological processes of classification, boundary construction and identification. Drawing on Mann's analysis of the development of nation-states in which subjects became culturally homogenized within an exclusive, legally bounded national community (see Chapter 2), she suggests that this was underpinned by a set of defence mechanisms which are best understood in psychoanalytic terms.

> Because national citizenship is an exclusive club based on social closure against those not seen as belonging to the nation (whether inside or outside the state) national boundaries provide a very powerful basis for the play of unconscious paranoid processes in which members of a nation are able to rid themselves of bad objects and destructive impulses by projecting them onto commonly shared and accepted external enemies. (Vogler, 2000, p. 30)

Neither Vogler nor Zizeck of course are the first to think critically about national identity along these lines, linking psychoanalytic ideas to sociological ones. From a perspective that was as much Marxist as Freudian, Adorno had earlier suggested that part of the appeal of nationalism lay in its mobilization of narcissism, in the comfort it could provide to those unsettled and destabilized by modernization or capitalist development (or crisis). As Finlayson explains, 'through identification with the image of the nation the modern subject can find a self-aggrandising sense of closure and stability. In advancing the nation and denigrating those not of the nation, the subject satisfies the demands of a narcissistic ego' (1998, p. 153).

Perceptions of 'our' national identity and that of designated 'others' can then become value-laden, and the promotion of the identity of one nation can involve the implicit or explicit denigration of another.[3] Indeed it may be argued that this risk is not only always present but that there may be a deeper logic at work, that the denigration of the other follows directly from nationalism's tendency towards exclusivity (Bowman, 1994), that, as Evans puts it, 'national identity is produced through a process of negation, the creation of a coherent sense of self through explicit rejection and denials' (1996, p. 33).[4] In nationalist discourse there is a recurring tendency to see those inside the nation as having special virtues, particular values and qualities which those outside do not and cannot share. They may (at best) have other virtues but these are always implicitly or explicitly of lesser worth or weight.

The embrace of such positive and negative perceptions requires mobilization of a particular kind. It is necessary, amongst other things, not only for there to be a sense of national identity as permanent but also for it to have a deeper or superordinate significance, for national identity to come first. It has to be prior not only in time but in order; other identities (if they exist) have to be less significant, less meaningful, have a lesser claim on people's loyalties. This is, as Stern has noted, a critical problem for national leaders, particularly when they need to mobilize for war and there is a potential conflict between this identity and others, and even (especially?) between this and self-interest. 'For the national effort to succeed, national identity must overcome other identities' (Stern, 1995, p. 113). Nationalism, he suggests, works here by 'pre-empting' rather than simply overriding or 'trumping' other identities. In explaining why so many people are prepared to sacrifice themselves for the nation (Anderson's question), he suggests that one of the key bases for the emotional appeal of nationalism is by tying national identity to those groups with which people do have the strongest and most deep-rooted links already, namely the family and community.

An important feature of this process (which is significantly gendered, as we noted in Chapter 2) is the way in which the nation is presented in a personalized form, so that the nation itself comes to be seen as if it has an identity in the same way as an individual. Ree (1998) has pointed how so many of the terms that are applied to individuals are applied unproblematically to nations in this way, how words such as 'character' or 'guilt' or 'survival' or 'self-determination' or 'interest' are freely used.

The production, reproduction and promotion of national identity along these lines can have real material consequences. In particular, once identity is yoked or linked to the state now or at some hoped-for future moment, it is no longer merely a matter of lifestyle choice, as may be sometimes implied by postmodernists. Once state power in particular is involved, the identification of and distinction between 'us' and 'them' has a real material significance. The boundaries between those inside and those outside the nation-state are not merely symbolic but material, involving not only cultural distinctions but concrete, physical borders, 'tools', as Tronvoll puts it, 'used by governments to create a distinction between the in-group, namely the "nation", and the out-group, those who belong to other communities and nations, the "others"' (1999, p. 1040). But they have also to be patrolled, to keep these others out, whilst rights (formal and/or substantive) can be accorded to those within. Claims of this or that national identity then may ground and give rise not only to distinctions of identity between but differential treatment of fellow-nationals and foreigners, citizens and aliens (see Chapter 4).

The inequalities and intolerance which can be associated with this may be hard to justify without some prior (and circular) sense that they are rooted in deeper, more profound, unchangeable and fixed differences. One way of doing this is to assert that national identity itself rests on the foundations of something more basic such as race or ethnicity.

Race and racism

Some writers have sought to insist that nationalism and racism have to be kept quite separate, that they are quite different in origin and implication. Anderson, for instance, asserts that 'the fact of the matter is that nationalism thinks in terms of historical destinies, while racism dreams of eternal contaminations' (Anderson, 1991, p. 149). Guibernau, too, claims that 'racism and nationalism offer radically different messages' (1996, p. 89). Both writers argue that racism does not cut across national boundaries but is rather focused internally on hierarchical differences between people living in one society. Both argue that racism is destructive, driven by hatred and fear, whilst they see nationalism as constructive, inspired by feelings of love and creativity, driven by aspirations and dreams for a better future (Anderson, 1991, ch. 8 passim; Guibernau, 1996, pp. 89–90).

It is difficult, however, to be persuaded by this attempt to distinguish the two so sharply, given how central racial categorization and racist discourses have been to the development of nationalism, particularly in the European context. The growth of nationalism in the nineteenth century took place after all in a context in which ideas of scientific racism were commonplace, informing many nationalist movements, particularly those with specifically imperialist pretensions and ambitions.[5] This was true both for nationalists in established empires such as those of Britain and France and for their more frustrated counterparts in Italy and Germany. In the latter case, a clear link can be traced between the exterminatory excesses of the worst forms of nineteenth-century imperialism and the Nazi implementation of racial logic in their version of nationalism in the twentieth century (Lindquist, 1998). However, as we argue in Chapter 4, the exclusionary logics of even apparently civic forms of nationalism in the contemporary world have also frequently taken a racialized form. When the supposedly civic nation has constructed immigrants as undesirable others, it has almost always done so on a racialized basis. Australians in the UK, Swiss in France, Austrians in Germany have never been seen in the same way as Bangladeshis, Algerians, or Turks.

It is difficult to account for this without some sense of a potential affinity between racism and nationalism, which has to do with the need to construct secure boundaries and categories of inclusion and exclusion, concerns which are common to both ideologies. In this sense, the force of Gellner's argument, that nationalism produces nations, has its parallel in the increasing acceptance by social scientists that racism produces 'races'. Without racism, there can be no concept of race. Since there is no scientific validity to dividing populations into biologically based races, then it is only with the emergence of racist discourses that certain biological differences can come to be seen as socially significant and be organized into the category of 'races'. As Stephen Castles has argued, racism is not *'an aberration or a result of individual pathology. It is a set of practices and discourses which are deeply rooted in the history, traditions and culture of modernity.'* As such, as he goes on to argue, it can play 'a crucial role in consolidating nation-states by providing an instrument for defining belonging or exclusion' (2000, p. 174).

This does not mean that nationalism and racism are identical, nor that they are always entwined to the same extent. The extent to which explicitly racist discourse can be integrated within nationalist ideology may depend on a range of historical, political and sociological factors.[6] It does seem that, in Europe at any rate in the aftermath of the Holocaust, it has become much more difficult to base nationalist ideas on overtly racist assumptions, although racist ideas have by no means disappeared from the political map. What is much more common is to find arguments for the distinctiveness of nations articulated not so much in terms of race as of ethnicity.

Ethnicity

By contrast with race, the concept of ethnicity is relatively new, emerging in social science discourse only in the twentieth century (McCrone, 1998, p. 22). Malik (1996) has argued powerfully that the concept itself, even or particularly in its culturalist form, was only developed when overt racist ideology became first theoretically untenable (since scientific evidence of the existence of races was impossible to produce) and politically unacceptable (certainly after the experience of Nazism).[7] The purpose and logic of the replacement concept, ethnicity, was, he argues, essentially the same, to counter the universalist aspirations that originated in the eighteenth-century Enlightenment by explaining away persistent inequalities (first in Europe and later in the colonies, enslaved by imperialism) as consequences of immutable, deeply rooted difference. Given this, there may be good reason to doubt that ethnicity (and, as we shall see, other related arguments based on the cultural distinctiveness of social groups) can, any more than race, bear the weight that some social scientists and (ethnic) nationalists wish to place upon it.

Yet the argument that national identity has an ethnic basis, that preceding and structuring the development of national identity is an ethnic one, is and has become an important one. This is not only because it forms a key part of some versions of nationalism as an ideology (see the discussion of ethnic nationalism in Chapter 4) but because it is taken seriously by some major contemporary theorists of nationalism. It can take a number of different forms, depending in part upon how ethnicity and ethnic identity is itself conceptualized. At one end of the spectrum there are those who argue for real genetic continuity as constituting the basis for ethnic groups, and therefore ultimately for nations. It is certainly the case that many people popularly ascribe elements of their character or personality to their 'Latin' or 'Celtic' or 'Jewish' blood. However, there are no credible grounds for believing that meaningful connections at this level can be made. As Chapman puts it with admirable directness in his critical analysis of the 'myth' of the Celts,

> 2000 years of coming and going must make nonsense of the notion that the nameable 'ethnic' groups of pre-Roman, northern and central Europe have any privileged biological connection with nameable 'ethnic' groups of the modern day ... The naive view from many works on the modern Celtic peoples that they are 'descended' from the Celts of the Iron Age can be summarily dismissed. Viewed at that distance, everybody is descended from everybody. (1992, pp. 81–2)

Most academics who take ethnicity seriously have largely abandoned arguments of this type. Instead they have turned to a conception of ethnicity in which beliefs and culture rather than biology play a central role. As anthropologist Stanley Tambiah summarizes this conventional view:

> Ethnic identity above all is a collective identity ... It is a self-conscious and vocalized identity that substantializes and vocalizes one or more attributes – the usual ones being skin colour, language, religion, territorial occupation – and attaches them to collectivities as their innate possession and their mythico-historic legacy. The central components in this description of identity are ideas of inheritance, ancestry and descent, place or territory of origin, and the sharing of kinship, any one or combination of which may be invoked as a claim according to context and calculation

of advantages. These ethnic collectivities are believed to be bounded and to be self-producing and enduring through time. (1994, p. 430)

Thus Anthony Smith, for example, thinks it is possible to identify an ethnic community or ethnie which 'must be sharply differentiated from a race in the sense of a social group that is held to possess unique hereditary biological traits that allegedly determine the mental attributes of the group' (1991, p. 21). The reason that such ethnies are, he argues, often confused with races is because of the 'widespread influence of racist ideologies and discourses' which he wishes, understandably, to reject.

The construction of ethnicity

Smith lists six main attributes which he considers central to an ethnic community. These are as follows:

- a collective proper name;
- a myth of common ancestry;
- shared historical memories;
- one or more differentiating elements of a common culture;
- an association with a specific 'homeland';
- a sense of solidarity for significant sectors of the population (1991, p. 21).

Three of these also figure in or overlap with his definition of national identity, whose features include:

- an historic territory or homeland;
- common myths and historical memories;
- a common, mass public culture (Smith, 1991, p. 14).

There are a number of problems with Smith's arguments which to some degree we have already rehearsed in our discussion of the concept of identity itself. In the first place, it assumes that what is distinctive to the ethnic community is prior to and independent of the construction of boundaries between one ethnie and another. As Bauman argues, however, 'it is the ethnic boundary that defines the group not the cultural stuff that it encloses . . . the very identity of the cultural stuff . . . is an artifact of the firmly drawn and well-guarded boundary' (1992, p. 678). Secondly, the construction of such boundaries, involves crucial processes of selection. This is a major focus of Barth's work. As he says,

We can assume no simple one to one relationship between ethnic units and cultural similarities and differences. The features that are taken into account are not the sum of 'objective' differences, but only those which the actors themselves regard as significant . . . some cultural features are used by the actors as signals and emblems of differences, others are ignored, and in some relationships radical differences are played down or ignored. (1969, p. 14)

In the case of a common history, for example, it is hard not to be struck by the circularity of Smith's argument. Appiah has pointed this out quite sharply in a related discussion of race, asking

whether a common history is something that could be a criterion that distinguishes one group of human beings – extended in time – from another . . . the answer is no . . . sharing a common group history cannot be a criterion for being members of the same group, for we would have to be able to identify the group in order to identify its history . . . History may have made us what we are; but the choice of a slice of the past in a period before your birth as your own history is always exactly that: a choice. (1991, pp. 50–1)

This process of selection is not random. For some, the acquisition or taking on of an ethnic identity may be a matter of calculation and advantage among those seeking to secure scarce resources in competitive situations. In these and other situations, however, there are issues of power and inequality in which some have rather more to say about what is to count than others. As Brass (1991) argues (see Chapter 2), elites play a key role in mobilizing masses to believe that it is in their interest to see themselves as different in crucial and fundamental ways from others, learning to assign and accept stereotypical (and value-laden) norms. One way of doing this of course is to suggest that these differences have always been there, since time immemorial, in a word to reify them. Of course, once brought into existence, once constructed and reproduced, it is the case, as Comaroff notes, that 'ethnic identities may take on a powerful salience in the experience of those who bear them, often to the extent of *appearing* to be natural, essential, primordial' (1995, p. 250). Such reification does not mean, however, that the ethnie of the past is the same entity as the ethnic group, let alone nation of today, that any of the ingredients, territorial, mythical, or cultural have the same meaning today for people that they had before, even if we could fix them at any one moment in time. Treating cultural categories as the same, for instance simply because they share the same name, is to mistake nominal similarity with real similarity. There may certainly be real consequences in people's minds and behaviour owing to the sharing of an ancient name but it is precisely the consequences of these perceptions that require our critical attention, as we shall see.

What these kinds of arguments about the ethnic basis of the nation obscure is, as Weber pointed out a long time ago (see Chapter 1), that ethnicity in the sense of a belief in common ancestry is a consequence of political action not a cause of it (Weber, 1978). Ethnicity becomes salient not as a result of deeply rooted or primordial ties, let alone some fictitious genetic continuity, but as a result of political and sometimes economic processes.[8] Failure to recognize this in the case of ethnic identifications in the past makes it in turn harder to think critically about the processes at work in the construction and maintenance of national identifications in the present.

One further question about ethnicity is inescapable. If a writer like Smith sees ethnic and national identities as highly overlapping concepts, can we make a clear distinction between them? Thomas Eriksen, who has made one of the most systematic attempts to address the relationship between ethnicity and nationalism is forced to conclude that they are 'kindred concepts' (1993, p. 118). For him the majority of nationalisms (but not all) are ethnic in character. But only some ethnic groups are proto-nations and form ethnonationalist movements. 'A nationalist ideology is an ethnic ideology', he writes, 'which demands a state on behalf of the ethnic group' (p. 118). In practice this distinction is often blurred. On the one hand, some nationalisms, as in the USA or Mauritius, are based on other civil ties or on multi-ethnic groups. (We discuss the validity of the distinction between civic and ethnic nationalism in Chapter 4.) On the other hand, many movements that we may wish to classify as nationalist have demands – for greater autonomy or recognition within an existing state – which fall short of demands for full independent statehood (see Chapter 6).[9]

Culture, belief and national identity

If ethnicity often seems to rest on relationships that are infused with structures of power and inequality, is there then some other way in which we can explain the basis of national identity? Many writers have turned to the idea of culture as an explanatory tool for this purpose. Indeed it is often implicit in concepts of identity and ethnicity themselves. We have seen above, for example, how Smith emphasizes the importance of beliefs and culture in the construction first of ethnic then of national identity. Although many modernists reject the ethnic part of this argument, they nevertheless take very seriously the idea that there are a set of beliefs and a national culture, common to and shared by all members of the nation, which form the basis of a given national identity. The argument is articulated differently by the various schools of thought on the modernity or otherwise of the nation.

For primordialists (and indeed many of the adherents of nationalism themselves) certainly, the cultural continuities of the nation are of crucial importance. The modern nation has a long formation through a developing national or ethnic culture with a long, unbroken (although sometimes suppressed) history. This idea is often accompanied by ideas of blood and descent which strengthen the cultural bonds or vice versa.

However, for perennialists or ethno-symbolists such as Smith or Hastings, culture is important too. Smith poses the question of where the 'inventions' of modern nationalist imaginings come from, claiming that at worst modern nationalism involves innovation on the basis of pre-existing cultural roots, rather than invention of any (arbitrary) kind. How can they be successful, he asks, how can they strike a chord in the population, were it not for their rootedness in older ethnic cultures and groups? He points out, against Gellner, that the intellectuals who were responsible for romantic, cultural nationalism antedate the modern national education systems and need to get their ideas, their languages, their stories, from somewhere. Culture is thus central to his explanation but it is the culture of pre-existing, historic, even ancient ethnie which lie at the roots of modern nationalism. Modern nations can only successfully sustain themselves on the basis of older ethnic ties, but if they lack these, Smith suggests, then such ethnic roots will have to be (re)invented. (The use of the term 're-invention', however, seems partly to beg the question of the extent to which these roots ever existed, whether they were entwined with many other roots, or whether the newly discovered roots were actually part of the same tree!)

'Early modernists' such as Greenfeld (1992) and writers such as Llobera (1994a), Reynolds (1984) and, most recently, Hastings (1997), who stress the existence of nations well before the advent of industrialism or other aspects of modernity, see cultural changes with the growth of vernacular languages in particular as critical to their arguments. Indeed many of the sources of their arguments are derived from literary or other textual sources.

Culture has been a key element too for modernists such as Gellner and Anderson. Gellner, as we have seen in Chapter 2, suggests that nationalism arises from the functional requirements of a newly mobile industrial society with a more complex division of labour. The state promotes the new common, high culture through a mass education system and this combination of common education and culture through the state's action produces modern nationalism and the nation-state. In the case of Anderson, it is relatedly the spread of mass literacy through 'print-capitalism' accompanied by changing conceptions of time – a new sense of simultaneity – which makes possible national imaginings. In both cases there are perceived crucial cultural prerequisites for nationalism, related to the prerequisites for a modern industrial society, in Gellner's case, or for modern industrial capitalism in Anderson's. Even Anthony Smith (1991), in his more modernist mode, partly agrees with Gellner, conceding that territorial or civic nationalism involves the state having a vital role in educating its citizens into a homogeneous culture.

Finally, postmodernists' focus on the various discourses of the nation is overtly concentrated on the cultural. This has led in some cases to a focus on nationalism as text, on the national narration. Anderson's account already tends in this direction but while stories of the nation are only part of what he is analysing, they are very much the focus of Bhabha (1990), whose aim is 'to study the nation through its narrative address', and the nation 'as it is written' (see Chapter 2).

With the partial exception of the postmodernist position, all of these approaches to nationalism tend towards a reified view of culture which sees it as 'a discrete, bounded and integrated "package" of traits, values and practices' with an assumption that its elements are shared by all its members (Vertovec, 1996) and that all individuals within a given nation are shaped or moulded by what is taken to be the nation's cultural identity. At the same time, issues of how boundaries between cultures are constructed and maintained, the processes of cultural transmission of culture, and the value-laden assumptions underpinning conceptualizations of culture are rarely if ever problematized. It can be argued that just as ethnicity was developed as a replacement for race, serving the same anti-universalist purposes and outcomes, so 'culture' has ended up here playing the same role, a value-laden way of reifying difference, occluding the processes at work and legitimizing otherwise unpalatable political consequences (Malik, 1996; Stolcke, 1995). Although there is no space here for a detailed and considered examination of the concept of culture, 'one of the two or three most complex words in the English language' (Eagleton, 2000, p. 1), we have to recognize that it is a highly contested one. For our purposes there are two important uses on which to concentrate here. First, there is a general anthropologically derived concept of culture as 'an array of beliefs locked together in relational patterns' (M. Douglas in Goody, 1994, p. 250) or 'a system of symbols and meaning' (D. Schneider in Goody, 1994, p. 250). These beliefs and symbols and the processes that produce and reproduce them form an important component of the production of national identities and of the affective underpinnings for the appeal of nationalism. Feelings and emotions are at least as important here as more intellectually based belief systems and philosophies. Secondly, there is the term 'a culture', 'comprising the patterned behaviour of a particular group, tribe, nation, class, locality' (Goody, 1994, p. 250), used both in social science and common-sense discourse. As Keesing (1994) argues, this idea of 'a bounded universe of shared ideals and customs' (p. 301), derived *inter alia* from Boas, has too easily led to a reified and essentialized notion of culture which has led to the promotion of 'tradition' or ethnic or national culture as an unproblematic and timeless inheritance from the past.

A key idea here has been that of a 'common culture', understood and shared by the members of a given nation, perhaps the most commonly articulated justification for the existence of a given national identity. This is a claim made both by modernists and their critics. For the latter, we may turn again to Smith who presents 'a common, mass public culture' as one of the 'fundamental features of national identity' (Smith, 1991, p. 15). For a modernist view, we may turn to Gellner who argues

one of the most important traits of a modern society [is] cultural homogeneity . . . *Citizens must be equal in culture* as well as in basic status . . .
This idea, the new imperative of cultural homogeneity, is the very essence
of nationalism. (1994, pp. 104–5; emphasis added)

Yet how common in fact are cultures? To what extent are they genuinely
shared by all within the putative nation? The very idea of a common culture
has significant political undertones or associations. It brings with it traces
of egalitarianism – sharing a common culture implies that all have the same
or equal access to it, equal ownership of it, have equally contributed in making
or creating it.

Closer inspection of this common culture reveals it to have certain conditions. In Gellner's version, for instance, it is, after all, not just any form of
culture that comes to be shared but a 'high culture' rather than a 'low' one,
a 'high' culture moreover which has had to be 'forged' and 'defended' both
internally against the 'expansionism of the old one' and externally against
both 'rival cultures' and 'bloodless cosmopolitanism' (1994, pp. 111–12). Is
not the outcome of these struggles, at least in part, the existence not of a unified
common culture but of majority and minority cultures (which may or may
not correspond to Gellner's high and low distinction), or of dominant and
suppressed (or sub-) cultures? Does not the assumption of a common culture
itself constitute a political stance, at least implicitly in opposition to the idea
or possibility that there may be different (multi-) cultures inside a given
polity, nourishing and interacting with each other, shaping and reshaping each
other over time? Does not the opposition to multi-culturalism so evident for
instance on the European right in recent decades (from the Front National
to the British Conservative Party), in part derive some of its force from prior
assumptions about the existence of a common culture allied to beliefs about
the inherent incompatibility of different cultures (Stolcke, 1995)? Those then
who apparently wish to bring into the nation 'their' own culture are seen as
a threat to the pre-existing national culture (Seidel, 1986).

The mixture of defensiveness and aggression that we can see in this
case is neither merely theoretical nor by any means unique and certainly not
confined to Europe. In Taiwan, for example, the KMT devoted considerable
efforts to construct and impose its own highly selective version of a supposedly
traditional Chinese culture in an effort to forge an effective hegemony over
an understandably resistant population. As Allen Chun has shown, this 'was
not a spontaneous discovery of traditional culture. It was a systematic effort
to redefine the content of these ideas and values, to inculcate societal consciousness through institutional promotion . . . to lead people to believe that
this spirit of cultural consciousness was the key to the nation . . . to directly
engender national solidarity' (1994, pp. 57–8).

As the Taiwanese case makes clear, a key element in this project is the
necessary reification of the culture that is to become common. Within a

nationalist context, the consequence if not purpose of such reification is then, as Eriksen has noted, 'that it enables people to talk about their culture as though it were a constant' (Eriksen, 1993, p. 103). Similarly, Penrose argues that

> The perception that culture as a particular way of life is essential helps to explain why the 'cultural bases' which underlie secessionist and irredentist movements are so powerful. . . . I think that the additional source of power is the reified concept of the nation which continues to be legitimized by intellectual culture through a process [of] 'ideologically motivated essentialism'. (1995, p. 405)

What can then easily become obscured is the process by which what is not originally shared by very many at all eventually becomes so. Both Llobera (1994a) (see Chapter 2) and Smith, for example, seem implicitly to recognize that there is an issue over specifying or explaining quite how and when a given culture did become common. They are constrained to recognize that key elements of this culture were not always or at particular times held by the whole of the population, but they then seem to brush the problem aside. The potential political and ideological conflicts which may be part of the process of establishing an 'ethnic community', with a supposedly shared culture, are indicated, we suggest, in Smith's formulation:

> An ethnic community, on the other hand, can be distinguished by just these attributes [a myth of common origins, shared historical memories, a sense of solidarity or an association with a designated homeland], *even if they are firmly held and clearly enunciated by only small segments of the designated population* . . . (1991, p. 21; emphasis added)

If such a minority can constitute other people as part of an 'ethnic community', they can surely only do so successfully through an essentially political process – of persuasion, of ideological struggle and, sometimes, perhaps, of coercion.[10]

In the rest of this chapter we intend to subject to critical examination some of the cultural processes that have been portrayed as crucial to the construction of the nation and to national identity, and in particular to selected components of what some have indeed seen as a common culture.

Components of the national culture?

Issues of language, memory or history or myth, and territory bulk large in discussions of the relationship between culture and national identity. The language of the nation is claimed to be the particular and indispensable medium in which intellectual, spiritual and artistic activity is expressed, consciously or sub-consciously, through which the world is classified, meanings are shared and values and beliefs transmitted. The memory or history or myths of a nation are ways of apprehending and articulating what is held to be the past development of a nation's unique civilization, its works and practices, its customs, conventions and habits. What is claimed to be the nation's own or designated territory is the physical space within which such expressive activity is said to take place.

In what follows we examine each of these elements in turn, highlighting the contested and political nature of what are often or largely treated as purely cultural matters yet which are used, unproblematically, to provide the basis for national identities. We will suggest in each case that they appear as material which has been deployed by the nationalist imagination, manufactured in particular ways for mainly nationalist purposes. For, to the extent that Anderson is right to identify a nationalist imagination (but see Chapter 2), we then need to know, as Bryant (1995) has suggested, whose imagination this is or who precisely does this imagining, with what (selected) materials, whom it and they address and what consequences then flow or follow.

The role of intellectuals

As much of the literature acknowledges, a key part of the answer to the first question lies with intellectuals. It is intellectuals who 'discover' identities, who research and standardize languages, who write the relevant histories, who uncover artefacts that locate the relevant territory and thus 'prove' the timeless quality of the nation. The role of intellectuals in providing the cultural meat for the nationalist meal has been well documented in a number of places (Connerton, 1989; Hroch, 1993; Karakasidou, 1994) and they have clearly been central to both the creation and reproduction of nationalist ideologies (Anthias and Yuval-Davis, 1992). In the nineteenth century especially, in what Anderson calls a 'golden age of vernacularizing lexicographers, grammarians, philologists and litterateurs' (1991, p. 71), intellectuals played a major part in identifying and drawing apparently clear boundaries between distinct languages, codifying them in dictionaries and grammars. For their part, of course, historians have played a key role in furnishing the materials for a particular vision of a national past, constructions that have generally been, as Fentress and Wickham put it 'linear in their conception of time, and indeed teleological: very explicitly, all of them lead up to and legitimise the present situation' (1992, p. 134).

For Hroch (1993), such activity has been characteristic of what he identifies as phase A of nationalism, a period in which intellectuals worked away in relative isolation in pursuit of particular projects. This was followed, he argues, by a second phase (B) in which the materials excavated by intellectuals were then taken up by nationalist movements. Yet many such intellectuals were heavily involved in political activity, scarcely unwilling to see their work taken up in this way and for such purposes. A number of historians, for example, played important roles in politics in Central and Eastern Europe in the nineteenth and early twentieth centuries (Deletant and Hanak, 1988). The case of German historiography is perhaps quite instructive but by no means unique in this respect, as Stefan Berger has recently argued.[11] He has provided compelling evidence for what he identifies as 'a longstanding and self-conscious commitment by German historians to nation building . . . to uphold national honour and glory and create national identity' (Berger, 1997, p. 3). This commitment began in the early nineteenth century, and was both shaped by and integral to the growing nationalist political movement which culminated in the unification of Germany in 1871.

In many ways indeed this commitment was central to the academic discipline of history as it was developed by historians in the modern era. Emphasizing the role of German professional historians such as Ranke in particular, Suny (1999) has argued that their 'focus on and location in the nation' was hugely influential throughout Europe and North America. 'Like the national historians of ruling European nations, American historians worked to legitimize the particular form of polity and national community in which they lived' (p. 22). In non-national states this activity could of course cut both ways, with historians in Imperial Russia engaged in the production of state patriotic historiographies whilst their Czech and Armenian counterparts worked to provide historical evidence to support claims of non-ruling or subject nationalities to states of their own.

Such enthusiasm on the part of intellectuals undoubtedly made it easier for powerful political forces within the state and society to use their work, to seek to impose visions of the nation so constructed on others. For intellectuals did not and have not worked alone or in isolation in contributing, consciously or not, to the (re)development or construction of nationalist ideologies. Without the intervention of political forces, these intellectual products, however politically motivated or loaded, would be of only limited interest. Kedourie (whose focus was after all very much on the role of ideas) himself pointed this out some time ago:

> It is absurd to think that professors of linguistics and collectors of folklore can do the work of statesmen and soldiers. What does happen is that academic enquiries are used by conflicting interests to bolster claims, and their results prevail only to the extent that someone has the power to make them prevail. (1993, p. 120)

It is political actors and agents of varying kinds, inside and outside the state, who have characteristically used the work of intellectuals in identifying, excavating and elaborating core components of a 'national' culture (a given nation's language, its memories, its history, its myths, its territory) to encourage nationalist sentiment and to mobilize nationalist forces.

Language

Language has frequently been seen as crucial to the nationalist project, as can be seen in the central role it plays for both modernists such as Gellner and Anderson and primordialists such as Fishman. Ever since Herder put forward his romantic view of cultural nationalism, language has been perceived by many to be the very embodiment of the national character and its genius, the main marker of national identity (Edwards, 1985).[12] Language in this view is seen as a link with the glorious past and with the authentic nature of a people (Fishman, 1972). However, to say different language communities define or require the existence of different nations may be to render unproblematic precisely that which is problematic (Billig, 1995).

There are a number of reasons for this. To begin with, it is easy to suppose that people 'naturally' speak different languages yet the idea of clearly distinctive languages is in many ways a relatively modern one. In any case, distinctiveness is not the same as exclusivity. As Anderson notes,

> language is not [in itself] an instrument of exclusion: in principle anyone can learn any language. On the contrary it is fundamentally inclusive, limited only by the fatality of Babel: no one lives long enough to learn all languages. (1991, p. 134)[13]

We might add, too, that texts can be translated, thus rendering them accessible to even more people. What needs explaining is quite why, given this potential inclusivity, perceptions of and attitudes to languages are so often couched in exclusivist terms. How is it that languages become used as markers of differentiation, distinguishing between us and them, setting off one community from another, delineating those speaking the same language as friends and those speaking a foreign language as enemies? It certainly was not always so. As Hobsbawm has noted, historically 'language was merely one, and not necessarily the primary way of distinguishing between cultural communities' (1992, p. 58).

Part of this process involves prioritizing one form of speaking and/or writing over others, distinguishing and privileging languages on the one hand from dialects on the other. This may, perhaps must, be fraught with political significance and be the outcome of struggles of various kinds. It certainly requires judgements about what counts as a significant difference, processes of selection (and de-selection), and enforcement, prohibitions and the use of injunctions against any continuing use of alternates (J. Hall, 1996, p. 164). Particularly in an epoch of state-sponsored nationalism, it has often been the deliberate policy of both ruling elites and putative counter-elites to seek to delegitimate rival linguistic claims, sometimes in quite openly opportunistic fashion.[14]

The recognition of identifiable, discrete, exclusive national languages then is not a simple, organic or spontaneous development. If such languages are not (always) exactly invented, then a strong case may still be made that they are, in Hobsbawm's words, 'semi-artificial constructs' and 'the opposite of what nationalist mythology supposes them to be, namely the primordial foundations of national culture' (1992, p. 54).[15]

The creation of such mythologies, however, has served particular purposes. However much nineteenth century intellectuals may have imagined or presented themselves as pure theorists, engaged in the politically innocent or neutral activity of cultural and linguistic 'revival', their efforts were quickly seized upon by ideologues, nation-builders and state elites and deployed in the interests of nation-state-building. So far from language 'reviving' naturally or spontaneously, great efforts have been put into spreading the word, as it were, encouraging, cajoling or simply coercing people to adopt what has been ideologically defined as the essential and necessary national language. A key role has been played in this by what Hobsbawm identifies as 'a minority of sufficient political weight' (p. 60), anchored or seeking to anchor itself inside a modernizing nation-state apparatus. There have been, as he argues, identifiable 'classes which stood or fell by the official use of the written vernacular . . . the socially modest but educated middle strata . . . the battle lines of linguistic nationalism were manned by provincial journalists, schoolteachers and aspiring subaltern officials' (1992, p. 117).

In the case of nineteenth century Greece, for instance, a major effort went into what Kitromilides calls the 'linguistic hellenisation' of Albanian, Vlach, Turkish, Bulgarian, Ladino, Armenian, Arabic, Kurdish and Syriac speakers. The state embarked on

> a crusade of national education . . . a drama [which] amounted to expanding the symbolic frontiers of Greek nationality through incorporating into it social groups which, by virtue of their language or religion, could be taught to identify with the broad imagined community of the Greek nation. This process was carried out through the activities of two complementary institutional networks, one directly under the control of the Greek state, the other operated by the local Greek-speaking or Christian Orthodox communities, but both staffed by cadres trained in Athens. (Kitromilides, 1990, p. 44)

The immediate beneficiaries and most enthusiastic proponents of this policy were teachers, lawyers, doctors and journalists. It may be popularly supposed that national languages are deeply rooted in the past, and a common written language may well be functional for (amongst other needs and purposes) intra-elite communication, the conduct of public administration, and a mass education system. But these myths and needs serve purposes and interests in the short as well as the long term.

All kinds of complexities and difficulties can then arise. Attatürk's re-engineering of the written Turkish language provides one instructive example. The Roman alphabet replaced the Arabic one which had the advantage of preventing a newly literate generation from reading the largely religious books published before his secular revolution. In addition, Arabic and Persian words were purged from the Turkish language and replaced with European ones. This had the advantage of furthering Attatürk's modernizing vision of the nation but was justified by reference to a theory that alleged that all European languages were derived from Turkish. Thus the changes were legitimized by an appeal to tradition and authenticity (Fentress and Wickham, 1992; Fishman, 1972)!

In the rather different 'modernizing' project of the early Soviet Union, Yuri Slezkine has demonstrated the central role played by the manipulation of language in the Soviet nationalities policy of the 1920s. Newly modernized, 'official' languages were codified, simplified and purified – purged of 'alien ballast' (cited by Slezkine, 1996, p. 215). For each recognized nationality was to have a distinct and different language (based on Stalin's theory of the nation and nationality). In the process books were published in more languages – 66 in 1928 compared to 40 in 1913 – but the borders and boundaries of these languages were patrolled and controlled with vigour. The ultimate goal was to be a 'total coincidence of national and linguistic identity' (p. 216), regardless of the wishes of the populations concerned.

In Ireland, on the other hand, language only became a focus after the failure of the earlier nationalist projects of first the non-sectarian United Irishmen and then Daniel O'Connell's campaign for Catholic Emancipation (Mezo, 1994). The revival of the Irish language was part of the cultural nationalist movement at the end of the nineteenth century and spearheaded by urban intellectuals and their political allies. It was seen by nationalist elites as an alternative to religion and a way of uniting all Irishmen and women, of all creeds, classes and origins, against the British (unsuccessfully, as it turned out, in the case of Protestants). After the settlement of the early 1920s, the government of the newly independent Irish Free State (later to become the Republic of Ireland) instituted an education policy in the schools which attempted to enforce Gaelic as the national language of the Irish people and of the Irish state. In the Herderian vision of De Valera, the Irish Taoiseach (or prime minister) for sixteen years, language had to play a major role in a nation-state-building project, a homogenizing tool, albeit one that would tend to exclude non-Catholics and non-Gaelic speakers.

> The only way to hold our nation . . . is by securing our language as the language of the Irish people. . . . The best way to preserve the philosophy

of life, to preserve the distinctive and spiritual and cultural life, of the people is through the language. It is the best way to keep pure Irish tradition. (De Valera cited by Dowling, 1997)

Thus in 1926 exclusively Irish language instruction for infants was imposed regardless of the language of the home (or in many cases the linguistic knowledge of the teacher)! The language was seen as the link between past culture and the future development of the nation. However, only a minority of the citizens of Ireland spoke Gaelic; government business was conducted in English and the Irish language, associated by many with poverty and lack of opportunity, continued to decline. As a practical tool for nation-building in the 1920s and 1930s, linked to an education system largely in the control of the Catholic Church, it failed to have the modernizing impetus of Attatürk's project and enjoyed little success.[16] In a summary of research on forty-seven language contexts, Edwards (1985), who makes extensive use of the failure of Irish language instruction as a case study (pp. 53–65), concludes that, although nationalists have made repeated and strenuous efforts to force people to change languages, these policies have generally been pursued without much popular consent (or even consultation). In fact, language shifts occur quite frequently, whether nationalists want them to or not. Language appears in this account as an element of identity very susceptible to change, 'a negotiable commodity' without the central symbolic status with which nationalists wish to burden it (Edwards, 1985, p. 98).

Language may also be used to further rather narrower special interests. In Taiwan, the KMT, fleeing from defeat at the hands of the Communists in mainland China, determined to use the people and resources of the island as a base from which to regain power back on the mainland. The interests and rights of the islanders themselves were brushed aside and every effort to claim these from below was suppressed. Part of this suppression involved the outlawing of Taiwanese and intense efforts to force everyone to speak only Mandarin, as part of a political project to assert continuity of KMT rule over the 'whole' of China, even though Taiwan had only been ruled by the government of China for a short spell in the late nineteenth century, having been occupied by a succession of imperialist powers. Efforts to maintain Taiwanese as a language in the face of this regime then became a key task for the democratic movement.

The case of Taiwanese is an example of the association of a language with the expansion of democratic rights and freedom rather than more narrowly with nationalism (see Chapter 5 for a further discussion of this relationship). For there are differences in the ways nationalists and democrats prioritize language issues. For nationalists, the emphasis is on the past not the future, the aim not to expand rights and enhance freedom but largely to exclude, to draw boundaries that were not necessarily there before, or to fortify them. Differences that may have already pre-existed political attention are then exaggerated or highlighted to suit political purposes and to strengthen divisions that were appearing for different reasons. Language differences are magnified to act as further barriers between people, 'treated', as Anderson suggests, 'by *certain nationalist ideologues* as emblems of nation-ness ... [used for] building in effect *particular solidarities*' (1991, p. 133; emphasis added).

The case of Serbo-Croat in the latter days of Yugoslavia provides a recent and tragic illustration of this. Here there were steadfast attempts to emphasize and construct such linguistic differences in the *wake* of national and ethnic 'awakenings' not as a defining characteristic of them (Rieff, 1995). There were in this case no regular linguistic differences between all competing groups which could (yet) provide an adequate framework for the national narratives, myths and imaginings which needed to be immediately deployed for divisive purposes. What is striking in the Yugoslav case is that language differences were inflated and invoked in a very particular context, that of war between groups hitherto living (in the Bosnian case especially) side by side, in mixed communities. Prior to the war, Serbo-Croatian was, as Sucic has noted,

> a single standard language with two major variants (the western or Croatian and eastern or Serbian variants) and two varieties (that spoken in Bosnia-Herzegovina and that in Montenegro). The variants contain many words exclusive to themselves, while the varieties blend elements of both variants ... Put in a room together, people from Serbia, Croatia and Bosnia have no problem communicating ... But today the people of the former Yugoslavia must answer that they speak Serbian, Croatian or Bosnian – even though they can't necessarily explain how it is that these 'different' languages are mutually intelligible. (1996, p. 4; p. 1)[17]

During and after the wars, nationalist forces on all sides embarked on a sustained policy of linguistic demarcation to match the ethnic cleansing that had taken place on the ground. A series of bizarre proposals were made to force people to speak and write in approved ways. In one case, a bill came forward to the Croatian parliament which would 'have turned the Croats into an illiterate people who would have to learn their new language virtually from scratch' (Sucic, 1996, p. 3). Despite the obvious absurdities of this process, linguistic differences which simply did not exist before, or certainly did not correspond to national differences,[18] have become hardened, institutionalized, promoted by state elites to justify murderous and divisive policies of ethnic cleansing.

Memory, history, myth

Alongside the idea of a clearly defined common language, a key component of nationalist ideology is the invocation of a unified national past, a unity which is 'passed' down in various ways. This is often formulated as an apolitical claim that 'we' all share a common past, a collective memory of a set of decisive and linked events which have in some way made us what we are as a nation. This argument generally takes one of two forms, depending on how such memories are conceptualized or understood, whether what 'we' remember is supposed to have actually happened or not. In the first case, we are dealing with claims about the supposed actual history of a given nation. In the second case, we are dealing in myth, with what people believe or would like to believe to have occurred even though it may not or is highly unlikely to have done so. The distinction between history and myth is not always a hard and fast one, of course, and for some, either or both will do. We may recall for instance that 'common myths and historical memories' together form one of the central features that Smith attributes to national identity (Smith, 1991, p. 15).

There are, however, a number of difficulties with both sorts of claims. In particular, there is a pronounced tendency in both nationalist ideology and in much writing about nationalism and national identity to minimize certain aspects of both nationalist history and nationalist myth, the extent to which both are constructed and the purposes for which they are deployed.

The idea that there could ever be one given, fixed, accepted, let alone objective account of the past is problematic. Any version of the past, narrative or otherwise, is bound to be selective, constructed according to a set of criteria of what counts as important or significant. What these criteria are and where they come from, in any given case, are often among the most interesting or important questions, perhaps nowhere more so than in the case of histories of the nation. Here, perhaps more than elsewhere, we have to understand the context within which those who construct accounts of the past operate. For, as Alan Munslow reminds us after all, while 'history is written by historians, [it is] best understood as a cultural product existing within society, and as a part of the historical process itself' (1997, p. 10). Where this process is understood in national terms, there is a temptation to assume what needs examination. This then may mask the considerable degree of invention often involved in constructions of the past.

This was famously the burden of the seminal collection (precisely on the 'Invention of Tradition') edited by Hobsbawm and Ranger. Defining tradition as 'a set of practices . . . which seek to inculcate certain values and norms by repetition, which continually implies continuity' and emphasizing that its 'object is invariance' (1983, p. 1), Hobsbawm suggested that nationalists were especially keen to construct accounts of a suitable historic past as an integral part of an exercise in social engineering. It is certainly possible to point to some very overt inventions of traditions and rituals for instance, and even to a number of cases of fraud and forgery in the service of nation-building (Ben-Yahuda, 1995; Trevor-Roper, 1983). However, as nationalist movements have become once again more politically effective, this more critical approach to nationalist historiography has itself come under attack. Some argue on postmodernist grounds, for instance, that all history is in some sense 'invented', that there is no truthful account waiting to be revealed, and that therefore singling out some traditions as 'invented' obscures the fact that all are (K. Jenkins, 1995). Others have argued that any distinction between myth and history is problematic. As David Archard puts it, this 'presupposes there is a true historical account waiting to be told rather than a variety of possible stories from different perspectives and serving distinguishable purposes' (1995, p. 478). He claims that 'historians do presume and have consistently presumed the existence of nations in their constructed narratives'. This ignores the many who have not done so. His recognition that 'far from being general demythologisers, they have often been the servants of particular national myths' points rather to the importance of their political role (p. 478).

Others have suggested that the kind of approach taken by Hobsbawm and his colleagues is too crude or implies too conspiratorial a view of the world, and that, whilst it may be the case that what is believed to have occurred in the past may not actually have done so, this is in some way beside the point. Just because a tradition or myth is invented does not mean that it cannot have powerful consequences. Neal Ascherson, for example, suggests that:

> To demonstrate that tradition is wrong or invented does not put an end to this story. A claim to national independence does not fall simply because its legitimizing version of national history is partly or wholly untrue – as it often is. The sense of belonging to a distinct cultural tradition, or 'ethnic identity', can be subjectively real to the point at which it becomes an objective social-political fact, no matter what fibs are used for its decoration. (1995, p. 274)

To argue, however, that it makes no difference whether the cultural claims are true or false seems less than compelling. It is not entirely clear why an obviously false account of the past should be preferred, other things being equal, to a more accurate one, even if the latter is not the final word on the subject. Whilst the falsity of claims about the past may not of itself undermine a claim to national independence, it may fatally weaken the claim to *historic* nationhood, leaving behind rather more pragmatic justifications which then have to be looked at in their own right. It may well be the case, to quote the famous aphorism from the American sociologist W.I. Thomas, that 'if men define situations as real, they are real in their consequences' (cited in

Sills, 1968, p. 3). But the real consequences of an imagined past surely need to be subject to critical analysis rather than uncritical celebration.[19]

We need in particular to look at how beliefs about the past are developed and the role such beliefs play in the present. If, as anthropologists have reminded us, we should certainly be wary about adopting too judgemental an approach to myths, we nevertheless need to think critically about their structure and function in a given society and polity. The Durkheimian emphasis on the functions of myth in strengthening social cohesion and legitimating the social structure is clearly significant here. Whilst it may be unhelpful to see them merely as irrational (though this is hardly irrelevant), we need also to understand their connection with power, how particular myths of identity especially are equally myths of alterity, how mythical constructions of the national self are also implicit or explicit constructions of others (Overing, 1997). Similarly, attention to myths directs us towards the ways in which nationalism and national identity are sustained by emotional attachments beyond the rational.

There are a number of ways in which national myths may work in this respect. In an interesting taxonomy, George Schöpflin (1997) has highlighted a number of functions of nationalist myths, pointing to their potentially deleterious or negative implications. Myths relating to territory can make political negotiation impossible. Myths of redemption and suffering in which fatalism and passivity become virtues can be used to foster the unquestioning acceptance of hierarchy and authoritarianism. Myths of election can underpin claims to moral and cultural superiority. Myths of rebirth and renewal can be deployed to disclaim responsibility for past injustices. Myths of ethnogenesis, antiquity and kinship can be used to justify the primacy of one group over another in a given polity or to exclude those thereby deemed not to belong.

Clearly we do not have space here for an extensive discussion of each and every type of national myth but it may be helpful to point to a few recent examples of the ways in which nationalist assumptions or purposes have structured and conditioned the elaboration and deployment of some of these. In an interesting study of the Celts, which throws considerable doubt on one powerful myth of continuity between ancient ethnie and modern nations, Chapman (1992) suggests that the origin of ideas that there was one Celtic ethnic group lies with Greek ethnocentrism and its concerns with the maintenance of boundaries between what were perceived as more or less civilized parts of Europe. There were no groups in early Europe who actually conceived of themselves as Celts.[20] Only in modern times, from the activities of nineteenth century philologists onwards, has there been a sustained and largely romantic search for Celtic roots and a propagation of Celtic culture, pursued largely by those who profit from it. At the same time, there are political implications in the present to be drawn from the dissemination of this particular myth. There are important elements of Celtic mythology in both Irish and Scottish nationalism which have, Chapman argues, distorted Scottish historiography in particular. Thus differences between Picts and Celts are downplayed because so much of Scottish identity has been constructed out of difference with England and the English. It is for the same reason that historically the Highlands and Highlanders with their Celtic forebears and Gaelic culture have been seen as defining Scottish identity rather than the Anglo-Saxon lowlanders of South-East Scotland who were much more culturally similar to the English.[21]

Herzfeld's work on the construction of the modern Greek nation reveals similar features. He writes 'the formulation of a Greek national identity in terms of cultural continuity was something of a novelty to the largely illiterate country people' (1982, p. 17). In his view, the process of ethnological justification for the new Greek state in the nineteenth century only set in after the event. In studying the more recent period, Karakasidou has focused on the sustained attempt to foster the idea of a continuous Greek ethnic history going back to Philip II and Alexander the Great. She has linked this to a concerted political campaign to assert a Greek cultural homogeneity, designed on the one hand to deny the existence of a Slavic Macedonian population in Northern Greece and on the other to underpin hostility to the new Republic of Macedonia for use of the name which is felt to be indelibly Greek. Opposition and indeed debate on this issue has been stifled by those holding institutionalized power in Greek universities who have waged a campaign against those who have challenged what is seen as a 'sacred' truth of national history (Karakasidou, 1994).

The past is not of course only the preserve of historians, and archaeology too has been important in developing ideas about the past. Indeed it can be argued that the rise of modern archaeology has been intimately bound up in many cases with the development of nationalism. The whole panoply of nineteenth-century archives, museums and libraries grew up alongside what Diaz-Andreu and Champion refer to as 'the consolidation of essentialist nationalism' (1996, p. 10). Whether it be the excavations at Masada and their exploitation for constructing Israeli nationhood (Ben-Yahuda, 1995), or Korean archaeology's obsession with a bogus idea of Korean ethnic homogeneity (Nelson, 1995), or the clash of Azeri and Armenian interpretations over the pre-history of the Caucasus, archaeology has proceeded on the basis that there can be found evidence of an unbroken history of peoples and ethnic groups in a given national territory. These political uses of archaeological findings need not be confined to the very distant past. In a nation with no possible ancient ethnic core (or at least not one that can be seen as the ancestor of the modern nation) like the USA, presidential tombs, Colonial Williamsburg and Washington itself became 'national' monuments (Zelinsky, 1988). Later, the National Parks Service expanded its role in developing historical sites that celebrated the development of the nation and told its story in particular ways.[22]

What is recalled or remembered in such cases is often highly selective. Long ago, Ernest Renan pointed out that it may be more important to nations that people forget as much if not more than they remember: 'The essence of a nation is that individuals have many things in common but have also forgotten many other things' (1996, p. 51). Alongside (and a condition of) the shared memories is often a shared amnesia or collective forgetfulness. Yet both the remembering and the forgetting involve reconstructing (or deconstructing) the past, activity which is subtly obscured by invocations of sharing. Memories, to put it another way, may have to be jogged or suppressed in various ways. At one level this may appear automatic, as Billig (1995) has argued. At another level, it may be much more overt.

Thus, in the declining years of Yugoslavia, the Serbian leadership set out quite deliberately to invoke 'memories' from both the distant and recent past with the aim of securing and consolidating an ethnonationalist political base. The defeat of a Serbian army in June 1389 in Kosovo at the hands of the Ottomans was turned into a mass mobilization 600 years later by Milosevic as he sought to take over the Yugoslavian federation or create a Greater Serbia under his own political control, linking historic memory to immediate political objectives (Judah, 1997; Silber and Little, 1995). For his part, the Croatian nationalist leader Tudjman sought to suppress memories of Ustashe atrocities in the war, both by downplaying estimates of mass murders, and by seeking to relativize them (Silber and Little, 1995). Of course, Tudjman was not alone in his efforts to suppress memories – arguably one of the crucial flaws in Tito's strategy of sidelining nationalist forces was that it denied people throughout Yugoslavia the right and need to mourn and work through the trauma of these experiences, so that when memories were recalled (or denied) later they had an explosive charge. As Tim Judah puts it, 'the effect . . . was not to make people forget, as was the intention, but to leave the wounds unhealed' (1997, p. 132).

Bette Denitch has written brilliantly on the different ways in which what she calls the 'symbolic revival of genocide' was then used by nationalist ideologues for the political project of dismembering Yugoslavia to their own advantage. While noting how 'traumatic memories on both sides became instruments of the power struggle', she asks how it is that personal traumatic memories (held after all only by survivors) become the collective memory of those who did not experience the original actual trauma. Part of Denitch's answer is that collective activity was orchestrated by political leaders and organizations (with the assistance of other supposedly non-political organisations such as churches), offering the connection between the individual survivor and others, as it offered a connection between the past and the present. Nationalist ideology here 'involves the exploitation of symbolic processes that mediate the communication between leaders and populace invoking them to think, feel and act according to its premises. [This is] the manipulation of symbols with polarizing emotional content' (Denitch, 1994,

p. 369). The invocation of a common past, the claim that there are shared historical memories, then became a key element in an effective nationalist discourse, designed to bind together some against others, identified as essentially hostile and dangerous in order to prepare the ground for and justify a murderous political project (see Chapter 5).

Territory and landscape

At the same time, such myths are rarely abstract. For a major focus of historical memory, and one which is often invested with religious significance, is territory, for which, fuelled by 'shared memories', people may be persuaded to fight, die and sacrifice themselves and others. Smith sees this as central, identifying 'an historic territory' as the first of his 'fundamental features of national identity' (1991, p. 14). He writes of the importance of landscape, of 'poetic spaces' – or rather of represented and imagined landscape in the formation of the nation. Painters, poets, musicians all contribute, he argues, to what he has more recently termed the 'sacred territory' of the nationalist homeland. Yet this cultural appropriation of territory is more problematic than it may first appear. For it is not simply a matter of hills and mountains, valleys and streams. Landscapes are often invoked to symbolize the nation, its values, its culture, and even its 'national character'. But why exactly does an attachment to a particular landscape or piece of land or type of 'nature' (itself thoroughly produced by culture and society) necessarily or automatically involve a *national* identity or attachment? Why is identity necessarily territorialized at all? If territorialized, why not to a more local or parochial area of attachment? Might it indeed be possible to have a deep attachment to a landscape without the baggage or superstructure of the nation as well? There is, too, a paradox here concerning the city and the countryside. Sacred territory is usually rural; yet the majority of people live in towns. It is unusual for the sacred territory of the national imagination to be a sprawling suburb, a shanty town, or an industrial estate! Is this connection between the nation and a vision of a rural idyll a nostalgic attachment to something from which one has been alienated, quite literally?

Michael Ignatieff argues, somewhat mawkishly, that 'land is sacred because this is where your ancestors lie. . . . Land is worth dying for, because strangers will profane the graves' (1994, p. 93). But where are the graves of those who died in Auschwitz or Srebenica or Rwanda? In the history of the worst excesses of ethnic nationalism, graves are something of a scarce commodity.

As our preceding discussion of historic memories might suggest, however, the idea that an identified area of land belongs over time to a particular group may not be politically innocent, and that we do not have, simply, sacred territories, but territories which have been sacralized, made sacred. Thus, for example, the Polish communist leader Gomulka made a speech near Wroclaw in Silesia a year after the end of the Second World War (which had seen Poland's borders shifted westward to fit in with Stalin's interests in the East and the desire to contain Germany), in which he attempted to claim the new boundaries and link them to a sacred past.

> Great historic events have let our generation return to the soil of our ancestors, the soul of our fathers . . . there is no way of Germanising history. Nothing and nobody can deny the fact that Polish Slavic Piast tribes lived here many years ago. Nothing and nobody can deny the fact that our ancestors, the landlords of this soil, defended it against belligerent German invaders at the battle of Glogow or Wroclaw. (Racczkowski, 1996, p. 209)[23]

Sacralization has been accompanied if not preceded by quite extensive coercion as borders have been allocated and demarcated by and between states. As O'Dowd and Wilson have reminded us, 'national boundaries are rooted in coercion, in practices of forcible exclusion and inclusion' (1996, p. 6). This coercive activity has both caused and taken place in a wider context of extensive and continuous mobility and migration. As Castles and Miller have noted, 'the post-1945 migrations may be new in scale and scope, but population movements . . . have always been part of human history. Warfare, conquest, formation of nations and the emergence of states and empires have all led to migrations, both voluntary and forced (1998, p. 48).[24]

Sacralization obscures the reality that borders are fluid and changing. Europe for instance, as O'Dowd and Wilson argue, 'has never had settled boundaries . . . Only 10 states (the largest being Spain), had the same boundaries in 1989 as they had in 1899' (1996, p. 7).[25] It may well be the case indeed that the most fervent claims to 'historic' ownership of a clearly marked out territory are often articulated by those with the least or weakest comparative claims on these grounds, the noise and fury of the claim being in inverse proportion to the evidence that can be mounted in its favour. This is certainly the view of two recent historians of Bosnia–Herzegovina who claim that 'as an integral territory, including Herzegovina, Bosnia has had more durable and widely recognized borders through the centuries than either Serbia or Croatia [which] have been laying claim to parts of Bosnia on ethnic grounds' (Donia and Fine, 1994, p. 7). If this is a case where rival claims are being made on the same (fluid) territory, there are other cases where the absence of rival claims does not necessarily mean the claims of the sole sitting tenant are politically unproblematic. In many parts of Eastern Europe, for example, large Jewish populations (which had lived there for centuries and surely constructed a distinctive culture) disappeared through extermination during the Second World War. Many towns, cities and villages in Lithuania, Latvia and Poland thus became distinctively monocultural only in the wake of the loss of significant sections of their 'historic' population (Mayer, 1990).

Thus there can be no recourse to an unproblematic notion of a sacred territory as the heart of the national homeland. Nor can one escape from the essentially political nature of claims to historic territory by way of simple cartography. For the drawing of maps themselves is not, as Anderson, following Thongchai, has reminded us, a politically innocent and objective recording of physical markers. Imperialist cartography provided a discourse (at more than one level) to serve as a paradigm for administrative and military operations, and, we would add, the political purposes that lie behind them (Anderson, 1991, pp. 173–4). The brandishing of maps indeed, as recent events in the former Yugoslavia have reminded us, may be an inevitable accompaniment to the descent into armed conflict that flows from rival claims to 'historic territory'.

Destiny

Such claims are not, however, only justified by reference to a historical or mythical past. For the future looms just as large in the nationalist imagining. The nation is also an imagined community of destiny, as Bauer (1996) noted, oriented towards the future. There are important links here between nationalism and religion, links which a Durkheimian approach with its focus on sacralization, rituals and symbols, is particularly well suited to illuminate. Certainly there are a number of cases in which the religious notion of the chosen people (notably adumbrated in the Book of Exodus) figures prominently in conceptions of national identity. Many writers (Greenfeld 1992; Hastings, 1997; Hayes, 1960) have traced the roots of English nationalism, for instance, to ideas of the Chosen People taken from biblical sources and expounded in the writings and speeches of Milton, Cromwell and others. In turn, core aspects of American nationalism are rooted in the concept of Puritan election and the notion of a unique destiny for the new chosen people who have made their own exodus to the new promised land (Smith, 1991, p. 150). Zionism and Afrikaaner nationalism are only two examples of other nationalisms which draw on similar ideas.

The purpose for which this or that people are chosen may of course vary. For the Children of Israel, it may be to go and establish a nation in order to provide a moral example to others; in Mazzini's vision, it may be that different nations have distinctive contributions to make to humankind; or, in the case of Nazism, it might be that the destiny of the nation is the establishment of a Reich that will last a thousand years. In any event, this destiny makes it possible for individuals to imagine themselves as part of the future, even or perhaps especially when they themselves are dead. Their own lives may in some sense then be redeemed or made more significant by the deeper purpose and meaning thus attached to the collectivity of the nation. They may then be able to think of themselves as living on in a sense after they are dead, achieving a kind of immortality. Perhaps more importantly, they may then have died to and for some purpose.

The links between nationalism and religion seem particularly strong here and again help us to account for and think critically about its appeal. For nations do demand and require sacrifice from their members in ways that are often associated with religions. As Hayes argued, people are now born into nations as they were into religions (and whether they are born with the nation's blood or on its soil makes little difference here – but see Chapter 4). They can then be called upon to fight and die for it, when their passing will be commemorated in a host of ceremonies, employing a raft of rituals and symbols of the kind noted above. As they are so sacrificed, they not only kill the other whose threat is so near the surface in the nationalist imagination, but their own death, it may be argued, serves further to consolidate the unity of the nation they have laid down their lives to protect.

> The flag in high patriotic ritual is treated with an awe and deference that marks it as the sacred object of the religion of patriotism . . . the soldier carries his flag into battle as a sign of his willingness to die, just as Jesus carried his cross to show his willingness to die . . . in both Christianity and nationalism, the violently sacrificed body becomes the god renewed – in Durkheimian terms, the transformed totem . . . is the soldier resurrected in the raised flag. On the basis of his sacrifice the nation is rejuvenated. (Marvin and Ingle, 1996, p. 2)

Many writers, such as Benedict Anderson, have been deeply impressed by the way in which so many people have been prepared to sacrifice themselves for love of nation (see Chapter 2). But we may also feel, more critically, that this love comes at quite a high and dual price, the killing of others and of selves, if it is to protect and fortify what we have suggested here is the problematic identity of the nation.

CONCLUSION

The fact that so many have been prepared to pay this price is of course testimony to the immensely powerful appeal the nationalist invocation of national identity has been able to make. In this chapter we have sought to think critically about what is involved in this invocation. We suggested, to begin with, that the use and even the construction of the concept of identity in relation to the nation was by no means straightforward, and that it is important to consider how national identity is presented and invoked, particularly in relation to the existence and possibility of other (multiple, overlapping) identities. We then highlighted some important arguments relating to the claimed depth and centrality of a national identity, particularly in relation to contested and contestable links with and conceptions of ethnicity and culture. Questions were then raised about some core claims relating to the national character of language, the nationalist use of history and myth and the problematic place of memories of the past and claims about the future, especially in relation to territory. Many if not all of these issues may be thought about as factors that explain the appeal of nationalism, although that has not been our primary concern here. Rather what we have sought to focus upon is what is involved when national identity is invoked, as opposed to other kinds of identity. Of course national identity can be invoked in many different ways and in support of many different kinds of nationalism. It is to some of the major ways that these nationalisms have been conceived and analysed that we now turn.

FURTHER READING

Interesting discussions of identity and ethnicity from an anthropologically informed sociological perspective are to be found in Jenkins (1996) and (1997). Social psychologists Reicher and Hopkins (2001) discuss national identity from a different disciplinary perspective to ours but similarly stress the ways in which national identity is essentialized, and they highlight the contribution made by academic psychology to such essentializations. Michael Billig's (1995) excellent discussion of 'banal nationalism' is a salutary reminder of the taken-for-granted ways in which national identity comes to be embedded in everyday life. Malik's *The Meaning of Race* (1996) traces the rise of racial thinking and the new cultural racism and its relationship historically to nationalism. On the cultural construction of nations and nationalism, Hobsbawm (1992) and Hobsbawm and Ranger's (1983) *The Invention of Tradition* are classic works. On the role of myths in the nation see Hosking and Schöpflin (1997). Although his perspective is different from ours, Smith's (1999) collection of essays is strong on bringing to the fore issues of myth, landscape and the sacred in the analysis of nationalism.

NOTES

1 A similar argument has been brought forward by Inden (1997) in relation to the work of Erikson, the key modern user and popularizer of the concept of identity (and identity crisis). Inden has suggested that it is important to locate Erikson's work (which equally fails to problematize the national) in the particular context of postwar America and the Cold War. Erikson was trying to deal with what may be seen as two related issues: how individuals come to participate in society, particularly through the critical phase of adolescence, and how immigrants

could be assimilated into America. The nation-state (or more specifically the idealized American nation-state) was the assumed pivot upon which much of his argument implicitly relied, in that it supplied the emotional glue that could attach both to society, without undermining the principles of freedom, rationality and individualism. As Inden points out, 'the place of the nation-state in this scheme was both crucial and problematic' (Inden, 1997, p. 69).

2 This is, of course, true of all forms of classification to some extent, and is even arguably central to any kind of meaning or social order at all, as Mary Douglas, drawing *inter alia* on Durkheim, argued many years ago (Douglas, 1966). See the helpful discussion in Woodward (1997, pp. 33–5). There are, however, particular implications for inclusion and exclusion in the case of national identity, as we shall see.

3 This is not to argue that the process of the constitution of a hostile other is an inherent part of human nature or necessarily present in all human societies, which Malik (1996) suggests is a problem with the use of this term. Rather the construction of the other is a social and political process which is (re)constituted historically.

4 Evans (1996) bases his argument in part on a more general claim that all identity is 'produced through the rejection of what is marked out as low, repulsive, dirty and contaminating' (p. 34).

5 As Miles (1993) points out, racism and nationalism were entwined in the ideas of nineteenth-century ideologues such as Knox and Gobineau.

6 For analyses of the racialized construction of the boundaries of the national collectivity in Britain, see Anthias and Yuval-Davis (1992, pp. 40–58) and Miles (1993, pp. 65–78).

7 See also Todorov (1993), especially pp. 156–7.

8 European colonialism frequently produced situations that created new ethnicities. Thus, the loosely defined social and occupational groupings of Hutu and Tutsi in Rwanda and Burundi became solidified into distinctive ethnic groups under the colonial administrations of Germany and then Belgium who treated them as separate 'tribes'. Divide and rule tactics in the colonial state then ensured the development of patterns of resentment and hostility that would be played on by ethnic leaders with catastrophic results culminating in the 1994 massacres of Tutsis by Hutus (Gourevitch, 1999; Mamdani, 1996). More generally, Eriksen has argued on the basis of examples from Mauritius, Guyana, Malaysia and elsewhere that 'ethnicity must be understood in relation to the colonial division of labour' which recruited certain groups to distinct tasks in plantation economies (Eriksen, 1993, p. 82).

9 For a questioning of the 'assumption that nations either have states or seek them' see Ramos' (2000) discussion of the case of the James Bay Cree within Canada.

10 A full discussion of this issue is clearly beyond the scope of this book and would take us into broader considerations of ideology, hegemony and especially cultural integration (Archer, 1985; Schudson, 1994), issues which in turn are linked to some of the meta-questions of sociological theorizing, the existence of value conflict or consensus in society (Smelser, 1992).

11 Although German historiography is his focus, Berger (1997) is quite explicit on this point, pointing to similar relationships between history and politics in Eastern Europe, in France, in Britain and in Italy (pp. 9–10).

12 It is also worth pointing out that in Herder's case, and even more in Fichte's, the argument that language is central does not mean that the language of each nation was seen as of equal value. Herder once memorably instructed Germans to 'spew out the ugly slime of the Seine' whilst Fichte insisted that German was quite superior to French (cited in Edwards, 1985, pp. 24–5).

13 There is some confusion however in his own analysis of language. He recognizes that only some pre-existing languages come to be associated with nations (some are assimilated, others welded together, others simply dropped) but also seems to believe that languages themselves are 'primordial', ignoring the extent to which languages are moulded, shaped and transformed over time (Anderson, 1991, p. 144).

14 See Anderson (1991, chs 5 and 6), for a number of examples of this.

15 A modern example of the nineteenth-century construction of new languages for nationalist purposes is that of the Lazi, who live in modern Turkey, and the codification of their language by a German philologist and enthusiast for their cause, Feuerstein. This has involved the production of a dictionary for a language which had previously only existed in oral form. See the discussions in Ascherson (1995) and Hann (1995).

16 A much more successful example is provided by the American intellectual and lexicographer Noah Webster, the originator of the famous Webster's Dictionary. Influenced by German Romantic thought, his avowed project in the years after American independence was to inspire 'the people' with 'the pride of national character' (cited by Tarver, 1993, p. 88), with a conscious policy of creating an American English distinct from British English. 'As an independent nation our honor requires us to have a system of our own, in language as well as government' (cited by Tarver, p. 88).

17 As Glenny has remarked, the demand for simultaneous translation in such cases is 'akin to somebody from Glasgow requesting that a Londoner's speech be translated into Scottish English' (1999, p. 146).

18 Differences between Cyrillic and Latin scripts, for example, were rooted in religion not nationality (Sucic, 1996).

19 This is something that conservative nationalists might reject on the Burkean grounds that myths are vital to the well-being of the modern nation and polity.

20 Simon James, too, more recently has added the voice of an archaeologist to this debate, arguing against seeing the peoples who inhabited Iron Age Britain and Ireland as one people or as the same as the similarly reified 'Celtic' peoples of continental Europe (James, 1999).

21 It may be noted that such Celtic mythologizing is not confined to the British Isles. Dietler (1994) has demonstrated the usages of similarly false or distorted ideas of a Celtic past in furthering other nationalisms within a European state (France), in regional resistance (in Brittany) to French nationalist hegemony, and even in the construction of a pan-European identity within the European Union. It is also worth pointing out that this has not been confined to any one

part of the political spectrum. In France, for example, the former Socialist president Mitterand, his Gaullist and allied opponents Chirac and Giscard, and the Front National on the far right have all made use of references to ancient Gallic triumphs, especially in the person of Vercingetorix, who is supposed to have rallied the Gauls against the Romans.

22 Nor in the USA has this simply been a function of federal or state authorities. Private enterprise like the impressive Old Stourbridge recreation of village life in nineteenth-century Massachusetts depicts a world without class or ethnic conflict.

23 See also Tighe (1990).

24 The results of this history can be seen in the information cited by Stepan (1994) from the Ethnic and Linguistic Homogeneity Index developed by the Department of Geodesy and Cartography of the State Geological Committee of the USSR Academy of Sciences which suggests that out of 200 states in the world only eighteen were ranked 96 per cent or more ethnically homogeneous.

25 As Kedourie puts it, 'natural frontiers do not exist, neither in the topographical sense favoured by Danton, nor in the linguistic which Fichte preferred; . . . Frontiers are established by power, and maintained by the constant and known readiness to defend them by arms' (1993, p. 120).

4

Good and Bad Nationalisms

INTRODUCTION

A constant theme running through much of the literature on nationalism is the dualistic attempt to make clear and sharp distinctions between two kinds, one progressive and benign, the other reactionary and malign. Attempts have been made to distinguish between Western and Eastern, political and cultural, civic and ethnic, liberal and illiberal types of nationalism. We examine the roots of these dualistic approaches in this chapter and subject all of these claims to critical scrutiny, suggesting that these supposedly fundamental differences are better understood as differences of degree and emphasis rather than principle. We conclude that all forms of nationalism have to confront and may be vitiated by the fundamental difficulty of what to do about the other, in relation to which the nation has to be both defined and constructed.

The Janus-face of nationalism

In a famous and influential article, Tom Nairn suggested that 'all nationalism is both healthy and morbid. Both progress and regress are inscribed in its genetic code from the start' (1977, pp. 347–8) (see Chapter 2). Nairn was perhaps unusual at the time in trying to deal with the complexity and at times baffling variety of nationalist movements by seeing nationalism as at one and the same time both positive and negative, a legacy perhaps of his background in Marxism. Many other writers have adopted a more dualistic approach, distinguishing more sharply between different kinds of nationalism, marking out more clearly positive and negative poles of reference.[1]

This tendency, to split nationalism into two fundamentally different types, has a long history in the literature, going back at least to the seminal work of Hans Kohn (1965). It can take, as we shall see, a number of different forms, not all of them necessarily consistent or compatible with each other. Whilst this may not in itself be an insuperable problem, there are a number of major difficulties, both theoretical and empirical, with the dualistic approach which cannot be easily resolved.

The theoretical difficulties are partly methodological and partly conceptual. To begin with, distinctions are often formulated in terms of dichotomous Weberian-style ideal types, not existing in a pure form in practice, but useful for comparing against the complexity of political and historical reality. Too often this seems to lead to the complexity being lost sight of in the heat of analysis and to the ideal type or model coming to stand itself for the reality. An analytical distinction (itself problematic) thus comes to be treated as real. At the same time, it can allow for, if not actively encourage, a certain slipperiness in argument, as writers attacked for overdoing a distinction between, say, civic and ethnic nationalism can retreat into a defence that they are only making analytical distinctions and that of course most nationalisms are a combination of both. Thus Anthony Smith writes that 'modern nations are simultaneously and necessarily civic and ethnic' (1995b, p. 99). Meanwhile the dichotomy establishes itself thoroughly in the literature.[2]

At the same time, the categories used by different theorists often overlap in ways that confuse and blur the distinctions between good and bad. What are held to be virtues in some accounts are vices in another. More seriously perhaps, the virtues themselves, what is held to make a particular form of nationalism good rather than bad, may have nothing essentially to do with nationalism itself. These supposed virtues may, in other words, be conceptually independent, stand or fall on their own account. Mixing them up with nationalism in one form or another may be both unnecessary and even counterproductive.

Empirically, certain sharp distinctions do not stand up to close scrutiny. Some of the often-cited classic historical examples of one type or the other appear to fall rather less than clearly into one side or other of a dichotomy than is often claimed. In the contemporary world too, and perhaps especially, a number of the distinctions are difficult to apply with any conviction. In relation to Western liberal democracies in particular there is a tendency to downplay certain features of nationalism and the nation-state whilst maintaining a full critical stance towards other manifestations of nationalism.[3] This is partly due to an ethnocentric bias which privileges the West, and partly due to a blindness to some of the contradictions in liberal nationalism itself. As a result, there seems to be a utopian character to the work of a number of writers as they fail to take account of (to borrow Bogdan Denitch's telling phrase) 'really existing nationalism' (Denitch, 1996).

Ultimately this dualistic approach, we argue, raises more problems than it solves. Whilst it would clearly be mistaken to assert that nationalisms are all exactly the same, or to deny that nationalism can take different forms across time and space, it may be more serious to underestimate what apparently different forms of nationalism have in common and the problems they may all pose. For at the heart of nationalism as a political project, whatever form it takes, is a logic that tends towards exclusion. There must after all always be people who are not part of the nation; the nation is always framed with the presumption of the existence of the outsider, the other, against which the nation is itself defined and constructed. The problem of the other is common to all forms of nationalism, constantly creating and recreating the conditions in which supposedly 'good' forms of nationalism turn 'bad'. The problem of dualism is that it obscures and cannot explain this continual slippage, and creates the illusion that somehow or other it can be avoided, when so much of the evidence points the other way.

One, two, many dualisms

It is possible to identify a large number of dualistic distinctions in the literature which have these characteristics. A cursory list would include all or some of the following:

Western	**Eastern**
Political	Cultural
Staatsnation	*Kulturnation*
Civic	Ethnic
Liberal	Illiberal
Individualistic	Collectivist
Voluntarist	Organic
Rational	Mystical/emotional
Universalistic	Particularistic
Patriotism	(Chauvinist) Nationalism
Constitutional	Authoritarian

Historic nations
Nationalism of the oppressed
Women–emancipation nationalism

Non-historic nations
Nationalism of the oppressor
Patriarchal nationalism

Some of these distinctions in the literature are more influential than others; some are overlapping; some refer to specific writers; others refer to more general tendencies. Whilst there is clearly not space here to provide an exhaustive treatment of all of these, we can highlight and analyse a central set which are closely related in terms of their foci of concern, and which may be understood in a sense as part of the same basic matrix. The contrast specifically between West and East, between the political and the cultural, between the civic and ethnic, between the liberal and the illiberal, are all, we may argue, hewn from the same rock. They emerge to some degree sequentially and to some degree as successive reformulations. Separately and collectively they are arguably at the core of the dualistic enterprise, seeking to arrive at the same point, at a clear and unambiguous point of distinction and contrast. If this point cannot in fact be reached even by these routes, it may be argued, perhaps it cannot be reached at all.

West and East

One of the earliest distinctions may be thought of on the face of it as more geographical than conceptual. This is the distinction between nationalism in its Western and its Eastern forms. Although less obviously in vogue today, it has played a prominent role in the work of some major writers on nationalism, from Kohn to Plamenatz and the late Ernest Gellner, writers whose work has spanned some sixty years and still remains influential today. Of course, this distinction could never be, and was never intended to be, merely geographical. Rather the words, West and East, functioned as containers, to be filled with a particular (and value-laden) content. According to Kohn (1965), nationalism developed in the West first and along singular lines. It was the product of the Enlightenment, of the age of reason, an essential expression of the confidence of rational (and especially) bourgeois individuals wishing to pursue their legitimate interests. Eastern nationalism by contrast developed in a profoundly different environment, along quite different lines and, importantly, in reaction to the success and confidence of the West. Plamenatz in turn identifies in the West a

> nationalism of peoples who for some reason feel themselves at a dis-
> advantage but who are nevertheless culturally equipped in ways that favour
> success and excellence measured by standards which are widely accepted
> and fast spreading, and which first arose among them and other peoples
> culturally akin to them. (1976, p. 33)

In contrast to this, the Eastern model represents

> the nationalism of peoples recently drawn into a civilisation hitherto
> alien to them and whose ancestral cultures are not adapted to success and
> excellence by these cosmopolitan and increasingly dominant standards.
> This is the 'nationalism' of peoples who feel the need to transform
> themselves, and in so doing to raise themselves; of peoples who come to
> be called 'backward', and who would not be nationalists of this kind
> unless they both recognized this backwardness and wanted to overcome
> it. (1976, pp. 33–4)

Both writers seem to suggest that the Eastern model is characterized
by an inferiority complex which produces an impatience and intolerance
that is a far cry from the rationalistic, constitutional Western model. A similar
sense that the West is the model to which others aspire (or ought to) and
to which they will sooner or later gravitate underpins Gellner's notion of
the different nationalisms of different time zones steadily moving westward
as they go (Gellner, 1994) (see Chapter 2).

There are a number of perhaps obvious objections to this whole
approach. The West/East dichotomy may be only a metaphor, but it is, even
on its own terms, a somewhat crude and inaccurate one, and liable to cause
disagreements even among its proponents. Is Germany located in the East?
It may be, if one starts in Britain or France. For Kohn it is Eastern, while
for Plamenatz it is Western! But what then of Ireland, which Kohn puts in
the Eastern camp?

More serious than any difficulties in acknowledging that the world is
after all round not flat, or, more accurately, a globe, is the problem of the
set of heavily value-laden assumptions that underpin the use of the concepts
of backwardness (Plamenatz), inferiority (Kohn) and incompleteness
(Gellner). These may be rooted in what Stuart Hall has called the discourse
of the 'West and the Rest', developed over hundreds of years of unequal
contact, imperialism and colonialism, founded on elements of power and
coercion (Hall, 1992b).[4] This discourse has deep historical origins in the form
of the opposition between East and West, going back to Roman and Greek
hostility to the barbarian others from the East, to the schism in Christianity
between Eastern Orthodoxy and Western Catholicism, to Christianity's
struggle with Islam, and to the contempt of some Enlightenment thinkers
for the East (Davies, 1997). This perception of cultural backwardness has
been a major factor in the importance many nations give to being 'European',
and in being as near to Western or at least Central Europe as possible. (It
is noticeable, for instance, how the term 'East-central Europe' has become
popular since the fall of communism as one way of carving out more
differentiation among the countries of Eastern Europe.[5])

The profoundly ethnocentric sense of Western superiority which informs
this particular dualism can then all too easily blind writers to the deficiencies

of Western nationalism as they rush to denounce that of the East. For it is
not too difficult to point to a number of the characteristics of supposedly
'Eastern' nationalism which appear to feature in Western nationalism, enough
to make the distinction murky. Waves of resentment against others (for stealing
'our' jobs, or swamping 'our' culture) have been a staple feature of right-
wing (both extreme and mainstream) nationalist discourse in France, Britain
and the USA for many years; the fruits of intolerance have produced the
widespread occurrence of acts of racial violence in many parts of the 'West'
now for decades or more (Björgo and Witte, 1993). Even the emotionality
attributed to Eastern nationalism has been clearly visible in the West whether
in situations such as the Falklands War in Britain, or the more routine celebrations of the nation in sporting triumphs and national commemorations
(Billig, 1995).

Political versus cultural nationalism

One of the primary distinctions that filled the East–West containers was the
contrast between (Western) political and (Eastern) cultural forms of nationalism. In locating the origins of Western nationalism in the Enlightenment
project, Kohn saw it as a part of a more general movement 'to limit govern-
mental power and to secure civic rights. Its purpose was to create a liberal
and rational civil society' (1965, p. 29). Thus, for example, 'English and
American nationalism was, in its origin, connected with the concepts of individual liberty and represented nations firmly constituted in their political life'
(p. 30). Intimately connected then with the liberal revolt against absolutism,
with the opening up of society, and (it is claimed) with democracy, Western
political nationalism was progressive, modern, the creation of the present
if not oriented to the future. The cultural form of nationalism, which
according to Kohn emerged in the East, was a reaction to this, opposed to
its core values and driven by a quite different dynamic. It emerged 'in lands
which were in political ideas and social structure less advanced than the
modern West. There was only a weak middle class: the nation was split
between a feudal aristocracy and a rural proletariat. Thus nationalism became
. . . a cultural movement . . . [led] to oppose the "alien" example and its liberal
and rational outlook' (1965, p. 30). Cultural nationalism looked elsewhere
for its justification, finding it not in reason but in emotion, not in the present
but in the past, turning inwards, to the imagination, to tradition, to history
and to nature.

   The sharpness of the contrast between the political and the cultural
roots of different forms of nationalism is, however, hard to sustain when
we seek to apply it to particular cases. Nations that are purportedly models
of the political form of nationalism appear both (positively) to exhibit a signal
pride in the achievements of 'their' own culture, and (negatively) to experience

recurring anxieties about their health, security, even viability. Such pride may be seen for example to underpin the assimilationist assumptions of, for instance, the French model of republican citizenship. Mitchell and Russell have further argued that 'a logic of assimilation clearly underpins [this] ideal type. Cultural assimilation is the price that must be paid . . . for integration into the political community' (1996, p. 67).[6] However, one can also note an obsession with culture in France as the basis for national identity, which has little to do with republicanism. Martin Thom has shown how sustained attempts were already being made in the early nineteenth century to use culture to identify a distinctively French national identity as opposed to a supposedly Germanic or Celtic one, concluding that this 'suggests that historians have been in error in ascribing the invention of cultural nationalism to the Germans alone' (1995, p. 257). On the other hand, from another angle, pride may be replaced by something more negative, by fears that this culture is vulnerable, under attack, threatened by the diluting and sapping presence of particular minorities. Movements have thus arisen (such as the Front National) which, (however disingenuously) explicitly eschew the overt racism of predecessors such as the Action Française in asserting the need to defend French culture (Safran, 1993).

Whether this amounts to a new form of racism is not the issue here.[7] Rather, it is necessary to point to the importance of cultural underpinnings for apparently political nationalisms, underpinnings that have to be fortified and sustained against both external and internal threats. Thus for some the existence of supposedly distinct and different national cultures underpinning the identity of West European states poses a serious barrier to moves in the direction of further European integration (Zetterholm, 1994). For others, it is necessary to mount a sustained argument for the existence and defence of a distinct (if not static) national culture against the disintegrating appeals of radical multi-culturalists (Miller, 1995). This may also involve the imposition of significant restrictions on immigration in order not to stretch the education system and other mechanisms of cultural integration beyond their capacity (Miller, 1995, p. 128). At this point the line between 'open' political and 'closed' cultural nationalism may seem blurred indeed. In a recent work, Anthony Smith has gone so far as to suggest that nationalisms of the Western European variety can be 'every bit as severe and uncompromising as ethnic nationalisms', arguing that 'the pedagogical narrative of Western democracies turns out to be every bit as demanding and rigorous – and in practice ethnically one-sided – as are those of non-Western authoritarian state-nations, since it assumes the assimilation of ethnic minorities within the borders of the nation-state through acculturation to a hegemonic majority ethnic culture' (1995b, p. 101).

Such dynamics of pride and fear may derive from a profound sense that political nations cannot themselves exist without a vivid and strong sense of their own cultural identity. They may lead to forms of nationalist politics which bear little resemblance to Kohn's optimistic picture, but in which nation-states seek both to impose 'their' culture on (selected) others internally (through assimilation) or to defend their cultural identities by excluding or raising barriers against others.

Civic versus ethnic nationalism

If the distinction between a good political and a bad cultural form of nationalism is then problematic, one alternative may be to distinguish between a civic and an ethnic form. In some ways, this can be seen as an extension or reformulation of the political/cultural distinction, drawing out more fully the implications of the civic element in Kohn's original formulation and, following him, locating this firmly in the West. Thus for Smith, 'historic territory, legal-political community, legal-political equality of members, and common civic culture and ideology; these are the components of the standard Western model of the nation' (1991, p. 11). Or in Ignatieff's more popular work,

> civic nationalism maintains that the nation should be composed of all those
> – regardless of race, colour, creed, gender, language or ethnicity – who
> subscribe to the nation's political creed. This nationalism is called civic
> because it envisages the nation as a community of equal, rights bearing
> citizens, united in patriotic attachment to a shared set of political practices
> and values. (1994, pp. 3–4)

The civic nation is 'an association of citizens' (Schwarzmantel, 1991, p. 207), with rights and obligations. Within the borders of the civic nation, on its soil, all may be citizens, according to the principle of *ius soli*. Membership is thus in some sense open, or at least not closed off in any a priori way.

In the ethnic model by contrast, the nation is, as Smith defines it, 'first and foremost a community of common descent' (1991, p. 11). Nations are the product of history and, to the extent that people are born into them, in a sense of nature too. 'Rather than free associations based on residence, they [are] historically determined entities based on ancestry' (Jenkins and Sofos, 1996, p. 15). The nation is thus a given, a fate, from which none may escape. As Smith puts it, 'whether you stayed in your community or emigrated to another, you remained ineluctably, organically a member of the community of your birth, and were for ever stamped by it' (1991, p. 11). One cannot at the most basic level choose to join this or that nation. The nation is overtly exclusive, closed rather than open. 'No one can become Kurd, Latvian or Tamil through adopting Kurdish etc. ways' (Kellas, 1991, p. 51). Citizenship is acquired by birth, through blood, determined by *ius sanguinis* not by *ius soli*.

The classic European examples of civic and ethnic nations, again placed along West–East lines, are generally held to be France and Germany. There is a long tradition in the literature, going back to Kohn and forward to the recent work of Rogers Brubaker, for whom even today 'the opposition between French and German understandings of nationhood and forms of nationalism remains indispensable' (1992, p. 3).[8]

The intellectual origins of this distinction may be traced back to German intellectuals such as Meinecke on the one side and French writers such as Michelet and Renan on the other. Michelet was the great historian and advocate of the egalitarian and humanitarian principles laid down and broadcast to the world by the French Revolutionary nation. Renan's seminal lecture 'What is a Nation?' (Renan, 1996) is often taken as a basic text for the civic model, 'a vindication', according to Stuart Woolf for instance, 'of the voluntaristic definition that originated with the French revolution . . . against the insistence on blood and soil that was being affirmed ever more widely in Germany' (1996, p. 48).

There are a number of problems, however, with this conventional contrast. To begin with, neither Michelet nor Renan, nor their followers, were exactly clear-cut or consistent in their approach to the French nation. Michelet's arguments are at best contradictory, undermined by a rather crass chauvinism and at times overt racism. As Todorov shows, 'the image that Michelet seeks to give France belongs to the purest ethnocentric tradition, which consists in attributing superlative qualifications to one's own group, without attempting to justify them' (1993, p. 217). Renan's arguments are flawed by similar racist assumptions. He did claim famously that 'a nation is the actual consent, the desire to live together . . . The existence of a nation is an everyday plebiscite' (Renan, 1994, p. 17). This formulation, however, was developed in a particular and highly charged political context. At the time Renan was writing, French nationalists were seething with resentment at the recent annexation by Germany of Alsace–Lorraine. The citizenship status of the residents of that area could then, as Weil has suggested, be argued to turn sharply on competing conceptions of the nation, conceptions that could be articulated as respectively either 'French' or 'German'. One way of understanding Renan's lecture then may be as a political intervention, its dramatic invocation of plebiscites intended to counter other, German claims to this territory (Weil, 1996).

It is not wholly clear, however, how seriously we are intended to take the notion of a daily plebiscite. This seems more of a romantic gesture, part of a rhetoric which has closer affinities than might at first appear with the object of its own critique, rendering any division between (French, Western) rationalism and (German, Eastern) romanticism problematic. As Silverman has argued,

> an analysis of Renan's lecture shows that his concept of the nation is informed by ideas of the spirit and tradition. Much of the imagery he uses is in keeping with the so-called Germanist tradition . . . his reference to

the nation as a 'spiritual principle' invokes the counter-revolutionary discourse informed by the romanticism of Herder. (1992, pp. 20–1)[9]

Renan's arguments are, however, more than merely romantic. The nation, according to Renan, is not only willed in the present but also a matter of culture (suggesting again that the distinction between political and cultural nationalism is flawed), and from this angle rooted in the past. But culture is, as we have seen, a problematic basis for the nation, and often a cover for a more vulgar biological racism. Indeed, as Todorov points out, Renan was a 'willing practitioner of popular racialism' and something of an anti-semite (1993, p. 228). In reality, Renan's apparently political nationalism was based, as Sternhell (1991) has argued, on rather different premises, those of a 'cultural determinism strongly influenced by racial determinism' (p. 32).

This, as Sternhell has indeed suggested, may help to explain a major puzzle about the kind of civic nationalism developed in France. It is often argued that there was a fundamental, irreconcilable conflict between the ethnic nationalism of the right and the civic republican patriotism of the left. This culminated in the Dreyfus Affair, which was in part a dispute about who could and could not be French. The driving obsession on the French right was to reverse the democratic and egalitarian implications of the Revolution. The right was not only Catholic, where the Revolution had been anti-clerical, it was also anti-semitic, where the Revolution had granted civic rights to Jews. Nationalist ideologues like Charles Maurras and Maurice Barrès hated the Jews in particular, whom they saw as inherently alien, rootless, incapable of becoming French. National identity for them was rooted in blood and soil. Nationalist movements, from Boulanger to the Action Française, aimed to take over or bring down the hated parliamentary regime in the name of historic French values, in the interests of a French nation, with a sharply differentiated, discrete identity. How then was it, if the civic nationalism of the left was so different from that of the ethnic and racist right, that in 1914, barely a decade after the end of the affair, left and right could come together so readily in a united defence of the sacred territory of the French nation?

One answer, indicative of a key element in civic nationalism, is that the French left, as much as the right, had at its own core a concern with national unity, was committed not only to the notion but to the forced construction of a homogeneous nation. The state in the Third Republic in fact took great care and devoted considerable resources to ensure that French became the common, dominant language, that a particular under-standing of French history was taught to all, that French territory (including Alsace and Lorraine) was seen as eternal, that a common culture was imposed on all living under its sovereignty. Without these efforts, after all, how could peasants and others have been turned into Frenchmen, as Weber (1976) put it, ready not only to take revenge on the hated Germans but also of course to extend the (imperialist) power of the French state over so many others through colonial conquest (plebiscites, of course, not being for everyone).

For a key element in the civic nationalism argument is the idea that all are or may be citizens of the nation. This seems rather questionable in the case of France at the time of the Revolution, often taken as the beginning of civic nationalism, when there were after all rather severe restrictions on who was or could be a full member of the nation, not least in terms of gender. The promise of universal citizenship, as it turned out, was not supposed to apply to women (Hufton, 1992). On the contrary, a good argument can be made that citizenship was constructed on an essential difference between masculine citizens and female others (Sluga, 1998). This was no temporary omission; women only gained the right to vote in France in 1945.

The English example, favoured by other writers, may be no more persuasive. Liah Greenfeld for instance, who has developed a version of the civic–ethnic contrast, connected to the opposition between individualism and collectivism, uses England, as we have seen (see Chapter 2). For her, the transformation in the meaning of the word nation, linked to profound structural transformations in fifteenth- and sixteenth-century English society, produced a form of nationalism which 'elevated every member of the community which it made sovereign' (1992, p. 487). Within this civic individualist version of the nation, in principle all could be members of a homogeneously noble nation. In reality, as even Greenfeld recognizes, this principle was rather heavily compromised, historically, by the systematic exclusion of the vast majority of the population (such as women, servants, Catholics, the poor) from the full exercise of civic rights.

Much the same was true for a very long time after the American Revolution, which founded another favoured civic nation. Civic recognition was withheld, it transpired here, not only from women (Hoff, 1996), but from both native Americans and black slaves. Native Americans were explicitly identified as aliens in a court judgment as late as 1831 (Daniels, 1998, p. 42), whilst it took a Civil War still decades later for slavery (revealingly not actually mentioned in the Constitution) to be formally ended, athough that did not put an end to major inequalities and to the continuing denial of many of the rights of citizenship. As Balibar puts it pithily, 'the American "revolutionary nation" built its original ideals on a double repression: that of the Amerindian "natives", and that of the difference between free "White" men and "Black" slaves' (Balibar, 1991, p. 104).

The ideal of the civic conception of the nation was then, at its inception in these cases, perhaps honoured more in the breach than in the observance. The point here is not to apply anachronistic standards to the past, nor merely to point out the flaws, imitations, and exclusions that were present at the birth of the civic nation. The problem is that these flaws are not simply of historical interest; problems of exclusion from rights of citizenship continue to haunt these very different civic nations, and the problem of the alien other is still a feature of civic nationalism.

Ius soli *and* ius sanguinis

It is often argued that civic nationhood is more open, more inclusive, more expansive than ethnic nationhood. Since ethnic nationhood is defined in terms of birth, it is only open to those born into the ethnos and closed to those who are not. Different legal principles are supposed to underpin these different conceptions of nationhood. Under *ius soli*, citizenship may be ascribed to all persons residing within a given set of borders. Under *ius sanguinis*, citizenship can only be ascribed to children of citizens. It is, however, difficult to find clear, unambiguous and consistent applications of the principle of *ius soli* in many Western civic nations. Not France, Britain, nor the United States has held consistently and confidently to the principle of *ius soli* for complex reasons that in many ways go to the heart of the problem of the dualistic approach.

It needs to be pointed out, to begin with, that *ius sanguinis* is used even by civic nations. As Mertes has pointed out, '*ius sanguinis* is a rule in most places in the world; children of American parents, for instance, are citizens of the United States even if born abroad. *Ius soli* and, of course, naturalization, are *additional* ways of conferring citizenship' (1996, p. 27; emphasis added). Thus, as Brubaker notes, although based to some degree on the principle of *ius sanguinis*, citizenship law in France has supplemented this with significant elements of *ius soli*. He concludes nevertheless that France and Germany represent polar cases: 'French citizenship law includes a substantial territorial component; German citizenship law none at all. Most other Western European *ius sanguinis* countries include some complementary elements of *ius soli*, without going as far as France' (1992, p. 81). However, whilst this has been the case for much of this century, it was not always so, nor always for the same reasons.

National identity, immigration and citizenship: the French case

Historically *ius soli* in France, far from being the product of democratization, was the dominant principle in France before the revolution, under the Ancien Régime. It was then pushed back under Napoleon. As Weil notes, 'it was decided that birth within the borders of the country was *not enough to guarantee the loyalty* of the children of those foreigners born in France' (1996, p. 77; emphasis added). Simple *ius soli* was then rejected and replaced by citizenship based on blood ties. It was not until much later, in the Third Republic, that *ius soli* was *readopted*; again concerns about loyalty were uppermost in the minds of policy-makers. Now, in a context of sustained enmity between France and Germany, the presence on French soil of residents who did not possess French citizenship and were therefore not obliged to do military service, was seen to be both unfair to French citizens who were burdened by this duty, and potentially dangerous (Withold de Wenden, 1994). The *readoption* of *ius soli* in these circumstances may be better understood as a state project to ensure citizenship for the potentially recalcitrant. It was accompanied by a rigorous programme of socialization, involving what Brubaker himself calls 'moral and civic indoctrination' in a national educational system (1992, p. 109). This was arguably designed to make loyal citizens of them all, to instil republican loyalties where they did not spontaneously exist.

Whilst sections of the French right have continued to pursue exclusionary objectives, targeting first Jews,[10] and more recently immigrants from Africa, the nationalism of the republican left has not been without its difficulties. As the *foulard* affair (see note 6) demonstrated, its predominantly assimilationist tradition is contradictory, appearing to be universalist and egalitarian but on its own particularist and intolerant terms. If they are to become members of the French nation, immigrants must assimilate to a given, dominant, national culture.

This has a number of consequences. Amongst other things, it leads to a tendency in that culture to render immigrants in some degree invisible in the depiction of the nation's identity, whilst at the same time there is evidence of racist criteria at work in the ways the French state has in reality sought to regulate immigration in the supposed national interest (Noiriel, 1988). Racist views are not of course confined to the elite, republican or not, but powerfully influence dominant conceptions of national identity. Hargreaves has identified a 'broad hierarchical ordering of ethnic categories by the French public [which] has remained fairly stable during the postwar period', although these 'ethnicized categories against which French images of national identity are constructed are seriously at odds with both the *de facto* participation of immigrants and their descendants within French society and with their own sense of belonging' (1995, p. 155; p. 159). It has not been easy for the French left to meet the challenge of such sustained racist nationalism, effectively mobilized by movements of the far right, by asserting the principles of the republic when these are themselves so contradictory. Rather what has been required is a move beyond the sacrosanct categories of the national itself, a re-interrogation of republican principles. In fact, as Catherine Lloyd (1998) has shown, the anti-racist movement in France has been impelled to develop along precisely these lines, articulating a demand for a 'new citizenship' which is not rooted in terms of nationality so much as in participation on an equal footing in the polity, in the economy and in society. This movement, Lloyd argues, has been at heart internationalist, challenging and critiquing the inherently ambivalent notion of a French national identity, and seeking to decouple citizenship from nationality altogether (see Chapter 7).

National identity, immigration and citizenship: the British case

Similar issues arise when we consider the British case, although here the pull of an exclusionary nationalism has been rather more effective. *Ius soli* in Britain was a product not of a political decision but typically (given the absence of a written constitutional tradition) of common law and precedent. In this case, as Cesarani (1996) has pointed out, citizenship laws have developed in a confused and uncertain manner, tied up with shifting definitions of national identity. These have varied over time, depending in good measure on who at any particular point in time has been perceived to have been the feared other. For, as Caryl Phillips has put it, 'Britain has always sought to define her people and by extension the nation itself by identifying those who don't belong' (1997, p. x). This has taken various forms, from attempts to construct models of the 'true-born Englishman' to the forging of 'Britons', analysed by Linda Colley (1992), in the course of prolonged conflict with France. Whether English or British, this identity has been premised on the existence of a dangerous other, to be suppressed, fought or excluded.[11] Robin Cohen (1997a) has also argued that this national identity may have been shaped to a significant extent by exclusionary measures taken to reject or eject those deemed not to fit the prevailing definition. Over time, those so proscribed have included former French allies, Jews (more than once), Lombards, Hansards, Flemings, Calvinists, Catholics, Spanish agents, continental revolutionaries, Germans, Gypsies, Bolsheviks, and especially since the war, black commonwealth citizens. Here, as he notes, 'the Other is a shifting category . . . But all are victims of a nasty version of the old game of "pass the parcel" [which] gets dumped into the lap of that group the Self, or more exactly the defining agents and agencies of the British identity, most need at that time to distance themselves from and repulse' (1997a, pp. 372–3).

The formulation of the appropriate categories to define who is and is not British has not been easy. At times, it has involved more or less overt racism, as both Miles (1987) and Cesarani (1996) have argued. The attempt to racialize national identity is certainly discernible in a number of legislative initiatives from the 1905 Aliens Act (deliberately constructed to keep out Jews fleeing persecution in Eastern Europe) to the legislation of 1962, 1968, 1971 and 1981, the last of which, Cesarani argues, 'exceeded all previous legislation . . . by abrogating the principle of *ius soli* . . . Such legislation exposed the racialized character of British nationality, reflecting the bitterly polarized and at one extreme, racist understanding of British nationality in the mid-1980s' (1996, p. 67).

This understanding was often obscured if not hidden, as policy-makers struggled with the difficulties of formulating a coherent policy on migration in the aftermath of Empire. It had after all been the riches of Empire and the ideology of 'mother country' which drew or encouraged many to come to Britain in the first place. As Kathleen Paul (1997) has argued, this produced a fundamental contradiction between what was initially a formally inclusive legal nationality policy and an informal, exclusive construction of national identity. The resolution of this conflict over time and in sometimes halting stages involved, as she has shown, the construction and pursuit of quite distinct strategies in relation to at least four designated groups. In the immediate postwar period, despite a domestic economic crisis and a labour shortage, white UK residents were encouraged to migrate to designated parts of the Empire. At the same time (and in sharp contrast with the treatment of Jews fleeing persecution from Germany in the 1930s), quite major efforts were made, at considerable cost, to recruit and integrate Europeans from refugee camps. Alongside this, in a more ambivalent way reflecting the tensions of a desire in the wake of independence to both define them as still British but also alien, Irish migrant workers were both recruited and accorded citizenship, whilst being at the same time subjected to sustained discrimination. Finally, in the wake of an immigration encouraged for economic reasons (cheap labour being the uppermost consideration), black migrants from the colonies (particularly from the Caribbean and the Indian sub-continent) were identified as a major problem, requiring a complex but ultimately drastic revision and retraction of citizenship. A succession of Acts were passed (in 1957, 1962, 1968, 1971 and 1981) which 'transformed British citizens into immigrants and immigrants into coloureds' (Paul, 1997, p. 169). This racialization of national identity, which, as Rich argues, 'drew on deep traditions of nativist reactions' (1990, p. 106) had the effect of effectively 'controlling the migration of subjects of colour, while allowing white subjects to migrate at will' (Paul, 1997, p. 180).

In recent years, many of the arguments, debates and exclusions previously visited on 'immigrants' have been reprised in relation to refugees. The 1990s saw a growth in the number of those seeking asylum and a raft of policies designed to exclude as many as possible of those fleeing from political persecution, ethnic conflicts, or those marginalized through discrimination and poverty in the name of supposedly integrating those who remain. The means employed have ranged from attempts to prevent refugees from reaching Britain through action against road hauliers, airlines and ferry companies, through the use of a discourse which has continually sought to separate undeserving 'bogus' or 'abusive' asylum seekers or 'economic migrants' from the deserving refugees, to measures that might deter potential refugees from seeking asylum in the UK in the first place, ensuring that Britain is not seen as a 'soft touch' for asylum seekers.[12] Thus many asylum seekers are held in various forms of detention to prevent them from simply staying in the UK illegally despite the conditions from which they might have fled. In March 2001 the number of those detained was 1,436 with a further 307 in a 'reception centre'; as the Home Office Research Development and Statistics Directorate puts it, 'a total of 1,743 persons not at liberty'. Finally, the Labour Government introduced a system of support that involved the issuing of potentially stigmatizing vouchers rather than cash at rates well below the normal welfare benefit levels, plus a system of coerced dispersal of asylum seekers round the UK often to areas of deprivation where they faced isolation, lack of support and racist hostility from the existing residents.[13]

It is difficult to interpret this complex and tortuous history as the expression of a coherent civic nationalism, given the discrimination and systematic inequities which appear to have marked successive revisions of citizenship, or to have a great deal of confidence in the civic character of a nation that has felt impelled to define itself by keeping out so many others on such apparently uncivil grounds.

National identity, immigration and citizenship: the American case

Many writers have seen the United States as the model civic nation in its openness to others and in the construction of its national identity on the basis of subscription to a liberal political creed. (As we noted earlier, however, this openness applied only rarely, if at all, to native Americans and the African American descendants of former slaves. After the Fifteenth Amendment to the US Constitution gave blacks the right to vote, in the South in particular a range of restrictions were introduced in the form of literacy and property tests, poll taxes, and criminal disenfranchisement provisions which had the effect – and the intention – of excluding as many black people as possible from local or national political participation.[14]) Notwithstanding this, in many accounts, the United States was not only a nation of immigrants from the beginning but in some ways has always idealized the immigrant. The immigrant is the one who chooses to move, to make something of himself/ herself, to make a new life in America (Goodwin-White, 1998). This ideal, it is claimed, lay at the heart of the American Revolution, which was based on a fusion of democratic, liberal and cosmopolitan principles. For Reed Ueda, the United States was

> historically a country in which heterogeneity formed the basis of the state
> . . . the state arose from a democratic and cosmopolitan nation shaped
> largely by immigration. . . . The Revolution popularized a new conception
> of national identity in the struggle to separate from the English, a new
> people bred from the frontier and the mingling of several nationalities.
> (1997, p. 39; p. 50)

It is true that the scale and variety of immigration has been greater in the United States than anywhere else in the modern world. Between 1790 and 1970 it has been estimated that something like 50 per cent of population growth was due to immigration whilst even today it is estimated that one-third of population growth stems from the same source (Hatton and

Williamson, 1998; Keeley, 1993). However, this has not been a uniform or unproblematic development for a variety of reasons that are particularly pertinent here.

There has from very early on in America been something of what Perea calls a 'love–hate relationship' with immigration (1997, p. 66). Immigrants from North and West Europe were not always welcoming to others who wished to follow in their footsteps. A whole battery of legislation has been framed in relation to immigration, from the Alien and Seditions Act of 1798 onwards. (Indeed it has been suggested it was American legislation that some people in Britain took as their model at the end of the nineteenth century – Cohen, 1992). There have been great surges of national panic over immigration, focusing on a variety of targets from the 'savage' Irish in the 1850s to the Chinese in the 1880s, Jews and Catholics in the 1890s, and Japanese in the 1900s (Reimers, 1998). By 1917 the racialized focus of concern was all too clear, culminating in the legislation of 1924 hailed at the time in one newspaper as a 'victory for the Nordic race' (cited by Feagin, 1997, p. 25). This established ethnic quotas designed to encourage immigration from Northern and Western Europe and exclude others. It was only in 1965 that this racialized system was overturned. In the meantime, there were growing concerns, not new in themselves but particularly acute at the height of the Cold War about the dangers of ideologically 'unsound' or dangerous immigration (Jacobson, 1996). In any event, by the 1980s the consequences of a relatively non-discriminatory policy were beginning to be felt, with a significant influx from Asia and fears of a mass influx from the South, at which point another major campaign began to develop to restrict immigration. Its success in again restricting immigration may be seen as a part of the conservative backlash against the supposedly radical 1960s (Capaldi, 1997; Duignan and Gann, 1998).

There is much in this that puts into question the romanticized self-image of the identity of a nation that prides itself on being open to the other.[15] It may make more sense to think of this identity not merely as paradoxical but inherently contradictory (Jacobson 1996). On the one hand there is the articulation of democratic, cosmopolitan and egalitarian principles which are at least implicitly universalist. On the other hand, there is, from the very act indeed of separating from Britain, from the Old World, a move towards the particular, to the assertion of uniqueness, of the importance of selection if not even (in its Puritan formulation) of election.[16] Horowitz (1998) claims as its great virtue that, unlike even other republican nations such as France, the United States has no core identity because it is continually reshaped by immigration. As we have suggested here, this both overstates the continuity of immigration, obscures the selective criteria deployed to control it and understates the effort put in to define who can and cannot be 'American'.

Exclusion in a 'new' civic nation: South Africa

This is not to suggest that immigration poses a special problem for national identity in America, whereas in other countries national identity is more secure. All national identities, and the nation-states that shape and depend upon them, face the same problem to a greater or lesser extent, which even the new civic nation of South Africa is discovering, as Croucher (1998) has recently and persuasively argued. There is something painfully ironic here, inasmuch as the struggle against apartheid was conducted on a wider basis than the national, both on a pan-African basis and across continents. Since the collapse of the apartheid system, South Africa has apparently attracted significant immigration, although estimates vary wildly; in the case of illegal immigration, for instance, figures range from two to eight million (*Migration News*, 1998c). There is here the typical combination of push and pull factors that one might expect in a regional context of extreme differences in wealth. According to one estimate, South Africans may be thirty-six times richer on average than Mozambicans (when Americans are 'only' seven times richer than their neighbours to the south (*The Economist* 4 March 1995, cited in Croucher, 1998, p. 645). Croucher argues that immigration here poses a challenge to nation-building on much the same lines as we have suggested it poses an acute challenge to the civic nature of the nation-states of France, Britain and the United States. The forms of rhetoric and discourse she has identified certainly seem remarkably similar. There is a similar politics of resentment and hostility to immigrants, a similarly invoked sense of a 'nation' under siege, at risk of disappearing under a tide of crime and insatiable demand, a similar sense of overwhelming panic. What is perhaps more tragic than ironic in this case is that, not so deeply buried in such projections on to the negatively defined other, are elements of the very racism from which the people of the region have struggled so hard to escape. A recent report concluded from its survey data that 'South Africans are more hostile to immigration than citizens of any country for which comparable data is available' (Mattes et al., 1999, p. 8), whilst a recent survey found that both blacks and whites prefer white to black immigrants (*Migration News*, 1998c). A report by the Southern African Bishops' Conference in May 1995 attacked the prevailing level of xenophobia in South Africa and concluded that 'one of the main problems is that a variety of people have been lumped together under the title of illegal immigrants, and the whole situation of demonizing immigrants is feeding the xenophobia phenomenon' (cited in Human Rights Watch, 1998a, p. 2). As a result, support was found for forced repatriation of immigrants among 65 per cent of respondents in a recent survey (cited in Human Rights Watch, 1998a). In 1997 nearly 200,000 immigrants were deported, with the number having risen every year since 1994. According to Human Rights Watch,

Suspected undocumented migrants are identified by the authorities through unreliable means such as complexion, accent, or inoculation marks. We documented cases of persons who claimed they were arrested for being 'too black', having a foreign name, or in one case 'walking like a Mozambican'. (*Human Rights Watch*, 1998a, p. 3)

Immigration has perhaps not so much replaced race as the issue around which the new South Africa defines itself, as Croucher suggests, as subsumed it. Either way, it is clear that we have here yet another case in which a nation, even a supposedly civic one, may be seeking to define itself by those whom it excludes since 'it is by defining who they are not that South Africans are defining who they are' (Croucher, 1998, p. 656).[17]

Immigration, national identity and the nation-state

What immigration in all these apparently civic cases has done is to pose a very sharp set of questions about national identity. Questions about who may be included and who must be kept out, about who has rights and who does not, are about the composition and character of the nation, and about the nature of the polity itself. Immigration may periodically have been welcomed, indeed organized, if it has been perceived to be in the national interest, but care has always had to be exercised that immigrants were of the right type so that their entry would not subvert the existing, dominant and reified vision of national identity. In all of this the civic nation-state has played a central role. For, as Briggs has pointed out, 'in a world of nation-states, immigration control is a discretionary act of government. Regulation is thus directly linked to sovereignty over a particular land area' (1996, p. 3). Insofar as civic nations are defined in terms of their control over territory,[18] it can be argued that they are driven to control immigration. For Boyle et al., 'the civic conception of the nation has clear implications for migration. If membership of the nation is determined by place of abode . . . Unregulated immigration poses a major threat to such a nation, since it implies a loss of control over who can and cannot become citizens' (1998, p. 155).[19] However, in order to justify such regulation, apparently civic nation-states have had to engage in a set of mystifications, making arbitrary distinctions, and erecting a host of barriers and gates.

Distinctions, for instance, between legal and illegal, economic and political, voluntary and forced migration are not only conceptually prob-lematic (Lucassen, 1997) but, when used to discriminate, liable to lead to civic nation-states breaking their own norms (see Chapter 5).[20] At the same time, such discriminatory policies have led to a contradictory state of affairs with regard to citizenship within civic nation-states, involving distinctions between fully fledged national citizens, denizens (or migrants who have stayed despite assumptions to the contrary) and aliens (Barbieri, 1998; Castles and Miller, 1998; Hammar, 1990). It has been argued that such distinctions (particularly between citizens and denizens) cannot for a variety of reasons be sustained in the long run and are eroding fast (Jacobson, 1996; Soysal, 1994), but this seems somewhat overstated, if not from our perspective somewhat over-optimistic (see Chapter 7). There remains still today a signifi-cant set of distinctions within the optic of the nation, between the nation's own citizens with (at least formally) full rights; denizens who have some rights but few if any of a political nature; and aliens who have very few.

Citizenship and the nation: inclusion or exclusion?

Citizenship in the 'civic' nations of France and the United States, as well as in the new South Africa, is thus rather more problematic than the civic model suggests. It is no longer (if it ever was) so open. This, we may suggest, has to do with the way in which the category of the national has taken precedence over that of the citizen. For despite appearances, citizenship and nationality are grounded differently. Oommen has suggested that citizenship is about equality, a category whose internality to a given society is not questioned, whereas nationality (and he adds, ethnicity) are about kinds of collective identity which precisely raise the possibility of externality. Thus, 'while nationality and ethnicity as identities are exclusionary and could be inequality generating, citizenship can essentially be inclusionary and equality oriented' (1997, p. 35). Now of course it can be argued that, in its own various ways, citizenship too is exclusionary. Minors may be excluded on grounds of age; felons on grounds of their failure to observe the laws; tourists on the grounds that they are not staying long enough to take on the burdens that go with the rights of citizenship. Some would argue (see Chapter 7) that any conception of politics implies some sense of bounded space within which political activity can take place, within which people may be citizens. There is no necessary reason, however, why this space has to be articulated in national terms, why the grounds of exclusion have to be based on the idea of nation, on associated conceptions of national identity. The principles of exclusion from the nation-state, even from supposedly civic nation-states, are framed characteristically in terms of who is deemed to belong to the nation and who is not, who may or may not threaten the nation's identity, a closure which necessarily has effects not just externally (on those excluded) but also internally (on those included) as well as those caught between nation-states, the stateless (see Chapter 5). Repeatedly within civic nations there has emerged a recurring anxiety about the other, however defined and wherever located, responses to which expose fundamental difficulties with the construc-tion of civic rather than ethnic foundations for the nation. This anxiety may focus on the presence of 'foreigners' of dubious loyalty who may have to have citizenship forced upon them, or from whom it may have to be forcibly wrested. It may generate denial, whether that 'others' have always been 'here', or of 'their' rights once here. It may lead to the erection of barriers to keep 'them' out or to gates to regulate their controlled admission. However, as long as the other is perceived in inherently hostile terms that are also in a fundamental sense constitutive and defining of the identity of the nation itself, the distinction between civic and ethnic is hard to sustain or apply. To see recent policies in particular as merely contingent, the result of specific historically atypical political pressures in the present forcing hitherto impeccably civic nations to abandon or retreat from long-held beliefs or deeply cherished traditions, seems unconvincing. Rather they may be better understood in terms of a shifting repertoire of responses to a problem for which there is, within the nationalist frame of reference, no easy or 'good' answer. The drift back to ethnic criteria, if not all the way to *ius sanguinis*, may be understood as (at best?) a search for firmer ground, a more certain answer to a question that will not go away.

Is this inevitable? Is there not another form of nationalism in which this problem may be managed in a 'civilized' fashion, in which the other is neither denigrated internally nor externally. Can there not be a liberal form of nationalism, founded on respect for the rights and freedoms of all?

Liberal versus illiberal nationalism

In recent years, there has been renewed interest in the possibility and desirability of a form of nationalism, anchored in or tied to liberal beliefs and values. In this liberal version, nationalism is moderate in ambition and temperament, valuing loyalty to and identification with the nation but not in excess, and not to the extent that this would override other values and commitments. It sees national commitments as understandable and legitimate, not merely emotional, able to balance particularism (loyalty to this nation) with universalism (a recognition that all have rights of various kinds). The contrast here would be with an illiberal form of nationalism. This would be more demanding of the commitment of its members, especially emotionally, seeing loyalty to the nation as the supreme good, overriding other commitments, demanding if necessary the supreme sacrifice. It would thus be particularist rather than universalist.

This is not a wholly new contrast of course, as we noted in Chapter 1. In the first half of the nineteenth century, many nationalists assumed that liberalism and nationalism were not merely compatible but more or less synonymous. However, as we have also seen, particularly in the aftermath of the First World War, a number of liberals came to believe that liberalism and nationalism were fundamentally opposed systems of belief. Why then have more recent liberals sought to reinstate the connection, to claim, as one such writer puts it, that 'the liberal tradition, with its respect for personal autonomy, reflection and choice, and the national tradition, with its emphasis on belonging, loyalty and solidarity . . . can indeed accommodate one another' (Tamir, 1993, p. 279)?

For liberal nationalists, one answer to this is that we are all nationalists nowadays, that it is simply unrealistic to deny that people have to identify with and have some kind of loyalty to 'their' particular nation. For Miller, this particularism is real, whilst universalism is based on assumptions which are too heroic, beyond the capacity of ordinary mortals. People have 'natural sentiments' which predispose them 'so that the judgements we make about others must reflect their (and our) natural preferences for kinsmen and associates' (1995, p. 58). National identity is inescapable; it cannot be avoided; it is something into or with which we are born. The belief that we can choose our identities (what he calls the 'radical chooser' model) is an illusion. Although Tamir does leave some room for choice here, she still thinks that 'membership in a national culture is part of the essence of being human' (p. 36). We develop within particular, national social contexts which, whilst they help us acquire a sense of our own individuality, at the same time impel us to identify with our fellow-nationals, members of our national community first and foremost (Canovan, 1996b; MacCormick, 1982, p. 247). The nation provides a context or framework in which it becomes possible for individuals to become autonomous self-determining human agents. 'Life in a cultural environment that is familiar, understandable and thus predictable, is a necessary precondition for making rational choices and becoming self-governing' (Tamir, 1993, p. 84). Culture is here a primary good, a critical medium through which different ways of life may be conceptualized and pursued. Without a national culture, it has been claimed, we would be unfree, like slaves, 'in a moral and social wilderness' (Couture et al., 1996, p. 635). Liberal nationalists thus attach great significance to national culture, and see it needing to be both promoted and defended in various ways (Bonin, 1997). As Tamir puts it, 'liberal nationalism thus celebrates the particularity of culture together with the universality of human rights, the social and cultural embeddedness of individuals together with their personal autonomy' (1993, p. 79).

At the same time, these particular identifications and loyalties, whilst prior, must be balanced with others. For, as MacCormick (1982) recognizes, it would be morally intolerable to claim that the nation overrides all other claims on the individual. For Tamir, it is precisely the 'main characteristic of liberal nationalism that it fosters national ideals without losing sight of other human values against which national ideals ought to be weighed' (1993, p. 29). These include commitments to others, not just members of one's own nation. Indeed, MacCormick asks how 'could one learn to love mankind universally if one had not at first learned to love people in the concrete in the narrower range' (1982, p. 253)?

There are a number of difficulties with these arguments. Leaving aside the unargued (and highly conservative) assumption that internationalism is too 'heroic' for ordinary mortals, it has to be said, to begin with, that for many writers the idea that national loyalties do have to override others is precisely the point, just that which defines nationalism. Thus for Hroch nationalism is 'that outlook which gives an absolute priority to the values of the nation over all other values and interests' (1993, p. 6), whilst for Gellner nationalism promotes the view that 'obligations to the nation override all other public obligations' (1983, p. 1).

In any case, if Tamir is right to concede that liberalism comes into play, as it were, after nationalism, after national loyalties have been established, it is not easy to see why or how it can moderate nationalist commitments. It would seem, on the face of it, perhaps more likely that other kinds of more primary identifications, alternative or antithetical solidarities (such as class or gender for instance) cutting across, if not subverting, nationalist ones, would be more effective. Opposition to national wars have indeed often come from such quarters, as in the First World War from feminists such as Sylvia Pankhurst or from sections of the international socialist movement. Nationalist sympathies work rather to undercut these other, rival identifications (Dahbour, 1996).

The thrust of liberal nationalism, however, is not so much to modify let alone oppose nationalism as to 'translate' its arguments into liberal terms (Tamir, 1993, p. 14). This effort of translation, however, seems to involve rather significant accommodations to nationalism, particularly in relation to the assumed priority of national identifications. Behind the claim that individuals need familiar environments within which to develop is an assumption that this environment has to be national. Insofar as liberal nationalists concede the strength of communitarian arguments that individuals are not isolated, atomistic monads but exist and develop within social contexts, the latter are assumed to be pre-eminently national. This is not, however, quite as obvious as it seems. Children are, after all, born not so much into nations as into families (of varying kinds). Families exist within a variety of contexts, as individuals develop identities within (and loyalties to) a variety of groups, not only (or even) the nation. The assertion of the primacy of national culture, if not prone to reification, tends to obscure the existence of competing or alternatives sources of meaning and commitment, removing ambiguity or ambivalence.

In any case, if Anderson is right to emphasize the degree of abstraction required to imagine the nation, awareness of the nation comes later rather than earlier in this process. The thrust of the liberal nationalist argument is to assume that, as an abstraction, the nation is more accessible, more direct than others, such as class or gender or humanity itself. Yet, as Todorov argues, 'the nation is an abstraction with which we have as little immediate experience as with humanity . . . The family ensures immediate interaction with other human beings; its principle may be extended, in extreme cases, to all the people we know – but no further' (1993, p. 385). As far as interaction with others is concerned then, it is not obvious that we have more contact with fellow-nationals than others. Challenging this notion, Brighouse has argued that

> we interact as significantly with members of other nations as with our fellow-nationals. The Detroit autoworker interacts as closely with her Japanese counterpart as with the Vermont organic farmer. The Scots fisher-woman interacts more with the Icelandic fisherman than with the East Grinstead stockbroker. (1996, p. 388)

The nature of our interactions with fellow-nationals or others is in any case critical. Is it actually the case that we are always or everywhere moti-vated by a greater concern for fellow-nationals than others? Norman Geras (1998) has argued strongly against this, citing the instances where rescuers of Jews in the Holocaust were, in their own words, motivated by a concern for others simply as human beings. In such cases, solidarity with others, simply by virtue of their fellow humanity, was not hindered by an inability to identify with others because they were part of some enormous, unimaginable unit, humanity. If scale is a problem, then identifying, say, with 'my fellow Americans' would also be impossible. 'It is just not credible', as Geras again points out, 'that the significant threshold in this matter, where compassion and solicitude will go no further, lies somewhere beyond several hundred million people' (1998, p. 137).

Core liberal arguments turn of course on the idea that each individual has certain rights, such as freedom of speech, of association, of movement. It is the state which typically has been the main culprit in liberal eyes in the denial or removal of these rights. However, insofar as it is a nation-state, concerned with the national interest and with what it deems to be national security, it frequently asserts its own authority to curtail such rights. It is hard not to feel that it is the liberal nationalist unwillingness to challenge these kinds of considerations that has made it so easy for them, as Tamir herself has acknowledged, 'to circumvent such thorny issues as membership and immigration, as well as the more general question about how groups are structured' (1993, p. 139).

It is difficult to see how selective membership of the nation-state and related state controls on immigration can be justified on liberal grounds, just as there is no obvious reason to accept that culture is *ipso facto* national or that national identity is the main identity that matters. Rather it could be argued that it is precisely making these assumptions in the first place which motivates or drives the move to exclude, to keep out, to raise barriers in the defence of the nation, national culture and national identity. In the process, rights may be denied to those who find themselves outside the nation-state, whilst those who are not seen to fit in with the 'national' culture, who do not fit with dominant conceptions of the nation's 'identity', can become the targets of quite illiberal treatment.

CONCLUSION

Comparable processes of exclusion seem arguably implicit in all the different forms of nationalism we have looked at in this chapter. What this suggests at the very least is that there are certain deficiencies in the tradition of dividing nationalisms into two distinct types. The dualistic models which we have discussed are highly interlinked and depend on implicit or explicit assumptions that there are good and bad (or bad and tolerable) forms of nationalism. There are, however, a number of ways in which this sort of approach is flawed. As we have moved from East to West, from cultural to political, from ethnic to civic, from illiberal to liberal – and back again – we have seen the recurrence of a pattern that is common to all them. That pattern is the problem of the other against which all definitions of the nation are constructed. Nationalism, however benign in form, must always seek to define the nation by reference to something else that it is not. The problem of forming boundaries and defining who falls on one side and who on the other is still at the heart of the nationalist project.

FURTHER READING

Kohn (1965) gives one of the classic statements of the division into Western and Eastern nationalism. Smith's (1991) study *National Identity* makes extensive use of the distinction between civic and ethnic nationalism. For a discussion of the historical origins of this distinction in the French and German cases, Brubaker (1992) is indispensable, although he has now questioned this distinction himself (in Hall, 1998). Renan (1994) should be read by students of nationalism, but put into context by Todorov's (1993) study of French thought. There is a huge literature on the issues raised about migration and citizenship. Cohen's *Frontiers of Identity* (1994) is a very good historical and contemporary account of exclusions in relation to British identity. The collection edited by Cesarani and Fulbrooke makes some incisive and penetrating criticism of nationalism in this context, as do Jenkins and Sofos (1996). More theoretical discussions of liberal nationalism occur in Tamir (1993), Miller (1995) and, more critically in Canovan's interesting (1996b) study. A sharp and compelling critique of the illiberal manner in which nation-states have historically developed policies in relation to asylum can be found in Noiriel (1993).

NOTES

1 There are of course some prominent exceptions to this. Carleton Hayes moved from a simpler division into good and bad forms to a six-fold classification of forms of nationalism (Snyder, 1990). Giddens (1993) and Kellas (1991) provide three-fold classifications.

2 See, for example, Michael Ignatieff's popular book and television series *Blood and Belonging* (1994), or Raymond Breton's (1988) analysis of nationalism among French- and English-speaking inhabitants of Canada.

3 For a good discussion of this see again Michael Billig's *Banal Nationalism* (1995).

4 See too Edward Said's analysis of 'orientalism' (Said, 1985).

5 Thus, for example, Holy (1996), in an interesting recent account of Czech national identity from an anthropological perspective, has shown that the Czech view of the Slovaks associates them with the East rather than the West, and that this is associated with a whole set of binary opposites which sees the Czechs as associated with modernity, history, progress, culture and rationality, while Slovaks are associated with traditionalism, lack of history, underdevelopment, nature and the emotions.

6 This has been seen most clearly in recent years in the so-called *foulard* or head-scarves affair. This *cause célèbre* which arose out of the desire of three female Muslim school students to wear headscarves in school was treated by sections of the left as well as the right as an affront to French culture. Left intellectuals such as Regis Debray wrote a letter to the French education minister warning of 'the Munich of Republican education' (cited by Moruzzi, 1994, p. 659), an extraordinary analogy! In this dispute, as Moruzzi suggests, 'any insistence on serious cultural difference' was seen 'as a perverse refusal of French values, French identity, and the French republican tradition' (p. 660). Thus the assertion of political, secular and Republican values was at the same time an assertion of a homogeneous French culture (Moruzzi, 1994).

7 But see Martin Barker's analysis of the 'new racism' that affirms the inevitable (and 'natural') divisions arising from cultural differences, whilst avoiding the crudity of more overt assertions of inferiority and superiority (Barker, 1981). Paul Gilroy too has argued that 'race is now being defined almost exclusively through the ideas of culture and identity' (Gilroy, 1993, p. 57). See also Malik (1996).

8 But note that in a later essay Brubaker has criticized the distinction between civic and ethnic nationalism 'especially in the rather simplistic form in which it is usually applied' as 'both analytically and normatively problematic' (1998, p. 299).

9 Renan insisted in his memoirs on his great admiration for Herder, calling him 'my king of thinkers' (cited in Birnbaum, 1992, p. 379).

10 On the repeated assaults on Jewish citizenship throughout the life of the Third Republic see P. Birnbaum (1992).

11 The war with revolutionary France, central to Colley's (1992) account, was fought, it may be noted, with another civic nation and involved not only the conflict with a hostile other, but also the repression of radical groups. Colley suggests that the recruitment of volunteers into the militias, from all classes, to face a possible French invasion was a key moment in the creation of a popular British patriotism. To the extent then that the 'British nation' was forged in an explicitly

counter-revolutionary project aimed at a hostile other, one might argue that its civic character is at best contradictory, rooted in conflict not just with another civic nation but with large sections of its own population.

12 For a full account of some of the worst aspects of the treatment of refugees in the UK see Hayter (2000, esp. ch. 3).

13 These measures were heavily criticized by human rights organizations and voluntary bodies working with refugees. However, even the Audit Commission (2000) (which did not question the overall thrust of the policy of dispersal) admitted that its implementation was flawed, that community tensions had 'been raised by emotive and sensational media reporting' (p. 1), and that there were many barriers to asylum seekers getting the support that they needed.

14 This is not of course only of historical significance. Although many of these forms of exclusion were outlawed by the federal government in the 1965 Voting Rights Act, the 2000 Presidential election was marred by claims about the exclusion of African American voters in the deciding state of Florida. Among many factors one key issue was the exclusion of ex-felons from the right to vote in Florida along with more than ten other states. In Florida, as a result of this, and of the exclusion of those on probation or parole as well, 31.2 per cent of Black males were ineligible to vote (Human Rights Watch, 1998b)! When taking into account a host of other irregularities particularly affecting minority voters, noted by the chairwoman of the US Commission on Civil Rights, it is clear that the exclusion of African Americans crucially determined the outcome of the election (CNN, 2001).

15 Teitelbaum and Winter suggest that it is best to think about American attitudes to immigration in terms of an ambivalent romanticism (1998, p.145).

16 As Joel Kovel noted many years ago, there is in such Puritanism 'a powerful tradition of hating strangers, foreigners and subversives' (cited in Feagin, 1997, p.16).

17 Croucher concludes by making much the same general point about civic nationalism that we have here. 'Civic nationalism, laudable though the goal may seem, overlooks the reality that nationhood, civic or not, is an inherently exclusive concept' (1998, p. 657).

18 As Smith puts it, 'It is in the first place, a predominantly spatial or territorial conception . . . [such] nations must possess compact, well-defined territories (1991, p. 9).

19 The line between civic and ethnic concepts again becomes blurred at this point. Like Smith, whose definition here they follow, Boyle et al. end up blurring the very distinction with which they began. Since civic nations seem to require a common culture, they are led to conclude that 'modern civic nations have little choice other than to become committed to selectivity in international migration. Such a policy serves to bolster national self-identity and homogeneity, through the admission of certain ethnic, racial and religious groups and the exclusion of others' (1998, p. 156).

20 Noiriel (1993) points out that it is democratic states which have led the way in developing rules for the control of immigration, pointing to the examples of France in the 1880s and Britain in 1905.

5

Nationalism and Democracy

INTRODUCTION

It is often argued that there is an intimate relationship between nationalism and democracy, at least since the French Revolution, usually taken to be the starting point for modern nationalism. Since then, there have been a succession of struggles, supposedly simultaneously nationalist and democratic, against various forms of authoritarian rule, from absolutist monarchy and empire in the nineteenth century to communist totalitarianism in the twentieth. This has strengthened the belief that the democratic struggle for self-government and the nationalist struggle for self-determination are closely connected if not identical, particularly in the struggle for national liberation. At the same time, it has been argued that it is the nation-state that has provided the basic framework within which democratic rights have been most effectively demanded, accorded and sustained. In this chapter, we examine these claims, arguing that it is important to distinguish clearly between the different dynamics involved. Closer inspection, we suggest, shows that democracy and nationalism may have rather different logics, and point in rather different directions, and that there may be dangers in confusing the struggle for democratic rights with any kind of nationalist mobilization.

The link between democracy and nationalism

Although it is possible to see England or America as the birthplace of the modern democratic nation (Greenfeld, 1992), most writers identify the French Revolution as the key moment at which nation and people became one, as the point at which, as Jenkins for instance sees it, 'the principle of nationhood emerged from a struggle to redefine political sovereignty' (1990, p. 6). When they rose up in 1789 against the power and privilege of monarchy and aristocracy, the deputies of the Third Estate identified the people of France as the nation rather than the King. What had belonged to the King now belonged to the people as nation. The victory of the army of the revolutionary nation at Valmy in 1792, over the professional armies of the kings, queens, emperors and empresses of the rest of Europe, then had a profound significance, marking the dawn of a new age, as Goethe put it. In order to defend themselves against counter-revolution, the people had been impelled to mobilize their forces in a new way, calling upon the nation as a whole (in the *levée en masse*).

The final defeat of Napoleon's army at the battle of Waterloo in 1815 put an end not only to more than two decades of only occasionally interrupted war, but also apparently to the revolutionary epoch. In the decades that followed, it may be argued, the forces of progress which sought to challenge the reconstituted Ancien Régime were making demands which were simultaneously democratic and nationalist. Most notably in Italy, where Mazzini was the emblematic figure, but also for example in Poland, in Germany and in Greece, organizations were set up to pursue what appeared to be the intimately related aims of national independence and constitutional government.

It may have been partly because of this that Mill was able to assert (as we saw in Chapter 1) with such confidence that democracy was so wholly compatible with the sentiment of nationality. Claims of this sort assert a direct link if not a fusion between the nationalist demand that the nation should be free to determine its own fate and the democratic demand that the people should be sovereign over its own affairs. This assumption has continued well into the twentieth century. Brian Jenkins, for example, draws a direct link along these lines between the French Revolution at the end of the eighteenth century and anti-colonial struggles in the twentieth. 'In this original democratic sense, nationalism has been reproduced . . . in the context of national liberation struggles' (1990, p. 8). In his survey of nationalism, Peter Alter too has pointed to obvious parallels with what he calls Risorgimento nationalism:

> The intellectual and political leaders of the national liberation movements – men like Mahatma Gandhi, Ahmed Sukarno, Kwame Nkrumah, Leopold S. Senghor and Jomo Kenyatta – had mostly lived and been educated in Europe. They made no secret of the fact that they were using an ideology whose power to change, to emancipate and integrate peoples had been proved in Europe. In much the same way as Risorgimento nationalism in

Europe had been directed against existing structures of domination and the multinational empires, nationalism in the Third World was now channelled against colonialism and the political, economic and cultural imperialism of the Europeans. (1989, pp. 143–4)

Back within Europe itself, the same kind of link between nationalism and democracy has been identified in the successful movements that swept away communism at the end of the 1980s (Karklins, 1994; Senn, 1995; Taageperra, 1993). According to this line of argument indeed 'it was nationalism and its capacity to mobilize broad masses of citizens . . . that proved the decisive force in the unravelling of totalitarianism' (Diuk and Karatnycky, 1993, p. 1).

A connection has also been made more generally between nationalism, nation-states and the development and consolidation of democratic rights, institutions and citizenship. David Held, for instance, insists that 'nationalism was a critical force in the development of the democratic nation-state' (1995, p. 58), while Pierre Manent claims that 'democracy, as we understand it, came into being within the framework of the nation' (1997, p. 94).

The logics of democracy and nationalism

These inter-related arguments may, however, be more problematic than they first appear. To begin with, it is important to note that, if they have appeared at times to overlap, arguments for democracy and for nationalism are not identical. As with nationalism, there are of course numerous disputes about what democracy is or should be; democracy is after all one of if not the most essentially contested of all concepts (Arblaster, 1987). In a comprehensive survey of democratic ideas, Held (1987) has identified at least nine different 'models of democracy' with different principles of justification, key features and general conditions. Although it has been argued that there is an essential core meaning, 'the idea of popular power' (Arblaster 1987, p. 8) or 'a form of government . . . in which the people rule' (Held, 1987 p. 2), this only raises a whole host of questions, particularly in terms of the relationship between democracy and nationalism. These have to do *inter alia* with who the 'people' are; with how they are to rule or be represented; with the scope and extent of popular sovereignty (itself a contested concept – Hoffman, 1998); with the nature and desirability of participation; with rights (of individuals and collectives, of majorities and minorities); and with citizenship.

At the risk of considerable over-simplification, however, we want to suggest here, in the context of the issues we have raised in relation to nationalism and national identity, that notions of democracy over time have tended in important respects to open up, to broaden out, as the democratic idea developed from its origins in ancient Greece through the Italian city-republics, the Levellers in the seventeenth century, the American and French

Revolutions, and beyond (Dunn, 1992). Relatedly, democratic movements, as John Markoff (1996) has argued, have been driven largely from below, by those hitherto excluded, and involved the transgressing and elimination of some boundary or other. Arguments for democracy have then generally pointed in an inclusionary rather than exclusionary direction: for democratic principles and procedures to apply in more areas of social life; for more sections of the *demos* to participate in the polity; for more extensive rights (from the civic to the political to the social), to be granted to more and more people, not fewer and fewer; for citizenship to be conceived in a more extended and expansive sense. There is then a fundamental sense in which, as Beetham and Boyle suggest, 'democracy is a universalistic doctrine, emphasising the common human capacity for self-determination, which all share despite their differences' (1995, p. 25).

Nationalism, on the other hand, if it may at times appear similar, in demanding self-determination for a given nation, or seeking the inclusion in a given state of the whole nation, does so on slightly different grounds. It is a particular nation that seeks self-determination, or inclusion in a particular state. Nationalism is then, as Beetham and Boyle put it, 'particularistic, emphasizing the differences between peoples, and the value of a nation's distinctive culture, tradition and ways of living. *Nationalism tends to be exclusive whereas democracy is inclusive*' (1995, p. 25; emphasis added).

In the 'real world' of course there may be all sorts of problems with states, which claim to be democratic, abiding fully by this inclusionary logic. 'Really existing democracies' may fall short of the ideal in all sorts of ways. The form, scope and extent of popular sovereignty may be distorted or restricted in various ways; democratic procedures may be flouted or curtailed in significant respects; there may be formal or informal barriers on political participation; the rights of individuals and/or collectives may be denied; citizenship may be denied on various grounds. There may then be a considerable gap between promise and performance, between image (or self-image) and reality. A democratic state *per se* does not, however, require or posit the existence of an other, who has to be seen as different in some fundamental way, and who, by virtue of this difference, has to be excluded or barred. One could argue rather the opposite: that democracy, rather than fearing the other, thrives on the presence of diversity, on the existence of different interests and views which are essential to debate, discussion and choice.[1]

Again, this is not to deny that within democracies majorities can discriminate against minorities, even tyrannize them, as Mill feared. Such tyranny, it may be argued however, would be undermining of democratic principles, since what Saward has called the principle of 'responsive rule' means that there has to be some limitation on what majorities can decide, that a number of basic rights and freedoms ought to be guaranteed and protected from majoritarian decision-making (1994, pp. 15–17). At the same time, it is important to remember, as Arblaster has pointed out, that the 'will of the majority' is not the same as the 'will of the people' (1987, p. 68). In a democracy this will has to be discovered by debate, between different points of view, in the present. It cannot be assumed, it is not a given, it cannot be taken or handed down simply from the past.

As we have argued throughout this book, on the other hand, nationalism in all of its forms is necessarily preoccupied with boundaries, with a distinction between those within and those without, with a need to identify some as belonging to the nation and others who do not. Although both nationalism and democracy may appear then to share similar concerns, they do so from different angles and with different emphases. The nationalist emphasis on the over-riding importance of the sovereignty of the nation tends to lead to a focus on questions of security and power, typically in the form of a nation-state; the concern is not so much with participation as with membership (of some rather than others); not so much with accountability as identification; not so much on rights as on identity. More generally, rather than openness, nationalism is more focused on closure. Difference and diversity pose problems, threatening to unsettle or problematize what is given, even hallowed by the past.

From this angle, democracy and nationalism have different priorities, and arguably obey or exhibit different logics, which may be more likely over time to diverge than converge. There is no intrinsic or necessary connection between them, and indeed it may be that the two principles are in important respects antithetical, as Ringmar has argued, focusing on the issue of representation.

> Democracy does not entail nationalism, and nationalism can certainly exist without democracy. In fact, it could be said that the two principles are contradictory. In a democracy the only thing that should matter is how responsive political leaders are to the will of the people, yet who these leaders are should be irrelevant. According to a nationalist doctrine [*sic*], the opposite holds. (1998, p. 536)

There are then, he argues, two fundamentally different concepts of representation involved, one based on interest, the other on identity. 'While the principle of democracy makes those political leaders legitimate who represent what the people *want*, the principle of nationalism makes those political leaders legitimate who represent what the people *is*' (p. 545; emphasis added).

It is, however, not only a matter of representation but perhaps more fundamentally of who is to be represented in the first place and its implications for the polity, particularly when this takes the form of a nation-state. A similar kind of distinction, between what he calls 'the competing logics of democracy and the nation-state', has also been made by Alfred Stepan, focusing on the issue of citizenship rights. Analysing the case of newly independent Estonia, where a whole raft of decisions were made to bolster a sense of national identity through denying citizenship rights to the great majority of Russian residents (something like 40 per cent of the population), Stepan notes that this 'led to a shrinkage in the political and social spaces where Estonians and non-Estonians interact and compete democratically' (1994, p. 139). He suggests that 'to argue for a broader definition of political participation, rights and citizenship is virtually impossible within the logic of the nation-state. Rather, one must introdue the value and logic of democracy . . . [and] deliberately problematize the tension between the two logics' (1994, p. 135).

It may be argued that this is to obscure and underestimate the vital contribution that nationalism has made to the emergence and consolidation of democracy. Ghia Nodia has argued powerfully in this vein, claiming that nationalism and democracy are not separate things but that nationalism is an essential component of (at any rate liberal) democracy. He suggests that 'the idea of nationalism is impossible – indeed unthinkable without the idea of democracy. The two are joined in a sort of complicated marriage, unable to live without each other' (1994, p. 4). Accepting that nationalism is a fundamentally irrational phenomenon, whilst democracy is supposed to be a highly rational enterprise, he claims that nationalism is vital precisely for this reason to the democratic project, because it answers a prior set of questions which democracy itself cannot resolve – the question of who the people are and where they are to form a polity.

> Democratic laws ('the rules') may be consensual products of rational decision-making, but the composition and territory of the polity (the 'players' and the 'playing field') in which these laws have force cannot be defined that way . . . the criteria for deciding just who is a citizen and just where the borders are cannot be derived from any logic intrinsic to the democratic enterprise. (1994, pp. 7–8)

Nationalism has a vital function in 'molding [*sic*] democratic (i.e. self-determining) political communities . . . The political cohesion for democracy cannot be achieved without the people determining themselves to be a nation' (1994, pp. 7–8).

It is, however, difficult to find evidence in some key cases for 'the people' so determining themselves. If we look, for instance, at the way in which what Charles Tilly has called the 'original' nation-states of Western Europe were formed, it is by no means clear that this moulding was an exercise in self-determination, rational or irrational. Rather they were political communities constructed from above by largely absolutist states. Their boundaries were determined not by the will of the people living within those borders, the demos, but by the actions of coercive, expansive and extractive states. The states of Brandenburg–Prussia, France, England and Spain were, as Tilly has argued, constructed along the same lines through a mixture of 'conquest, alliance, bargaining, chicanery, argument and administrative encroachment, until the territory, population, goods and activities claimed by the particular centre extended either to the areas claimed by other strong centres or to a point where the costs of communication and control exceeded the returns from the periphery' (1994, p. 252). Here at any rate, it has to be recognized that states come first and nations second, that as Wallerstein puts it, 'in almost every case statehood preceded nationhood, and not the other way around, despite a widespread myth to the contrary' (Balibar and Wallerstein, 1991, p. 81).

Democracy and nationalism in the French Revolution

The subjects enclosed within the borders of such states were not for some considerable time to be citizens of a democracy. They were subjects of states, however, which had gained sufficient control to have become the kind of 'bordered power containers' conceptualized by Giddens (1985) as modern nation-states. Like other modernists, Giddens is sceptical about the existence of any wide-ranging sense of national identity at this time. State sovereignty did not depend on such sentiments, but was itself an effect of sustained processes of internal pacification and collaborative political decisions over borders between rival state powers. 'Common though it is to portray nationalism in "continuous states" as emerging in an inevitable way from the doctrines of sovereignty which they took up, there is little intrinsic association between them. A link was only forged subsequently' (Giddens, 1985, p. 119).

When the French Revolution occurred, however, and the people challenged the sovereign power of the king, the issue of the basis of sovereignty was posed anew and was to generate quite fundamental and far-reaching debates about who was to be included in the people and what this sovereignty entailed. In the first instance, however, the concept of the nation was neither clear nor arguably central to this discussion. At the outset, in the first flush of revolutionary democratic enthusiasm, the sense of a distinctive French nationhood was actually quite limited, certainly if we bear in mind the ambiguity and interchangeability of the key terms *nation, peuple, patrie* and *état* (Greenfeld, 1992).[2] The idea of democracy on the other hand was very much in the air, appearing in many of the *cahiers* of the Third Estate (Llobera, 1994a, p. 180). This is not surprising. The revolution as a democratic upsurge from below marked a fundamental break with the past and could not, by its very nature, invoke a national past to justify itself (Emsley, 1987, p. 41).

To the extent that a concept of nation did emerge, it came into contradiction in important respects with the idea of democracy. For Hannah Arendt indeed, the conflict between these two principles could be identified from the outset: it 'came to light at the very birth of the modern nation-state, when the French Revolution combined the Declaration of the Rights of Man with the demand for national sovereignty' (1966, p. 230). Following Arendt then, it is possible to discern within the same revolution two different logics at work – one nationalist, the other democratic. On the one hand, there is the logic of inclusion, the impetus born of the demand of those hitherto excluded (the demos, those who were hitherto merely the 'common' people), engaging actively in politics for the first time and in the process transforming the modern history of democracy (Arblaster, 1987). On the other hand, there is a logic of exclusion, the drawing of a new boundary between nationals and foreigners, as in Brubaker's words, 'the Revolutionary invention of nation-state and national citizenship engendered the modern figure of the foreigner – not only as a legal category but as a political epithet, invested with a psychopolitical charge it formally lacked' (Brubaker, 1992, p.47).

At the heart of this contradiction lay two rather different sorts of answers to the question of what was meant by popular sovereignty. In an important study, Istvan Hondt (1995) has identified two kinds of answers formulated during the Revolution, one associated with Sieyès, the other with Robespierre. Sieyès was of course the author of the famous pamphlet 'What is the Third Estate?', often taken to be a manifesto of the revolution, at least in its first phase. Sieyès was perhaps the first to identify the people so directly and unambiguously with the nation, arguing that 'all public powers without distinction are an emanation of the general will, all come from the People, *that is to say, the Nation. These two terms ought to be synonymous*' (cited in Schwarzmantel, 1991, p. 32; emphasis added). Sieyès and his co-thinkers, however, were, in Sewell's words, 'reluctant democrats [who] envisaged a political order in which public service would be performed by an enlightened and public spirited elite on behalf of the nation' (1988, p. 121) Amongst other things they proposed to limit popular sovereignty, to restrict the franchise to the better-off by distinguishing between active and passive citizens. At the same time, however, Sieyès insisted on the unity of the nation, opposing federalism for example on the grounds that 'France must not be an assemblage of little nations' (cited in Hondt, 1995, p. 199). A very different view of both popular sovereignty and the nation was put forward by the radical left and by Robespierre in particular. Robespierre began by attacking the distinction between active and passive citizens, seeing it as a distinction invented to cover the spoliation of the poor (Sewell, 1988). At every stage until the crisis of 1793, Robespierre backed insurgency from below, the democracy of the *sociétés populaires*, the *sans-culottes*, the Commune and the sections against the privileged, the elite and their representatives. Insofar as he was a democrat, Robespierre was a proponent of popular sovereignty, of the participation of the hitherto excluded, of the accountability of institutions to the people, of the extension of rights. In this vein in particular, he saw (long before Arendt) a fundamental contradiction between nationalism and democracy. The identification of people and nation was fatally limiting, would mean that the declaration of the rights of man had 'been drafted for a human herd planted in an isolated corner of the globe' (cited in Hondt, 1995, p. 207).

This line of argument inevitably brought Robespierre into conflict with others, such as the Brissotins, who sought war between France and other nations (Emsley, 1987). For Robespierre, the real war was not between France and other nations but between the revolution and its enemies inside as well as outside France. 'What sort of a war can we see ahead? Is it a war of one nation against other nations? Or a war of one king against other kings? No, it is the war of the enemies of the French Revolution against the French Revolution' (cited in Gauthier, 1987, p. 31).

It is true that, within a relatively short space of time, propelled into power by the *sans-culottes*, Robespierre became a member of the Committee of Public Safety that would prosecute the war with implacable vigour. In the process, he came to adopt a rather different language. By the beginning of 1794 he was declaring that 'I hate the English people (applause). I will increase the hatred of my compatriots as much as I can. What do I care what they think? My only hope is in our soldiers and in the deep hatred, which the English have for the French' (cited in Hondt, 1995, p. 225). He had thus come to assert that national differences were primary, that it was now not a question of social divisions but of national conflicts. This shift occurred at a time when the beleaguered republic was taking greater and greater powers into its own hands, adopting terror as state policy (motivated at least in part by the terroristic threats of their enemies), seeing enemies everywhere to the left as well as the right, searching out conspiracies fostered by the external forces of counter-revolution.

Hondt (1995) has argued from this that a radical conception of democracy necessarily culminates not only in terror but also in an extreme nationalism. However, it may rather be that it was as radical democracy began to falter that nationalism regained the initiative. If we follow what Woloch (1994) has elsewhere called 'the contraction and expansion of democratic space' we can see that the lines on the graph, as it were, go in opposite directions, that as democracy flourishes, nationalism withers and vice versa.

Driven by the exigencies of war, the Jacobins centralized power in their own hands.[3] This fatally undermined a democratic movement which, as Soboul argued, had been pressing for more and more control over elected officers, and established the principle of the right of the people to dismiss their chosen representatives. However, 'the demands of war resulted in practices that were contradictory to [this] form of democracy' (Soboul, 1980, pp. 251–2). This had the paradoxical effect of undermining the Jacobin's own popular base in the process, so that when Robespierre was challenged by his enemies on the famous 9th of Thermidor, he was unable to call on the *sans-culottes* to support him (Guerin, 1977; Soboul, 1980).

The adoption of nationalism instead of democracy was arguably therefore not only part of the tragedy of his fall but also revealed early on a contradiction between democracy and nationalism. In prioritizing nation over people, in identifying as intrinsic enemies those who had earlier been offered support and encouragement, the revolution as an exercise in radical democracy came to an end and a different form of politics developed. For after Thermidor, two dynamics began to unfold in earnest and in harness. On the one hand, there was a rapid contraction of democratic rights, with restrictions on the franchise and a sustained effort to take power away from and tame the *sans-culottes*, culminating in what Lucas calls 'the complete exclusion from power of the *classes dangereuses*' (1988, p. 282) which itself paved the way for Napoleon's imperial regime. On the other hand, at the same time, there was a visible and palpable shift towards an annexationist rather than defensive war. This, Florence Gauthier has argued, was a fateful step which ran directly counter to Robespierre's earlier arguments. In this sense, she concludes, 'the nationalism of the French as conquerors was due to the *failure* of the revolution of the rights of man' (1987, p. 26; emphasis added). To put it another way, as nationalism expanded, democracy withered.

For the wars of annexation that post-revolutionary France as a nation-state then waged, from Thermidor through to Napoleon, were precisely of the type that had been explicitly renounced at the outset of the revolution, that is, in its democratic aspect (Emsley, 1987; Johnson, 1987). They were marked, as Blanning points out, by an 'increasingly strident insistence . . . on the superiority of the Grande Nation and the way in which a sense of national superiority was flaunted without inhibition' (1996, p. 247). It was then precisely the experience of the nationalism of the French as conquerors which fuelled the next phase of nationalism in Europe and marked out a template which was to be followed with increasing frequency over the next two centuries. For 'nationalism is never generated by purely endogenous forces but develops dialectically in confrontation with the other' (Blanning, 1996, p. 247). What he calls the 'mutual detestation engendered by the French conquest of Europe' was sooner or later to shape the main contours of nationalism in Germany and then elsewhere.

What the French state had been able to do was to turn the equation of people and nation to its own advantage, to present its own interests as those of the whole people, to identify this people as a nation united, opposed to and always threatened by other nations. The vocabulary of nation had become what Jenkins accurately describes as the 'key agency of political mobilization', different in key respects from the democratic ideology that had fired the earlier revolutionary movement, substituting passive obedience for active citizenship, imperialism for self-determination (Jenkins, 1990, p. 51) Others were soon to see the possibilities, to see how, at least in this respect,

> effective the innovations of the revolution could be as *tools of power politics*. The success of the French patriotic army was seen as a combination of patriotism and the thoroughly homogenized unity of the French state

behind it. The way forward was to persevere in *the quest for national power* with the policy of unification and homogenization which had begun with the absolutist monarchies and been preserved and reasserted by the French revolutionaries. (Hondt, 1995, p. 22; emphasis added)

Germany and the failure of liberal nationalism

German nationalism specifically was developed in this context. For Sheehan, 'the most important impact of the French conquest was not on German national identity, but rather on the politics of the various states' (1992, p. 48). Humiliated by defeat at the hands of Napoleon's armies, their rulers sought, as Hughes puts it, 'to acquire many of the benefits of the French Revolution without the inconveniences' (1988, p. 51). Amongst these inconveniences would of course have been democracy. (Or, as the Prussian moderniser Hardenburg put it, 'we have to do from above what the French have done from below' [cited in Brubaker, 1992]).

This again casts a slightly different light on the argument that German nationalism with its focus on ethnic identity, on language, culture and descent, was radically different from the French form with its emphasis on politics and citizenship (see Chapter 4). In important respects, some of those most involved in the construction of German nationalism were following a similar logic to their French counterparts in seeking to develop a political ideology that would assert the over-riding importance of national identity over others in the construction of a powerful nation-state. This is not to minimize the contribution made by cultural nationalists in Germany from Herder to Fichte and beyond in articulating particularistic conceptions of cultural identity, but rather to locate them in a political and historical context.

Whatever their intentions, the work of cultural nationalists at first had little resonance in the wider society and may well have been largely ignored in a different political context. As in France, there is little evidence initially of a mass interest in nationalism (Hughes, 1988; Minogue, 1967). When nationalism emerged in Germany, it did so in the context of disappointment with the French Revolution and resentment against the occupying French armies (Greenfeld, 1992). However, such resentments were primarily articulated by a minority within a framework of concerns about state power.

Liberal nationalism in Germany (as perhaps elsewhere at this time) was largely confined to the better-off, eschewing much concern for the poor (a large part of the *demos* after all at that time). Liberal nationalists were constrained 'by a fundamental mistrust of the masses and unwillingness to mobilize them in support of Liberal aspirations' (Hughes, 1988, p. 93). They were preoccupied too by considerations of power and prestige, if necessary at the expense of other liberal values: 'the majority of Liberals, faced with a choice between national unity and power or Liberal freedoms, opted for the first' (1988). This became clear in 1848, when liberal nationalism was at its zenith, particularly in relation to the central issue of self-determination. This principle, it now turned out, was only to apply to Germans and not to Danes, Poles, Italians or Czechs whose suppression by counter-revolutionary (but Germanic) Austria was a cause for celebration. More generally, as Langeswiehe shows, German nationalists in 1848 were 'prepared to cooperate with counterrevolution to advance their interests against other nations' (1992). Significantly, the only opposition in 1848 to this came from radical democrats and the extreme and internationalist left (including Marx) (Hughes, 1988).

After 1848, liberal nationalism in Germany lost much of its appeal and nationalism became increasingly identified with concerns of state power, notably in the form of the shape, scope and identity of a putative German state. This, as is well known, was achieved not from below by democratic means, but from above, by military conquest or, in the evocative phrase of its main architect Bismarck, 'by blood and iron'. What Bismarck offered was the fulfilment of the nationalist dream, a powerful nation-state but one in which (it was an Empire after all), there was little space for democracy. In these conditions, German nationalism took a radically anti-democratic turn. Democratic forces, notably on the left, were often attacked as enemies of the nation (Allen, 1992, p. 143). What the state demanded was that German interests came before all others, that loyalty to the nation be overriding. When war came in 1914, German nationalism was hegemonic, whilst democracy remained a chimera.

The defeat of Germany in 1918 was not accepted by German nationalists who refused to admit that defeat was anything but the consequence of a supposed 'stab in the back' by the internal enemies of the nation (the left and the Jews). Nationalism then played an important role in the destruction of the fragile Weimar Republic, with much of Hitler's appeal stemming from his successful attempt to project himself as the man who would undo the effects of the Versailles peace treaty and restore the fortunes of the German nation-state (Hughes, 1988, pp. 207–8). In this respect, despite the actual lack of unity in Germany, before and after 1918, a sense of national identity could play a significant part in Hitler's rise to power. As a result, as Breuilly argues,

> in times of crisis the national idea – an idea which was almost universally accepted in some form or another – could be turned against government and parliament. The national idea meant national unity whereas parliament meant division; it meant strength whereas the republic was weak . . . Hitler's success was predicated on the basis of a near-universal acceptance of the nation-state as the political norm. (1992, p. 16)

When democracy did finally establish itself more securely in (part of) Germany after the Second World War, it was accompanied significantly by something of a general 'rejection of the nation' (Alter, 1992, p. 156). This may have had more to do with the catastrophic consequences of Nazism for the German state (defeat and now division), rather more than any widespread shame connecting nationalism with Nazism.[4] However, in the Federal Republic there was a sustained attempt to anchor the new state in a wider frame of reference (notably the European Community), whilst this occurred perforce also in the East, given the Soviet Union's commanding not to say imperial position. The idea of a single German nation-state was put on the back burner in many ways. The right in the Federal Republic was more concerned with anti-communism, while the social democrats had moved (with Brandt's Ostpolitik of the 1970s) to some kind of acceptance of the reality if not legitimacy of the GDR. As a political force, it could appear that nationalism was largely confined to the margins of the far right. It was argued that Germany had become what Bracher called 'a postnational demo-cracy among nation-states' (cited in Winkler, 1996, p. 59).

On the other hand there was a renewed effort on the right in the 1980s to force attention back to the question of national identity, to assert a link between the West German state *qua* nation-state with its German prede-cessors, in part by seeking to relativize the atrocities of Nazism. The debates this generated among historians, the so-called *Historikerstreit*, had some political impact in reprioritizing the issue of national identity (Maier, 1988). Meanwhile, in the GDR, in an effort to provide some legitimacy, the one-party communist state sought to link itself to a German past, claiming both Luther and Frederick the Great as forebears. What did much more than any of this, however, to restore the salience of nationalism and national identity were the events of 1989–90.

German (re)unification: the return of democratic nationalism?

The collapse of the communist East German state and its absorption into the framework of the Federal Republic meant that, as in 1871, there was now only one German nation-state. Once again, it seemed the national principle had triumphed. This time, however, it was claimed, a nation-state had been created (or re-created) in a quite different, essentially democratic manner, from below peacefully not from above violently (R. Evans, 1987).

The East German revolution had in many ways a dual character. It was undoubtedly a movement for a radical change to the political system, the economy and society. On the one hand it involved democratic mobilization from below and active participation in a revolutionary attempt to reclaim power for the *demos*. On the other hand, it involved flight, the mass escape to the West, to another state largely identified in national terms (as West

Germany). There were two different forms of politics at work – the politics of voice versus the politics of exit, to borrow Hirschmann's terms (Hirschmann, 1970). The balance of power between them shifted over time, from an emphasis on the democratic to an emphasis on the national. This was dramatically illustrated in the switch of slogans on the demonstrations in the fateful month of November from '*Wir sind das Volk*' to '*Wir sind ein Volk*'. This was no trivially semantic change. Rather, as Stephen Brockmann has noted, 'the mere change from the definite to the indefinite article implied the move from a revolution based on democratic principles to a revolution based on ethnic togetherness, a shift from *demos* to *ethnos*' (1991, p. 6).

The democratic character of the process was thus undermined in a number of important respects. First, the adoption of nationalist demands had an implicitly demobilizing effect on the population of the GDR. The momentum that had brought growing masses onto the streets led by independently organized oppositional movements was cut short, as political leaders from the West German state intervened directly and openly.[5] The fragile space that had been opened up briefly by the independent democratic movement, shrank and narrowed. Rather than pursue a political project of democratization, the majority of the citizens of the GDR responded to what critics such as Habermas (1994) dubbed 'D-mark nationalism'. The East German population thus renounced their (developing) sovereignty by entering wholesale (in more than one sense) into the intact, unmodified structures of the West German system, without having to exhaust themselves in independent activity. As Philipsen puts it, this transformed 'the exhilarating search for a new democratic beginning into a muted turn [the German term is "*Wende*"] *directed largely by others*' (1993, p. 6; emphasis added). The constitutional mechanism through which unification was accomplished furthered this process of demobilization in both the East and the West. The GDR was effectively absorbed via article 23 of the Basic Law into the existing political structures of the Federal Republic, stymieing the call, if unification was now inevitable, for the use of article 146, which would have necessitated a debate not just about the future of the GDR but also about the nature of the democratic basis for a new, unified Germany. As Habermas (1994) has argued, this was no merely procedural issue. Rather it closed off, in both the East and the West, any discussion about the character of a united Germany as a *democratic* polity, both in relation to the past and in the present. Both the Nazi and communist periods were constructed predominantly as exceptions, implying that West Germany as a democratic state was connected umbilically not only to the democratic West but also in national terms to Germany's pre-Nazi history.

This invocation of a historic national identity, as a call for re-unification, was predicated on assumptions about the nation across time, that had profound implications for residents within the borders of both old and new German states. This discourse, as Torpey has put it, 'consecrated a primordial, trans-historical concept of the nation that places that entity *utterly beyond the power of a state's citizens to alter'* (1995, p. 174; emphasis added). For, however 'popular' the demand for unification, however inclusive its logic from one angle, there were inevitably those (particularly in the West) who were excluded by the nation. Whilst, for instance, supposedly ethnic Germans could now claim and be welcomed into full citizenship by virtue of their biological descent, millions of 'foreigners' who had lived, worked and raised children within the country for decades remained excluded (Wilpert, 1993).

There was then a reaffirmation of the overtly exclusionary character of the German nation, with citizenship continuing to be based, as it had been ever since 1913, on *ius sanguinis* (see Chapter 4). The stability of this structure was, however, shaken by this upheaval, and violence flared against already resident 'foreigners' (*ausländer*) but also against asylum seekers (Jarausch and Gransow, 1994), whilst resentment also began to develop too against incoming ethnic Germans from the East (*aussiedler*) (Räthzel, 1995). This opened the way for the development of different exclusionary discourses: one which welcomed the latter within a racialized conception of the nation based on blood; the other, hostile with an alternatively racialized conception of the nation based on culture, language and behaviour.

These tensions led to pressure to change the very constitution which had been used to cement unification, and to a party compromise on tightening the asylum law. These changes pointed in a largely exclusionary direction with severe restrictions on asylum seekers, whilst also setting some limits on the number of foreign-born ethnic Germans allowed to enter (Jarausch and Gransow, 1994).

If these restrictions had the desired effect in sharply curtailing the number of asylum places,[6] they did not provide a secure resolution to all problems of immigration and citizenship. The new Red–Green governing coalition revised the 1913 legislation to incorporate elements of *ius soli*. Whilst this has the undoubted advantage that it does at last recognize the reality that Germany is a country of immigration, it may do little to ease the pressure on asylum seekers, according to migrant advocates (*Migration News*, 1998b), and in any case has been sharply contested by the right-wing opposition. The new legislation may have the effect of bringing Germany more into line with (some of) its European partners and in this way, as Joppke (1997) has suggested, Europe may be used as a way of resolving some of Germany's particular difficulties in this area, although how stable the situation is there is open to doubt, as we saw in Chapter 4. In any case, it may also simply displace the problem to another level (see Chapter 7).

Overall, the effects of nationalism in this case do not seem to have been unambiguously democratic. Rather it was nationalist ideology in its various forms which appears to have largely dictated and structured the terms of debate, marginalizing democratic demands for equal rights within a multicultural postnational society, incorporating others into the nation on selective criteria, whilst constructing a range of new barriers and gates.

Nationalism, democracy and postcommunism

It would be a mistake, however, to focus too heavily on the German case here, as a similar divergence between the logics of democracy and nationalism emerged elsewhere in Eastern Europe after the collapse of communism.

In the newly independent Czech republic, for instance, the issue of citizenship in a re-democratized state was also posed. In this case, it was the Roma who were the objects of nationalist displacement. It has been estimated that at least 75,000 (something like one-third of the total Roma population) have been deprived of Czech citizenship since the 'Velvet Revolution' of 1989 (when communist autocracy ended) and the 'Velvet Divorce', when Czechoslovakia split into two separate nation-states.[7] Many were driven into Slovakia where they have been met with further ill-treatment at the hands of Slovak nationalists (Bauman, 1998). The Roma have been the target of a campaign of stigmatization, portrayed as lazy, undeserving, essentially criminal and unworthy of membership of the Czech nation. The legality of the measures taken to deprive them of their rights within the polity has been somewhat dubious, involving the use of retroactive legislation (Jarabova, 1998) and uncomfortably reminiscent of the ways found by the Nazis in the 1930s to deprive the Roma of citizenship (when they had also been classified as criminals) (Beck, 1994).

It may be argued that the treatment of the Roma in this case is not unusual either comparatively or historically, that they have been repeatedly and throughout the region the target of what is essentially racist rather than nationalist hostility. It is nevertheless striking how levels of hostility have grown, not only since the fall of communism but as the national character and independence of the state has been emphasized. However, the denial of citizenship to the Roma is not a unique or isolated case in the politics of post-communist Eastern Europe. For elsewhere in the region, related invocations of national identity have also worked to weaken democracy in this respect.

In the Baltic states, nationalists have identified substantial minorities as, in some sense, to a greater or lesser degree, 'alien' intruders, and thus a 'threat' to the core identity of the nation and its state. These minorities did and do vary in size[8] and the measures taken to deal with the supposed 'threat' they posed have also varied from case to case but it is possible to identify a common nationalist logic at work throughout. In Estonia a 1938 law on citizenship was re-enacted with some minor amendments, restricting citizenship to those who were residents before the Soviet occupation and their descendants, with a two-year period of residence required for others before citizenship could be applied for, one further year of naturalization and some proof of knowledge of the Estonian language. This was followed by a very restrictive Law on Aliens (Kionka and Vetik, 1996). As a result of these restrictions, all Soviet-era immigrants were effectively barred from voting not only in the September 1992 national elections but also in the June 1992 referendum on the constitution. In the town of Narva, for example, only 6,000 out of the population of 77,000 were eligible to vote (Pettai, 1993)! In Latvia, similar legislation initially required a much longer period of residence (sixteen years) before this was reduced after protests from within and without to a mere ten years. It was accompanied too by a quota system whereby only 2,000 non-citizens could become citizens each year. This too was modified after protest, but even then, it will take until 2005 before all those who might wish for citizenship can be naturalized (Smith, 1996). Moreover, according to the law, they needed, *inter alia*, competence in the Latvian language, a knowledge of the lyrics of the national anthem and of Latvian history, to have a legal income, and they had to swear allegiance to Latvia and to defend Latvia with their lives (Nørgaard et al., 1996). Policies of this kind resulted in the effective 'disenfranchisement of most Russians' (Gray, 1996, p. 79). Only in Lithuania by contrast was the so-called 'zero option' adopted, whereby all resident in Lithuania at the moment of independence could become citizens (Senn, 1996). It could be argued in defence of such measures that they were designed to correct historic injustice. It is certainly the case that a wave of Soviet state-directed Russian immigration, accompanied by harsh repression, followed the occupation of the previously independent Baltic states by the USSR after the infamous Nazi–Soviet pact of 1939. This immigration was a central element in an imperialist project of colonization and subordination. The citizenship measures may therefore be presented as essentially reactive and defensive of the supposed democratic right of each nation to restore its independence and re-establish its identity, imperilled both in the past by annexation and the 'asymmetrical bilingualism' of the communist period (Muiznieks, 1993) and in the present by the continued presence of the Russian minorities. (The larger the minority presence, the greater the need for such measures: hence the difference between Latvia and Lithuania.) However, the nationalist version of history that is propounded here is selective and has been utilized to some extent to legitimate exclusion. For the region in question has, over many centuries, been the site not of one (state-sponsored) immigration but of multiple (including substantial Russian) migrations (Gray, 1996), which render problematic any easy invocation of a simple or straightforward 'return to independence' (Taageperra, 1993), or a fixed, 'previously existing ethnic balance' (Vebers, 1993, p. 181).

Perhaps more significant than any of these considerations is the fact that there was, to begin with, strong evidence of a commitment to staying in the Baltic Republics among many Russians, and an identification with the language of the new republics (Nørgaard et al., 1996). In this context, the definition of others as a problem of incorporation, rests on a prior definition of the polity according to exclusivist nationalist criteria, which may undermine the possibility of pluralism in the present.

The wars over Yugoslavia

It is, however, in Yugoslavia that the divisive potential of an exclusionary nationalism has been most fully revealed. The first Yugoslavia, which came into existence after the First World War according to the selectively applied principle of national self-determination, was riven with conflict between (primarily Serbian and Croatian) nationalists. It was then dismembered by the Nazis, who engineered with the collaboration of Croatian nationalists the creation of a separate, puppet Croatian state. The ensuing civil war was won by the communist Partisans led by Tito, who defeated the rival nationalist forces (Chetnik Serbs, Ustashe Croats) and ostensibly sought to create a new Yugoslavia on the principles of 'brotherhood and unity'. According to Tim Judah,

> in the interests of restoring Yugoslavia, Tito's policy was to draw a line under the past. Everyone who died in the 2nd World War had either been a collaborator or a victim of the Axis powers and their satellites. For the sake of balance, Chetniks and Ustashes were condemned equally by the new regime as the evil twins of the Serbs and Croats. (1997, p. 132)

In reality, Tito never broke fully with Stalinism, particularly in terms of the latter's conception of the national question (see Chapter 1), resulting in the selective and not wholly consistent identification of a number of nations in Yugoslavia, according to Soviet formulae. Rather than confronting nationalism, there was then a guarded suppression of its more overt expression, matched by efforts to balance power between the various nations (in the allocation of republics and autonomous regions) within an overarching structure controlled by one communist party and its supreme leader. The 1974 constitution then devolved further powers within a federal framework to the republics now defined as 'states based on popular sovereignty'. In the aftermath of Tito's death, and as economic crisis began to bite, the leaders of the republics engaged, as Vejvoda has explained, in 'a drive to constitute fully-blown nation-states on the basis of the republics (proto-states) . . . Powerful and deeply vested material and political interests were at stake . . . . The obvious tool for the regional political leaderships, as they strove to muster support, was national sentiment – the ideology of nationalism' (1996, pp. 19–20).

The prime but not sole mover in this process was the Serbian leader Milosevic. Seizing his opportunity in Kosovo, where he had actually been sent to dampen down Serbian nationalism, he instead invoked Serbian nationalist myths, fears and hatreds to mobilize support with which to unseat his former political patron. Using this newly acquired power, he proceeded to destroy independent sources of power not only in Kosovo but also in Vojvodina and Montenegro before launching a mass mobilization campaign evoking the supposedly historic resentments and grievances of all true Serbs (see Chapter 3). As Thomas has noted, this had the effect of homogenizing the population, and maintaining society in a 'state of permanent revolution' (1999, p. 5). Serbian identity was now projected as over-riding, within the framework of what became a project to bring all Serbs together in one nation-state. Although Milosevic was to face bouts of opposition, this was rarely to the core nationalist assumptions which underpinned his policy (Ramet, 1999).[9]

Whilst his intent may have initially been to cow his opponents into accepting his domination of the collective Presidency, it led to a series of conflicts which culminated in the series of wars that then engulfed Yugoslavia in (successively) Slovenia, Croatia, Bosnia and finally Kosovo itself. In Slovenia, Serbian nationalist forces (masquerading as the Yugoslav National Army) beat a retreat when it became clear that they could find no base within a population which saw itself as ethnically homogeneous. In Croatia, Serbian nationalism ran up against a rival nationalist project. Here an alternative elite, led by the ex-communist general Tudjman, had come to power, drawing on extensive support from the émigré community (Cviic, 1996, p. 206), claiming that the Croatian nation had an historic desire for an independent state, and invoking Croatian national identity in a manner almost designed to alarm the large Serbian population inside Croatia (Tanner, 1997).[10] Their response was to turn in growing numbers to the Serbian nationalist movement, the SDS, backed (if not organized) by Milosevic. The resulting polarization then divided Croatia into ethnically divided and warring sections dominated on either side by nationalists feeding off each other. As in Serbia, although there were periods when Tudjman's conduct of the war was criticized, there was little in the way of opposition to the nationalist assumptions underpinning either the setting up of the state or the ongoing war.[11]

The war over Croatia then spread to Bosnia where the stakes and issues were signally different. Here nationalist forces were not so easily hegemonic, in part because the presence of a large Muslim population had never made it easy to apply simplistic nationalist categories (although the Muslims were in fact officially deemed a nation in 1971, much to the chagrin of Serbian and Croatian nationalists). Political differentiation did then take place initially on what Bougarel (1996) identifies as a communitarian basis, with three main organizations emerging (the Muslim SDA, the Serbian SDS and the Croatian HDZ). They were nevertheless still able to form a coalition which, in the absence of aggressive and centrifugal pressures from Zagreb and Belgrade, might well have been able to survive, grounded in an attachment to the values of a multi-cultural, pluralist even cosmopolitan society (Campbell, 1998; Denitch, 1996; Donia and Fine, 1994).[12]

Neither Serbian nor Croatian nationalists could accept this, given the priority they attached to national identities, especially their own. Tudjman (1981) had long argued that Muslims living in Bosnia were essentially Croat. At a secret meeting with Milosevic in March 1991, the two nationalist leaders agreed to divide Bosnia up between them (Glenny, 1999; Meier, 1999). For both sides, the existence of a multi-cultural, cosmopolitan Bosnia not only deprived Serbia and Croatia of additional territory but also implicitly challenged the nationalist basis of each state. For as Ali and Lifschutz have argued,

> what was at stake in Bosnia were two visions of society and democracy. Those who came under assault in the newly-formed Bosnian state made clear that they stood for a society of equal citizens where the rights of all (Muslim, Croatian and Serb) would be secured under the law as a matter of constitutional right. This was a vision of a multi-ethnic society in the tradition of the European enlightenment . . . the opposing vision was the one promoted by the nationalist leaders of Serbia and Croatia. Insular, parochial, ethnocentric, this was a vision of a purified nation-state in which there was no room for the 'Other'. (1992, pp. xiv–xv)

This was no merely discursive strategy but had real, deadly consequences in the systematic efforts at 'ethnic cleansing' which then took place, culminating in the mass murder of the male Muslim population of Srebrenica, as the weakness of the United Nations 'safe havens' was tragically exposed.

Despite such atrocities, the ethnic cleansers were rewarded to a depressing extent by the subsequent peace 'settlement' at Dayton in December 1995. This was primarily engineered by the United States which threw its support behind Croatia, enabling Tudjman's forces to drive the Serbs out of Krajina, in yet another example of ethnic cleansing. At Dayton, despite provision for some of the trappings of a unified state, Bosnia was split along essentially 'ethnic' lines by Western powers committed to the view that this was a civil war between irreconcilable ethnic groups and (characteristically and self-interestedly) desperate themselves, as Ramet notes, to 'dam up the flow of refugees' from the area (1999, p. 209). Dayton was a settlement between nationalist forces both outside Bosnia (the Milosevic and Tudjman regimes) and within. Effective control in Bosnia clearly lay not with what remained of a multi-ethnic government. Rather, 'post-Dayton Bosnia encompasses one weak federal state, two more or less ethnically defined entities and three ethnic communities with mutually hostile armies and police forces' (Denitch, 1996, pp. 213–14).

The Dayton agreement, however, was also inherently unstable. It failed to deal with the *dynamics* of nationalism that had brought Bosnia to this pass in the first place. Serbian nationalism in particular had now been thwarted in Bosnia, and defeated in Croatia. Those who had mobilized it now turned back to their first objects – the Albanian population of Kosovo, generating renewed conflict. This is not to minimize the rise of separatist nationalism (the KLA) within the Albanian population (Glenny, 1999), but only to recall that Kosovo was where Serbian nationalism had first been successfully mobilized. If it had been thwarted in its other objectives, it could always console itself with tightening its grip here. Having risen to power by exploiting Serbian nationalism in Kosovo, Milosevic was now driven again to play the 'nationalist card' (Thomas, 1999, p. 425). The same intimidating and violent tactics that had been perfected by Serbian nationalists in Bosnia were now redeployed in Kosovo. By the end of 1998, it has been claimed that half a million Albanians had been driven from their homes in a campaign of terror (Schwartz, 2000, p. 141). Eventually, after abortive negotiations, NATO embarked on a bombing campaign against Serbia which was followed by a massive escalation of terror by Serbian nationalists, before the latter finally withdrew and NATO forces entered Kosovo itself. Kosovo, the core nationalist symbol of martyred Serbia (Anzulovic, 1999), was now the scene of another mass exodus, this time of Serbs, as the nationalist wheel came full circle. Finally, some months after the end of the conflicts that his nationalism had done so much to foment, Milosevic himself fell from power, as disenchantment with the consequences of his policies eventually found effective expression.

The end result of this decade of nationalist action and reaction has been a radical redevision of territory and population along national lines. Croatia, Serbia, divided Bosnia and Kosovo are now markedly more ethnically homogeneous than they were or indeed have been for centuries. The trauma of war and ethnic cleansing has polarized and poisoned relations between communities, flattened and simplified identifications, destroyed social trust and confidence, and constrained (at best) the development of democratic institutions. Each spiral in the nationalist violence, apart from the physical, cultural and moral destruction it has wrought, has come to an end not through democratic decision-making but through the price exacted by external military power, whether exercised or threatened, which has put some limits to the brutalizing nationalist exercise of sovereign state power. (We discuss some of the implications of this development in Chapter 7.)

As this brief survey suggests, this kind of nationalism has caused major problems for the development or consolidation of democracy in post-communist Eastern Europe. It may, however, be objected that this has to do not with all forms of nationalism but only one, *ethnic* form, characteristic of this region of Europe, of the East rather than the West, although we have already questioned these kinds of distinction (see Chapter 4). Are there not then cases where nationalism and democracy do go hand in hand, where the struggle for self-determination is simultaneously democratic and national? This, it is often argued, is the case with movements for national liberation, to which we now turn.

Democracy, national liberation and the right of nations to self-determination

The democratic principle of popular sovereignty, that political authority stems from the people, is often framed in terms of the right of nations to self-determination. 'The nationalist belief in the self-determination of peoples, each within its own state is' as Beetham and Boyle put it, 'closely akin to the democratic principle that the people of a country should be self-determining in their own affairs' (1995, p. 25). In situations in particular where one nation is oppressed by another, it is not difficult to see how democratic principles might seem to be central to the claim that the nation has a right to determine its own destiny. The struggle for national self-determination has been seen by many then as inherently democratic, a central feature of democratization in the modern world of nation-states.

In the nineteenth century, this argument was most famously advanced by the great Italian liberal nationalist Mazzini, for whom nationalism was not an aggressive doctrine but an open and generous one. His heart stirred at the success of other struggles for self-determination which would lead to the creation of a world (or at least a Europe) made up of a number of free and independent nations, each with its own distinguishing characteristics and calling, or mission. Relationships between these nations would be entirely harmonious as a result, as each nation would recognize the freedom of others to pursue their destiny, but also because the different missions in some sense complemented each other. Thus, as Alter explains, 'England's calling was to industrialize and create overseas colonies, Russia's to civilize Asia and Italy's to lead the world as a new Rome' (1989, p. 30). Whether past, present or future colonies, Asia or indeed the rest of the world, could share Mazzini's enthusiasm for these various missions may perhaps be doubted. In any case, when it came to specifying which or how many nations were to be included in his 1857 map of the new Europe, it appeared that space was rather restricted. As Mack Smith (1994) points out, the Irish, Danish and Portuguese for instance were to be denied entry, on the grounds that they lacked a positive mission for humanity.

It may of course be argued that the particular prejudices of this or that thinker do not in themselves invalidate the general line of argument. Conversely, it is difficult to see how much purchase Mazzini's vision, were we to make allowances for the odd if revealing inconsistency, has ever had on reality, or tells us very much about 'really existing' nationalism, past or present. Nationalist movements, if they may originally have found some inspiration in these ideas, have often been somewhat reluctant, particularly when they have secured state power in the form of the nation-state, to recognize the rights of others when these are perceived to conflict with their own interests.

This, it has to be said, was apparent almost from the outset. English nationalism, Greenfeld's original ideal model, was, as Kaiser (1994) has commented, under Cromwell brutally imperial in its treatment of Ireland, and suppressed other nationalist movements (notably the Indian) with similar ferocity throughout the following centuries. French nationalism, we have argued, became overtly annexationist quite rapidly, as the democratic momentum of the revolutionary process faltered.

It may not be enough to see both these early instances of the refusal to recognize the rights of other nations as failures of principle by already existing powerful states. For the same dynamic has recurred repeatedly once new nations have obtained or even come close to obtaining recognition.

In 1848, it was not only German liberals who, as we have seen, distinguished themselves with what Woolf describes as their 'contemptuous dismissal of the claims of other nationalities' (1996, p. 15). The so-called 'Spring of the Peoples' more generally was a severe disappointment for many, not just because of the failure of the liberal revolutionaries to defeat the forces of reaction but because it became rapidly apparent that more powerful nationalist movements could not resist the temptation to impose their will on weaker ones. In Kohn's words, 'the dream of the brotherhood of equal peoples in a universal order of democratic justice had given way to appeals based upon historical rights, the "reality of power", and the supposed vital or strategic necessities of the nation' (1965, p. 51). After the First World War, many of the newly recognized nation-states of Eastern Europe proved intolerant of nationalist movements in their own areas, Polish treatment of Ukrainians being a case in point (Brubaker, 1996a). However, this phenomenon has by no means been confined to Europe. The government of the People's Republic of China denies this right to the people of Taiwan even though Taiwan was regarded as a separate territory to which it was actually illegal to emigrate from China for centuries, has only been ruled (undemocratically) by China for very limited periods (especially this century) and was recognized by Mao as not part of China as recently as the 1930s (Copper, 1988; Murray and Hong, 1988; Snow, 1972). China's occupation of Tibet may serve as another example. Neuberger has provided an extensive list to illustrate his claim that 'the double standard is alive and well everywhere' (1995, p. 32).

Why then has self-determination been such a problem? Is it simply hypocrisy or inconsistency, or are there problems with the notion of national self-determination that render problematic any easy connection between democracy and nationalism?

There is certainly a serious problem of what we might call infinite regress. If the principle of self-determination is taken to be an absolute right, it can lead to an almost infinite number of claims, as the number of potential nations in the world (however we define nations) is bound to exceed considerably the present number of states. Again, this became apparent early on this century, as US President Woodrow Wilson, who contributed perhaps more than any one else to the legitimization of this concept, noted somewhat ruefully:

> When I gave utterance to those words ('that all nations had the right to self-determination') I said them without the knowledge that nationalities existed, which are coming to us day after day . . . You do not know and cannot appreciate the anxieties that I have experienced as a result of many millions of people having their hopes raised by what I have said (quoted in Cobban, 1969, p. 65)

Many of these hopes of course were dashed by Wilson himself, including those of the Irish, as he and his fellow Allied statesmen applied the principle with markedly greater enthusiasm to the territories of their defeated opponents than to their own. As Wilson explained, the Allies could not 'act upon the right of self-determination of any peoples except those which had been included in the territories of the defeated empires' (in Cobban, 1969, p. 66). This was, as Alfred Cobban tartly noted, 'equivalent to an acknowledgement that a moral principle was being enforced on the defeated states which the victors refused to apply to themselves' (1969, p. 66).

The problem, however, is not simply hypocrisy. The right of self-determination, understood as the right to form a nation-state, clashes with the same right conceived of from another angle, the right of the nation-state once formed to determine its own affairs, or the principle of sovereignty. From the viewpoint of the latter, the former appears as the threat of secession. From the viewpoint of existing states, this threat may be seen not just to threaten the sovereignty of particular states but the security of the international order. It is revealing in this context that the United Nations itself did not get round to formalizing the right of self-determination until the 1960 Declaration on Granting Independence to Colonial Countries and Peoples (Hannum, 1996), and insists nevertheless that it is not absolute but has to be qualified by other principles which affirm the territorial integrity of states (Moore, 1997, p. 902). The Organization of African Unity, made up of states which had precisely claimed the right of self-determination for themselves, was immediately preoccupied with the threat of secession and required its members to respect each other's (existing) territorial integrity (Alter, 1989; Calhoun, 1997).

There is in addition a problem with who exactly the 'self' is which is to exercise it, and who the people are, who are to determine themselves. Here we return to a critical problem. For not only are the boundaries which the nation claims for itself invariably determined initially on non-democratic grounds, but it is difficult to see how this could be otherwise. Historically, as we have seen, the first powerful nation-states in Europe were not the products of democratic consent (Tilly, 1994); nor were those states (selectively) accorded recognition by the Allies after the First World War the product of referenda or plebiscites (Hannum, 1996). More generally, recognition seems always to have had to be fought for, wrested as the outcome of violent conflict, rather than accorded in a context of discussion, negotiation, or in tribunals (Canovan, 1996a).[13]

The cause for which many such struggles have been fought, particularly since the Second World War (such as those in Algeria or Vietnam for example) has often been defined in terms of national 'liberation' from colonial rule. Clearly the presence and power of imperialism suppressed any form of self-determination other than that of the colonialists (although tensions always persisted between settlers and the metropolitan centre of command and could explode, as in the case of the rebellion of the United States against Britain).[14] The end of colonial rule, however, did not and cannot of itself resolve the difficulties of self-determination. Rather, as Lahouari Addi has argued, 'the overthrow of foreign domination and the triumph of nationalist ideology does not spell the birth of a nation, but only of a central power' (1997, p. 114).

It does not resolve the question of the identity of the people who are seeking to determine themselves. The struggle for national liberation against the imperialist has often occurred within the borders given (or better, dictated) by the colonial oppressor in the first instance. The identity of the *national* self at this level has in many cases been at the outset a colonialist datum. The 'nation' that seeks self-determination has no 'primordial' shared history, or at the very least its borders may be in some doubt. Rather there may have to be a complex effort to construct a national identity for the 'people' that can be both historic (despite the often immense territorial change mapped by imperialism) and new (despite what Anderson calls the 'isomorphism between each nationalism's territorial stretch and that of the previous imperial administrative unit' [1991, p. 114]). This is a difficult project on both sides. For the turn to a precolonial past may, as with all nationalism, invoke a history that is mythical rather than real, and in this instance may even be the product precisely of the colonialist mystification that it seeks to evade. Basil Davidson has argued compellingly that nationalists in Africa have generally worked within a nation-state framework actually 'fashioned from the structures and relationships of colonial states' (1992, p. 181). As a result, and to some extent by choice, they turned their backs on the various institutions and diverse cultures that had developed in Africa over several centuries, or at least what still remained of them after imperialism's destructive impact.[15]

At the same time, the 'new' national identity can over-ride, suppress and seek to eliminate others as it seeks to construct a homogeneity that was not already there. 'In the African context', Thomas has argued specifically, 'nationalism has come to signify the attempt to bring together peoples who were not linguistically, ethnically or culturally homogeneous within given territorial boundaries' (1997, p. 116).

None of this is to deny the fact that national liberation movements did succeed in developing and sustaining mass support. Without this, they would never have been able to overthrow the tenacious and violent grip of imperial rule. The problem here, in terms of the relationship between nationalism and democracy, lies with the longer-term political consequences of the conditions in which these movements developed, the state form of power at which they have aimed, and the different interests this has generated and secured.

The leaders of anti-colonial movements focused on state power in a particular way which helped them to adopt nationalism as their predominant ideology. Within this optic, as Nigel Harris has argued, 'national liberation . . . is the first step on the road to the creation of a new state . . . the militants of national liberation [are] single mindedly focused upon the conquest of state power' (1992, p. 18). In achieving a newly acquired and often fragile state power, these leaders then became rulers of nation-states, albeit with acutely limited resources, still economically at the mercy of imperialism, ruling over societies with arbitrary borders, endemic divisions between town and countryside, and easily bloated bureaucracies (Davidson, 1992). They were confronted immediately by potential enemies without, not only from the imperialist powers eager to retain or regain control over resources unwillingly surrendered, but also from the rulers of rival states, given the arbitrariness of the borders and the scarcity of resources throughout a given region. Nationalism, with its assumptions about the inevitable hostility of the other, was an obvious recourse. At the same time, the assertion within the nation-state of diversity, of different interests and especially identities, may also have appeared as a threat, so that the nationalist insistence on the unity and over-riding importance of the nation became equally attractive.

Many of the problems are certainly economic and focused on the desperate need to build up or develop a nation-state's economic base that can survive in a hostile global economy. In this respect, however, the unity of the nation may come under severe strains, for reasons that are well summarized by Harris.

> What begins in the springtime of national liberation as a great sense of popular emancipation becomes a new range of new and often heightened oppressions, those required for economic development . . . the nation liberationists of Jharkhand may cry '. . . we want a Jharkhand free of exploitation, a Jharkhand where those who work will eat and those who loot will go'. But the terms to achieve this end are not in Jharkhand and not within the grasp of the Jharkhand State. Many people, of course, do gain in the achievement of independence. Those that inherit the new State and come to constitute its new ruling order are some . . . But once the State settles down to the task of development, the majority of people may find conditions distant from the rhetorical promise of independence. Class struggle emerges from the supposed common interest, and the invitation to sacrifice for the nation is directed at one class by another. (1992, pp. 18–19)

In the process, of course, nationalism may become much more attractive for the postcolonial elite than rival ideologies.

In her close study of such movements in Japan and China for example, Germaine Hoston has traced the growing ascendancy of nationalist motifs over Marxist ones over the century, an ascendancy well entrenched long before the Maoists were close to taking state power. In Japan this culminated in the Tenko episode of the late 1920s which marked 'the massive defection of Japanese Marxists . . . to the national cause' (Hoston, 1994, p. 123). The difference between the two cases was that 'the surrender of Japan's Marxists [was] to an existing state power whose effective national myth [the *kokutai*] pre-empted and nullified appeals to nationalism from the Left' whilst in China the CCP, faced with a much weaker state, adopted nationalist ideology for itself in order to obtain state power (1994, p. 366). One way of reading the conflict between the Chinese Communist Party and the Guomindang was to see which was better equipped to be the director of the 'awakening of China' (Fitzgerald, 1996). The now quite evident and overt nationalism of China's rulers (see Unger, 1996) may, from this perspective, be better understood as the unfolding of a logic not of any kind of communism, however distorted, but rather of nationalism *tout court*.

Similar patterns appear in other liberated nation-states that have eschewed the peculiarities of Maoist Marxist–Leninism. What is common to them is the particular ideology of nationalism, a discourse of power in its own right, deployed to legitimize the rule of a postcolonial elite over a nation-state. One can see a similar development at work for example in India. Here, as Chatterjee has traced it, nationalism became in stages an effective if contested state ideology, evolving from Bankimchandra's inherently elitist exposition via Gandhi's utopianism to Nehru's more tough-minded and pragmatic version. In this context, the contrast he draws, between the aspirations, activity and directive role of nationalist elites and the necessary passivity of the mass of the population, is highly pertinent.

> Thus, while it was the Gandhian intervention in elite–nationalist politics which established for the first time that an authentic national movement could only be built upon the organized support of the whole of the peasantry, the working-out of the politics of non-violence also made it abundantly clear that . . . the peasantry were meant to become willing participants in a struggle wholly conceived and directed *by others*. (Chatterjee, 1986, p. 124; emphasis in the original)

Once the British had finally been forced to flee, having played a key role in fostering the communalist hatreds that culminated in Partition, Gandhi's successor, Nehru, was left to preside over a 'state [that] was in the hands of a nationalist elite' (Khilnani, 1997, p. 166). Nehru's primary focus was on building up the power, prestige and status of a sovereign nation-state (Chatterjee, 1986, p. 131). Although his own quite imaginative and experimental nationalism was tolerant and pluralist in spirit, it was inscribed within a regional framework of antagonistic nation-states (India, Pakistan,

China) all bent on securing their power, invoking supposedly historic national identities and projecting the other as a mortal threat against whom it was necessary to develop extensive armed forces. In many ways, as Khilnani suggests, Nehru's thought pointed in an internationalist rather than nationalist direction, and was in permanent tension with the dictates of *raison d'etat*. Inside the political framework of the Indian nation-state, however, Nehru like both his predecessor and successor, had to operate within a field defined by the gravitational pull of (primarily Hindu) nationalism. His daughter's swift deployment of overwhelming military might to 'liberate' East Pakistan not only exposed the hollowness of Pakistan nationalism but showed how useful nationalism could be as a source of legitimation.[16] This lesson was not forgotten, as Mrs Gandhi showed in 1980 when she crudely adopted Hindu nationalist themes to boost her flagging popularity (Khilnani, 1997, p. 54; Vanaik, 1990, p. 145).[17] This only opened the door for more and more exclusionary forms of nationalism that have come in recent years to dominate politics both regionally and nationally, making it more difficult to mobilize on the basis of other identities and solidarities.

These have always posed a problem for nationalist elites. We may see this, for instance, with regard to the women's movement, which has mobilized internationally behind the demand for women to be accorded equal rights, a struggle now, if belatedly, seen as a central part of the history of democracy (Dunn, 1992). This claim has been met with at best an inconsistent response from the leaders of national liberation movements.

Although women have played in many ways a central role in national liberation struggles, the outcome has proved to be deeply disappointing. Jayawardena concludes her classic study of the relationship between feminism and nationalism in twelve states across the third world with the judgment that 'the impulse to assert a national identity . . . which could serve as the basis for national aspirations [has] circumscribed the freedom of women' (1986, p. 257). In her account of women in national liberation movements in Africa south of the Sahara, notably in Mozambique, Stephanie Urdang too has noted how despite the apparently 'strong commitment to overthrowing not only the colonial oppressors but also the oppression of women . . . hopes and dreams [have] gone awry' (1995, p. 219).

Although highly contested, two factors in particular (both highlighted by Yuval-Davis, 1997, see Chapter 2) may have been key factors here: the control of reproduction and the (ab)use of cultural 'traditions'. In the first case, women have been required by nationalists to play a crucial role as biological reproducers of the nation, to produce future liberation fighters, to increase or alternatively to limit the number of children they may have for supposedly strategic or tactical considerations (Bulbeck, 1988, p. 107).[18] In the second case, women have been 'assigned', as Moghadam puts it, 'the role of bearers of cultural values, carriers of traditions, and symbols of the community' (1994, p. 4).

It could be argued that criticism of such positions bespeaks a Eurocentric or Westocentric first world arrogance and ignores the importance women in different contexts have attached (and continue to attach) to particular national identities. There is a demographic dimension to some struggles against colonialism (Palestinian activists would point to the Israeli state's own policies to encourage Jewish women to have children). The assertion of cultural values and traditions may be a form of resistance to modernization policies imposed from above by repressive, colonial or neocolonial regimes (unveiling made compulsory at times in Iran by the Pahlavi regime for example). However, it is by no means clear that control over the decision-making process within national liberation movements has lain primarily with women, who are after all most affected by these strategies. More generally, it seems that the significant (if hardly unusual) power imbalances that have obtained here have had some serious longer-term consequences. If the position of women has indeed deteriorated since the achievement of national liberation, this may be because, as Jayawardena argued, 'the seeds of this decay were inherent in the nature and organization of the women's movements during the period of nationalist struggle' (1986, p. 259). Whilst women played a major role in many struggles for national liberation, they were, in Abdo's view, 'largely excluded from taking an active leadership role in national struggles' (1994, p. 149).

It may therefore be no accident that, as she goes on to argue, 'in almost all liberation movements where women were actively involved, a general reversal of their roles became the fact of life after national liberation and the establishment of the nation-state' (Abdo, 1994, p. 150). Once the struggle for national liberation has succeeded, the role of women in it has generally been downplayed, the systematic depreciation of the role of the *moudjahidates* in the Algerian case being a particularly striking example (Bouatta, 1994).

This may be an expression of a deeper anxiety that the demand for equality is (at least implicitly) rooted in a solidarity that transcends the borders of the newly consolidated nation-state and may invoke (or have the potential to invoke) an alternative identity to the national. Or to put it another way, whereas nationalism has to insist on unity, on a commonality of interest founded in the over-riding importance of national identity, the feminist focus is on rights and the shared interests of women both within and beyond the nation-state. There may then be a growing divergence between the logic of the nationalist struggle for possession of a nation-state and that of the feminist struggle for equality. As Bulbeck concludes, 'their goals are not the same, and there is no reason why they should be' (1988, p. 115).

But the pursuit of nationalist goals may affect more than the rights of women. Any expression of different interests or points of view can become intolerable, challenging the authority of leaders who see themselves as representing if not personifying the unity and identity of the nation. It may be this which has led so many postcolonial elites to adopt forms of repression and exploitation characteristic of their former colonial enemies, stifling debate, censoring thought and deploying more or less extreme forms of violence, establishing what Thomas evocatively calls 'the state's right to violence and to silence' (1997, p. 123). This has involved *inter alia* the suppression of the right to vote, of freedom of expression, of freedom of association, as various forms of authoritarian rule, from one-party states and military dictatorships, have been imposed. The African experience has been particularly tragic in this respect, with the state 'in the most extreme cases . . . more or less reduced to its coercive apparatuses' (Olukoshi and Laakso, 1996, p. 10). Of course this experience has to be situated, as they observe, in the context of that continent's particularly traumatic experience at the hands of colonialism, but they also make it clear that the nationalism of top-down nation-builders has played a major role in a series of catastrophes from Somalia to Liberia, from Zaire to Cameroon. Further north, Addi has drawn attention to the way in which the army in particular has found nationalism a congenial ideology:

> military establishments typically see themselves as the guardian par excellence of nationalism. As officers work their way up the ladder of promotion, they draw nearer to the ideal type of the nationalist individual . . . the soldier is convinced that he is the shield of the country and as such the rightful holder of that legitimacy from which all political and administrative authority must flow. Yet all this is merely an ideological cover for political inequality . . . and impedes the emergence of citizenship. (1997, p. 121)

Rather than fostering democracy then, the predominance of nationalism in national liberation movements, in the struggle for self-determination, can have quite different effects. This is not only a conclusion that Western liberals or Marxists have drawn, but one that, for all their critiques of Eurocentrism, even radicals of postmodernist or postcolonial persuasion now appear to share. As Mufti and Shohat put it,

> that the great era of national liberation in the Third World that began in the years following World War 2 is now over has become more or less obvious. This is evident in even those struggles for nation-statehood and self-determination that continue into the 1990s, struggles that have consequently been marked by a deep sense of belatedness and anachronism. In large regions of the Third World, the powerful framework of nationalism, which held such enormous liberationist promise even twenty years ago, has begun to fall apart. In these countries, the slogans of nationalism, its mythos of home and heart, are now the property of national elites that have increasingly been revealed to be corrupt, capitulationist, undemocratic, patriarchal and homophobic. (1997, p. 3)

Nationalism, the nation-state and democracy

It may now be more difficult to see the nation-state as the optimal framework within which democratic rights may be accorded and secured. This, however, is the burden of some influential modernist accounts which have emphasized the importance of the emergence of the modern state for an understanding of nationalism (see Chapter 2). It has been argued, in particular, that democratic institutions have been developed inside nation-states not elsewhere, and that citizenship rights have been extended over time within the same framework. David Held, who has usefully summarized this general line of argument, sees this as a process driven both from above and from below, as elites sought new ways to legitimate their rule and masses demanded rights in return for the sacrifices they made for the nation-state, notably in wartime (1995, pp. 48–72). National assemblies or parliaments were established as the quintessential representative forums through which the people could express its views, and in which rulers were made accountable. Within the nation-state, citizenship rights have been extended over time on the basis of membership of the nation-state, from the civil to the political to the social. In relation to social rights in particular, David Miller (1995), a prominent advocate of a liberal nationalism (see Chapter 4), has argued forcefully that it is only the trust that obtains between fellow nationals that can make a welfare state work.

There are a number of problems, however, with this line of argument. To begin with, it must be noted that representative institutions have not emerged within every nation-state. There are a great number of nation-states both past and present which have dispensed with such institutions, or at least deprived them of any real power, often by invoking considerations of the nation's security. On the other hand, representative institutions have also developed outside the framework of the nation-state, at more local and regional levels, for instance, and as Held (1995) himself has argued, may now be developing (if they have not done so before) at supra-national levels.

Secondly, the citizenship rights that may have been accorded by national legislatures did not depend wholly on a shared sense of national identity and to the extent that they did, this may have raised as many problems as it solved. Marshall's somewhat evolutionary account of the extension of these rights laid more stress perhaps on difficulties thrown up by capitalist development than anything else, particularly in terms of class inequalities. His account has in any case been challenged on the grounds that it was inattentive to other forms of inequality, notably those relating to gender, disability and, most pertinently in this context, 'race'. Indeed, it can be argued that it was precisely because he took for granted the national frame of reference that he obscured the way in which the according of social rights through the construction of a welfare state for national citizens generated particular inequalities in this respect. As Lewis (1998) has argued, we need to think about the development of the welfare state not as the product of a sense of belonging to a given nation but as a central part of a process by which such constituencies of belonging were constructed. This process generated both a sense of inclusion and policies of exclusion, targeted at those deemed not to be part of the nation, according citizenship rights to some whilst at the same time depriving others of them. In the British case of course, imperial considerations bulked large in the evolution of such exclusionary policies (see also Chapter 4) but the distinction between the nation and the other is by no means confined to this instance.

We may need then to consider more critically whether the invocation of national identity in this context has in fact secured citizenship rights. As Yasemin Soysal (1994) has argued, there are good reasons for thinking that citizenship and nationality can and ought to be so decoupled. With migration especially, the presence inside many of the original nation-states of Western Europe of non-nationals has posed major problems in this respect (see Chapters 4 and 7).

This is not, however, a new problem. There is a critical sense in which, ever since the nation-state became hegemonic, the rights of significant numbers of people to participate as equals in social and political life have been seriously limited. This point was made by Hannah Arendt with a force scarcely dimmed by subsequent events when she identified a critical confusion between humanity and nationality in the Declaration of the Rights of Man at the time of the French Revolution. As she noted, this meant that 'the same essential rights were at once claimed as the inalienable heritage of all human beings *and* as the specific heritage of specific nations . . . The practical outcome of this contradiction was that from then on human rights were protected and enforced only as national rights' (Arendt, 1966, p. 230). This was to have and continues to have serious consequences. For what happens to people from whom a national identity is withdrawn, or to whom it is not available, or to whom it is denied?

This century in particular has seen civilian populations become a major if not the prime target of the violence of nation-states, with the Nazi conquest of Eastern Europe and the attempt to exterminate all Jews in their domain as perhaps the most appalling example. In this case, which may serve as a dismal paradigm, the attempt to escape from a murderous nation-state exposed most sharply the contradictions involved and may well have served as the inspiration for Arendt's reflections.

Deprived of their rights initially within the German nation-state, no longer members of that nation, the Jews suddenly found themselves, in a world of nation-states, outside any polity at all, without protection, without security, without rights. No other nation-state was keen to take them in, as was made clear at the Evian conference of 1938. This put them in an acutely dangerous situation. For, as Margaret Canovan explains, the rights lost by the stateless were much more fundamental than those traditionally listed in declarations of the rights of man. The problem was not so much one of equality before the law as of being recognized by the law at all; not so much that they lacked freedom, as that in their shadowy existence outside the legal community their actions and opinions were of no interest to anyone. The fundamental human right is therefore the right to *have* rights, which means the right to belong to a political community. (1992, p. 34)

When the political community is defined in national terms, as it has been so powerfully and repeatedly in the modern era, the withdrawal of such fundamental rights is often justified in terms that seem to turn reality on its head. It is those who are removed, those who lose their rights, who are often defined as the danger, as the threat to security and well-being, rather than the reverse. It was a central element of Nazi ideology that the very presence of Jews posed a mortal threat to the German nation (when it was the Nazis of course who posed precisely such a threat to the Jews).

Although the hostility expressed in this case had a particularly racist character, it may have deeper roots in the way in which nationalism 'solves' the problem of how a political community can come into existence in the first place. The threat posed by the Jews in that case, as perhaps by the Roma in Europe today, may have been that they exposed something problematic about this by virtue of their tendency or willingness to move from place to place, from state to state (Sampson, 2000). Bauman has suggested that this was indeed one of the sources of the hostility felt towards them, that

the sight of a large group of people free to flip at will from one national fortress to another must have aroused deep anxiety. It defied the very truth on which *all nations, old and new alike*, rested their claims: the ascribed character of nationhood, heredity and naturalness of national entities. (1989, p. 55; emphasis added)

At this level, there is perhaps, as Bauman has argued, an 'essential incompatibility between nationalism and the idea of free choice' (1989, p. 55).

CONCLUSION

Choice is, however, in many ways central to the idea of democracy. The will of the people cannot be asserted but needs to be discovered in the present, out of debate between different views, deriving from the pursuit of diverse interests and different conceptions of the public good. Nationalism, as we have suggested here, is rooted in a different set of values and points elsewhere, to the past more than the present, to identity not difference, to what is given not to what is to be chosen. As we have sought to illustrate in a variety of cases (from the French Revolution to the collapse of communism, from struggles to establish new nation-states free from colonial rule to the extension of citizenship rights in established nation-states), although at times struggles for nationalism and for democracy have appeared to converge, the link between them seems more contingent than necessary. In some key instances and in important respects, as we have suggested, their paths have diverged and their logics pointed in different directions.

FURTHER READING

Contrasting approaches to the issue of the relationship between nationalism and democracy are advanced in Nodia (1994) and Ringmar (1998). Stepan's early critique (1994) of how democracy was hampered by some postcommunist nation-states is illuminating and thought-provoking. Greenfeld's (1992) magnum opus is worth looking at for an exploration into the development of nationalist ideas in some circles in France and Germany, and indeed elsewhere, but needs treating with some caution. Some interesting reflections on German national identity after the Holocaust can be found in Fulbrook (1999). The nationalist conflicts that tore Yugoslavia apart have spawned a growing literature. Ramet (1999), Denitch (1996) and Thomas (1999) analyse different aspects of this complex and tragic history. For a wider perspective on nationalism in the region, see also Glenny (1999) and Pavlowitch (1999). Harris (1992) offers a sharp analysis of some of the arguments involved in various struggles for national liberation, whilst Jayawardena (1986) analyses the relationship between feminism and nationalism more generally in the third world. The development of postcolonial theory has thrown a new light on some of this – see for instance some of the essays in McClintock, Mufti and Shohat (1997). The arguments advanced long ago by Hannah Arendt (1966) still seem highly pertinent to us, as (similarly) do those put forward by Bauman (1989).

NOTES

1 Although this is not Chantal Mouffe's view, since she considers that democracy is based on what she calls the 'logic of identity' and is therefore opposed to such pluralism (Mouffe, 1998), her powerful arguments about the nature and significance of multiple identities, which we too noted in Chapter 3, do seem to point in this direction. (See Hoffman, 1998, pp. 60–2 for a discussion of this in relation to the idea of democratic sovereignty.)

2 Delegates to the Estates General were not only elected from provinces but saw themselves very much as representatives of the locality (Hampson, 1991).

3 This centralization included the attempt to force a French language on the people of France on the grounds that, as Barère put it, 'the language of a free people must be one and the same for all'. For the architects of linguistic uniformity, those who continued not to speak French were seen as enemies of the people, in the grip of the (usually clerical) forces of reaction. Significantly, Bell has noted that the linguistic reformers 'paid little attention to the problem of participation ... "The people must understand the laws to approve and obey them" wrote Gregoire in his report to the convention' (Bell, 1995, p. 1431).

4 The Greens, however, did make this an issue, arguing that after two world wars Germans should not want a sovereign nation-state (Winkler, 1996, p. 63). A profound sense of shame was also at the heart of Gunter Grass' eloquent polemic against German unification (Grass, 1990).

5 As one of the main opposition figures later put it, with some understandable bitterness, 'the West German political parties ... with their huge political machines, effectively killed all attempts in the GDR to articulate independent political ideas and to build independent political structures' (Sebastian Pflugbeil in Philipsen, 1993, p. 310).

6 By 1995 there had been a 69 per cent drop in applications compared with 1992 (Teitelbaum and Winter, 1998).

7 This has been viewed in some quarters as a further triumph for democracy. For a more sceptical view, see Spencer and Wollman (1997).

8 In Estonia at the time of the 1989 census 600,000 out of a population of 1,600,000 were non-Estonians, mainly Russians (30 per cent). In Latvia, only 52 per cent was ethnically Latvian, with Russians forming 34 per cent and Belorussians a further 5 per cent of the population. Only Lithuania among the Baltic states was relatively homogeneous, with 80 per cent of its population Lithuanian, the remainder including Russians (9 per cent) and Poles (7 per cent) (Dawisha and Parrot, 1994, pp. 338–9).

9 Much of the opposition in Serbia was more enthusiastically nationalist than Milosevic himself. As Thomas has demonstrated, nationalism in Serbia cannot be located at one end of the political spectrum.

> The importance of the national issue in Serbian politics cannot simply be seen in terms of the prevalence of blood and soil patterns of thought. Even political parties which were self-consciously 'civic' and 'democratic' in orientation felt themselves compelled to define and set limits on the borders of the state in which those values should operate. (1999, p. 429)

10 See the slightly disingenuous account in Goldstein (1999, p. 215) and for a rather more forthright view, Crnobrnja (1994, pp. 151–2).

11 Much of the opposition was to how the war was conducted, although there was also some opposition to the project (never openly articulated for tactical reasons) of dismembering Bosnia (see Tanner, 1997). For a critical view of the damage done to democracy in Croatia by nationalism, see Pusic (1994).

12 It is important in this context not to ignore 'the large number of people who chose not to join any of the three tribes, who described themselves as Yugoslavs,

who are secular cosmopolitans, or who are children of secular mixed marriages' (Denitch, 1996, pp. 182–3).

13 Again Cobban made both these points acutely many years ago.

> The success of national revolts in the nineteenth century, when they did succeed, is not to be interpreted as the triumph of democratic virtue unaided by force. On the contrary, nations only achieved their independence when they had the effective backing of a strong military power ... Moreover, the democratic elements in the movement were generally very restricted. (Cobban, 1969, p. 43)

14 These tensions are in many ways key to Anderson's account of the development of nationalism – see his chapter on 'creole pioneers' (Anderson, 1991, pp. 47–65).

15 Basil Davidson (1992) argues that some African traditions were a good deal more democratic than the nation-states that were now built. He gives as an example that of the Golden Stool of the Akan, a meaningful political system, with extensive checks and balances and an effective constitution, within which there was considerable and effective political participation (p. 56 and following).

16 Harris has commented on 'the striking speed with which a Bangladeshi nationalism was invented. It had no illustrious past [but] once the historians were unleashed, an extensive slice of history could be colonised (a parallel to the exclusive territory of the new State). ... Bangladesh was a tactic ... [and] adventurers were on hand to utilize the opportunities as they arose ... But, in the language of nationalism, the soul of the nation had now to be invented to make inexorable its advance to self-realization in a new State' (1992, p. 208).

17 Vanaik argues that Gandhi too had gone some way down this road, having 'made the National Movement a mass movement by substantially Hinduizing it' (1990, p. 142).

18 In China, for example, immense pressure has been exerted by the state on women to limit the number of children they have, indirectly encouraging practices of female infanticide in the process. In Nicaragua, the Sandinistas' need to conciliate the Catholic Church led to agreements with the latter on the issue of abortion (Moghadam, 1994, p. 5).

6

Nationalism in a Global World

INTRODUCTION

In this chapter we shall discuss the development of nationalist, secessionist and what some have termed neo-nationalist movements, in relation to what is seen by many as an increasingly globalized world. East and West, North and South, there appears to have been a resurgence of such movements. Francophones in Quebec, Basques and Catalans, Scots and Welsh, and the many ethnic and national movements in Eastern Europe and the former Soviet Union provide just some of the examples of groups who have asserted rights to national autonomy or independence in the past few decades. In addition, there has been an increase in political support for political movements of the far right, that have nationalism as a core component of their ideology, in Europe, Australia, the USA, and elsewhere. Whilst not all features of the resurgence of contemporary nationalism may be explained by reference to the concept or reality of globalization, the latter may nevertheless have significant implications for nationalism, particularly in relation to the contemporary salience and appeal of national identity, and the need for and viability of the modern nation-state.

By contrast, some of the literature on globalization, particularly that influenced by postmodernism, has argued that globalization itself is undermining nationalism through processes that produce more fluid, fragmented or hybrid identities. We therefore commence this chapter with a brief examination of the facets of globalization which are relevant to both these sets of arguments.

Globalization

Across a multitude of discourses both academic and 'everyday' it has become asserted that we live in a more globalized world. The process of globalization is alleged to have had profound implications for many aspects of our lives, and, in particular to have had a number of implications for nationalism, national identity and the future of the nation-state. First, we shall attempt a broad definition of its main features; secondly, we shall briefly discuss the issue of its novelty (or otherwise), and thirdly, we shall examine various facets of globalization, economic, political and cultural, and draw out their implications for contemporary nationalism.[1]

It would be impossible to attempt here a full account of the various definitions of globalization that exist in a literature that has grown apace over the past decade. Waters, for example, attempts to condense a number of issues from this literature when he defines globalization as 'a social process in which the constraints of geography on economic, political, social and cultural arrangements recede, in which people become increasingly aware that they are receding and in which people act accordingly' (2001, p. 5). For Giddens what happens to people in localities is increasingly influenced or even determined by a web of global relationships: 'Globalization can thus be defined as the intensification of world-wide social relations which link distant localities in such a way that local happenings are shaped by events occurring many miles away and vice versa' (1990, p. 64). Thus the peasant producer of coffee in Nicaragua will be part of a set of relationships which include the Tokyo stock market. Harvey writes of 'space–time compression'. The instantaneity of modern communications obliterates the constraints of space and distance; thus the world *is* getting smaller, and McLuhan's talk of a global village back in the 1960s is becoming a reality.

As we shall see, the various interpretations of globalization emphasize different processes and with differing accounts of causation. For many writers, what is involved is a complex process involving a dialectical relationship between, *inter alia*, the global and the local. Globalization, for the likes of Giddens, is not a one-way process of cultural, political or economic relationships. 'This is a dialectical process because such local happenings may move in an obverse direction from the very distanciated relations that shape them. Local transformation is as much a part of globalization as the lateral extension of social connections across time and space' (1990, p. 64). Or again, specifically discussing questions of political identity, Held argues that 'globalization can generate forces of both fragmentation and unification . . . Globalization can engender an awareness of political difference as well as an awareness of common identity' (1992, p. 32).

This characterization of ambivalence at the heart of globalization is perhaps what may be held to distinguish it from other concepts that have been around somewhat longer, concepts such as 'internationalization' and, in some contexts just as relevant, 'imperialism'. There is more at stake in this argument than an arid dispute about terms because the phenomenon to which globalization points is not necessarily a new one. Indeed, for Giddens it is one that is tied up with a Western dominated (so far) modernity more generally, whilst of course, Marx and Engels powerfully argued in the Communist Manifesto that capitalism was from the outset an international process that battered 'down all Chinese walls' (Marx and Engels, 1976).[2] The peasant in Nicaragua (or elsewhere in Latin America) was always at risk from the vagaries of the international market; it simply took longer for the effects to be apparent. However, it would be churlish to deny the speeding up of these processes in the past few decades. A further point, that has some significance for approaching the analysis of identity in these globalized times, is that it is all too easy for globalization to be assumed as a Western process. Wallerstein (1974), in Marx's footsteps, begins to date his 'world-system' from the sixteenth century with the birth of capitalism. However, others have pointed to the problems with the Eurocentrism of this approach. Janet Abu-Lughod (1989), in her fascinating work of synthesis, has argued for a world system in the thirteenth century, which was not centred specifically on Europe, but one in which East and West were in balance.

All this should be a salutary warning against coming to simplistic conclusions about the nature of globalization, let alone its consequences. But what in fact is being argued about globalization that has consequences for nationalism and national identity?

Economic globalization

First, there is discussion of economic aspects of globalization. Here, perhaps most clearly, we are dealing with a phenomenon that has been discussed over a long period. The 1960s and 1970s saw considerable discussion about the power of what are now termed transnational companies. One hundred and thirty UN states have smaller economies than the fifty largest transnational corporations (TNCs) (Cohen, 1997b). The world is increasingly one global economy, with a far-reaching international division of labour involving massive global movements of capital, and, of particular importance for questions of identity, of labour. This last has propelled millions of people to move across the globe, often over large distances, to settle, temporarily or permanently, in new lands, new nation-states. In their comprehensive survey of modern migration, Castles and Miller (1998) cite the estimate of 120 million international immigrants in 1994 by the head of the International Organization for Migration. Although representing less than 2 per cent of the world's population, this is still a large number. The implications of population movements on this scale are profound, in spite of the obvious fact that the majority of the world's population does not undergo such migration. The formation of transnational cultural, economic and political networks is none the less considerable. Thus by the end of the 1980s, for example, 'about half of all adult Mexicans were related to someone living in the United States' (Castles and Miller, 1998, p. 220). We discuss the implications of this for national identity later in the chapter. Thirty million of the recent immigrants were foreign workers who were estimated to be sending 67 billion dollars annually to their home countries, making this the second largest item in global trade after the oil industry. The globalization and acceleration of migration, its increasing feminization and politicization at a variety of levels (Castles and Miller, 1998), has also had profound implications for cultural changes which we shall discuss below. The existence of transnational communities as a result of migration is but one factor in this process.

One of the key debates about economic globalization has been over the degree to which such a process may have undermined national economies and the power and sovereignty of nation-states. Some writers have seriously challenged the view that nation-states have lost significant power over economic decision-making (Hirst and Thompson, 1996; Mann, 1997). Current fears of worldwide economic recession raise the possibility that protectionism and economic nationalism may yet be brought out of mothballs as attempted solutions to economic crisis. Supposedly global economic actors such as the IMF and the World Bank may be concerned not just with stabilizing global capitalism, but particularly acting in the interests of maintaining debt payments to Western banks. They may also act in the interests of the most influential and dominant national economies and nation-states.

Political globalization

The functions, scope and autonomy of the nation-state in an increasingly globalized world are central to the issues of political globalization. For some, this has to do with the emergence of a range of issues that cannot be dealt with adequately at a national level. Held (1995) has summarized some of these in terms of five major 'disjunctures'. These involve, first, the emergence of a body of international law; secondly, the internationalization of political decision-making; thirdly, the emergence of both hegemonic power blocs and the development of international security structures; fourthly, the globalization of modern communications (part of a supposedly 'global culture'); and fifthly, the internationalization of economic processes. In other words, the globalization process itself is undermining the adequacy of the nation-state as a unit of political authority in the modern world. Whilst Held et al. deny that 'national sovereignty today . . . has been wholly subverted' (1999, p. 81), they do argue that 'the locus of effective political power can no longer be assumed to be national governments' (p. 80), and that the life chances of individuals are now influenced by forces way beyond the scope of the individual nation-state to determine or to substantially control on its own.

Theorists of international relations as well as of politics have been concerned with these questions whilst a number of writers have pointed to the radical effects on the nation-state of increasing global interdependence. Perlmutter (1991) poses the question as to whether there is a global civilization; Rosenau (1980) distinguishes between state-centric and multi-centric worlds, the former associated with the nation-state, the latter with transnational organizations, movements, communities, problems, events and structures. Prima facie support for this is provided by the huge rise in intergovernmental organizations and international non-governmental organizations since 1945 (Held et al., 1999). More recently, Rosenau has argued that 'control mechanisms at national level are . . . yielding space both to more encompassing forms of governance [transnational] and to narrower, less comprehensive forms [subnational]' (1998, p. 35). Bull, as far back as 1977, suggested that we could be witnessing the development of a 'neo-medieval' form of world political order in which nation-states share sovereignty with both subnational or state authorities and supranational ones (Held et al., 1999).

Our concern here is not to resolve wider issues about the nation-state but to review some of the implications of these processes and arguments for nationalism. In Chapter 7 we discuss the EU as an example of a suprastate organization and also the potential for movements and communities that are global or at least transnational to represent an opposing principle to that of nationalism. However, we shall argue later in this chapter that some of these movements – such as those of religious fundamentalism, for example, probably represent similar phenomena to some modern nationalist movements, phenomena that are themselves partly a response to globalization. In a similar vein some nationalist political movements, as we discuss below, gain support on the basis of their programme of strengthening the nation-state in opposition to global forces and globalizing politics. In addition to the supranational threats to the power and autonomy of nation-states, there are other, more local ones. It has become a commonplace to suggest that the nation-state is threatened from above and below, from the global and the local, with the two very much interlinked. The second part of this chapter will deal with the rise of local or regional neo-nationalisms, which are a real or potential challenge to existing nation-states.

Cultural globalization

This brings us to the third aspect of globalization that we need to discuss and which forms much of the sociological and postmodernist writing on the subject, namely the cultural. It is here that we come to a literature that has raised fundamental questions about changing identities in the modern world, including political ones. It is here that we find, again, a close inter-relationship between political and cultural factors, and here that we look at the consequences for nationalism and national identity of globalization rather than those for the nation-state. The core of the claims in much of this literature, is, as we noted in Chapters 2 and 3, that identity has become much more fluid in the contemporary world; that people not only have multiple identities, but that they have more of a *mélange*, a mixture of identities, often referred to as the spread of hybridity. In addition, these new kinds of identity are not fixed or permanent; rather they are fluid and open to change. The modern (or, for most of these writers, the postmodern world) celebrates difference rather than uniformity. Globalization fits into this process in a counter-intuitive way. Whereas it might be thought that a process of cultural homogenization is set in motion by the actions of global media and communications, the reality is far more complex. There is, it is true, plenty of evidence for homogenization in global media (the dominance of US products in world television), in tourism with its international hotel chains and identical airport terminals, and in other aspects of consumption in the global market, such as the ubiquity of McDonalds and Disney. However, there is equally evidence of the opposite, in the rise of the 'ethnic' product, the quest for local authenticity in tourism, the rise of local radio and TV. Even McDonalds has some local variability – with salads in France, and regulations to ensure food is kosher in Israel, for example (Holton, 1998). What we, have instead is a more complex interplay between global and local, what some writers have called, in a hideous compound word, 'glocalization' (Holton, 1998; Robertson, 1995). Thus Appadurai writes, 'the central problem of today's global interactions is the tension between cultural homogenization and cultural heterogenization' (1990, p. 5). This distinguishes this approach from ones which stressed American global media dominance or employed the term 'cultural imperialism'. Rather, as Appadurai argues, 'the new global economy has to be understood as a complex, over-lapping, disjunctive order, which cannot any longer be understood in terms of existing centre–periphery models' (p. 6).

Much of this approach has come as a reaction against Marxism that is one feature of postmodernism. It has also emerged from the field of cultural and literary studies, alongside postcolonialism. At one pole of argument are those who eschew a material grounding for these cultural developments. Other writers, including Appadurai, wish to ground the cultural processes in other global developments, especially migration. In either case, central concepts have been those of transnational community, diaspora and hybrid identity. It is to an examination of these that we now turn.

Transnational communities and diasporas

The concepts of 'transnational social space' and 'transnational community' are rooted in anthropological and geographical discourses that have been concerned with linking global processes to migration issues (Basch et al., 1994; Faist, 1998). Basch et al.,

> define 'transnationalism' as the processes by which immigrants forge and sustain multi-stranded social relations that link together their societies of origin and settlement. We call these processes transnationalism to emphasize that many immigrants today build social fields that cross geographic, cultural, and political borders . . . An essential element is the multiplicity of involvements that transmigrants sustain in both home and host societies. (1994, p. 6)

Faist stresses the importance of trading links and economic flows in transnational social spaces which are characterized by *'triadic relationships* between groups and institutions in the host state, the sending state (sometimes viewed as an external homeland) and the minority group – migrants and/or refugee groups or ethnic minorities' (1998, p. 217). The idea of a 'transnational community' is seen by Faist as a concept that overlaps that of 'diaspora', a term that he wishes to retain for examples of traumatic or forcible exile and migration. Further, not all diasporas, for him, are examples of transnational communities, since not all 'develop some significant social and symbolic ties to the receiving country' (p. 222). In much of the contemporary literature, as we shall see, diaspora has come to have a wider meaning than this.

The concept of diaspora is an old one, deriving from the Greek words for to sow or scatter. It is defined in the *Shorter Oxford English Dictionary* as 'the dispersion'. It originally was applied to the scattering of the Jews after the fall of the Temple, and for many centuries diaspora and Jewry were interwoven terms. Over the centuries, Jews lived in varying kinds of tension with the communities among which they found themselves. They perhaps fared best in the multi-ethnic Arab world in north Africa and Spain, where they made considerable cultural as well as commercial contributions. In Eastern Europe, until the impact of Enlightenment thought, they maintained a highly separate identity, culturally and religiously distinct from the host society which in any case excluded them from civil rights, and unsympathetic to the early formations of nationalist sentiments in those societies. Under the impact of the Enlightenment and modernist political movements, such as socialism and nationalism, the Jewish diaspora experience and response became increasingly diverse and complex, presaging the issues which have come to the fore again in the late twentieth century with other diasporic groups. The new choices – of assimilation to a national community which was largely hostile, of class identifications through a labour and socialist movement intent on challenging nationalism and radically changing society, building socialism through claims to ethnic and cultural distinctiveness within the socialist struggle, or constructing an alternative nationalism based on the idea of a return to the biblical lands – all had their enthusiastic adherents (Traverso, 1994). There remained too the older solution – that of maintaining an orthodox religious separatism that ignored the modern world as far as possible and had little to do with any state structures and institutions.

In the original meaning diaspora implies forcible exclusion from a native land, but it is now being applied to the much wider range of situations produced by global migration.[3] Anthias (1998), in a recent critique, distinguishes between diasporas as 'social collectivities' as seen in the work of Robin Cohen, and diaspora seen as a social condition, exemplified in the work of James Clifford, but also more typical of postmodernist writing in general. Despite some problems identified by Anthias, Cohen produces a useful typology of diasporic situations, and the great strength of his work is that it is rooted in an understanding of the material realities behind diasporic dispersion, in particular, transnational migration. Cohen's summary of the common features of a diaspora includes a variety of reasons for original dispersal; a collective memory and myth about the homeland; a distinctive popular ethnic group consciousness involving an idealized view of the supposed ancient homeland, and sometimes a popular movement for return; and a commitment to its well-being, or even to its creation or recreation if it no longer exists; a difficult and insecure relationship with the host society; and 'a sense of empathy and solidarity with co-ethnic members in other countries of settlement' (Cohen, 1997b, p. 26).

Cultural diasporas, such as the Caribbean cultural diaspora in the UK, one of the particular types highlighted by Cohen, point to the existence of hybrid identities which we discuss below. These diasporas are seen as being advantageously placed to benefit from globalization, both in terms of trade and intellectual life. Thus Kotkin suggests that Indian, Chinese and Jewish diasporas have come to represent 'global tribes' whose members have the cultural and economic networks which, allied to their global dispersion, enable them to prosper in the global marketplace (cited by Holton, 1998).[4]

'A diaspora', Cohen writes, is 'well placed to act as a bridge between the particular and the universal' (1997b, p. 169). From the perspective of national identity diasporas point to alternative modes of identification. Identity becomes deterritorialized, no longer linked to one particular nation-state. Citizenship itself undergoes a transformation.

In contrast to the past . . . this new conception of nation-state includes as citizens those who live physically dispersed within the boundaries of many other states, but who remain socially, politically, culturally, and often economically part of the nation-state of their ancestors. (1997b, p. 136)

The process of deterritorialization is a crucial one for undermining traditional nationalism, and Appadurai, too, sees migration as a central way in which this has occurred:

Deterritorialization, in general, is one of the central forces of the modern world, since it brings labouring populations into the lower class sectors and spaces of relatively wealthy societies, while sometimes creating exaggerated and intensified senses of criticism or attachment to politics in the home state. (1990, p. 11)

Through the processes of globalization and the spread of diasporas, Cohen suggests, there is a fundamental undermining of the principles of nationalism:

What 19th century nationalists wanted was a 'space' for each 'race', a territorializing of each social identity. What they have got instead is a chain of cosmopolitan cities and an increasing proliferation of subnational and transnational identities that cannot easily be contained in the nation-state system. (1997b, p. 175)

Thus, just as the Jewish diaspora had tenuous links with any homeland through much of its existence, diasporas more generally can break down the seemingly inextricable links between people, nation, territory and history.

In contrast to Cohen's account, which stresses diasporic groups and communities, much of the postmodernist literature features diaspora as a cultural condition. It is as much about a critique of fixed identities as it is about the analysis of actual social groups. Thus Brah suggests 'that the concept of diaspora offers a critique of discourses of fixed origins, while taking account of a homing desire which is not the same thing as a desire for a homeland' (1996, p. 180). Or again, 'diasporic identities are at once local and global. They are networks of transactional identifications encompassing 'imagined' and 'encountered' communities' (p. 196). In this perspective diaspora is as much a metaphor as a reality. Cohen puts his finger on the heart of this when he writes that 'in this genre of analysis the migrant and the refugee have become the *träger* of the post-modern/late modern world: a means of globalization from below' (1997b, p. 133). Thus the migrant, the exile, the refugee become key players in undermining fixed national and ethnic identities. It is the idea of cultural dislocation which is central here (Gandhi, 1998). However, for Clifford, too, diasporas undermine nations:

'The nation-state, as common territory and time, is traversed and, to varying degrees, subverted by diasporic attachments' (1994, p. 307).

These ideas of the cultural flux and the shifting and fragmented identities that constitute the diasporic condition also find their expression in the idea of hybridity or hybrid identities. For Pietersee (1995), hybridity is a major feature of globalization. Others have used the term 'creolization', deriving from past colonial histories, to denote the same process of cultural inter-mixing. The intention here, again, is to counter fixed and essentialist notions of identity, particularly ethnic identity. As such, the focus is on the ways in which globalization breaks these down in favour of cultural syncretism and synthesis. It is thus possible for a wide variety of cultural mixtures and syntheses to develop on a global basis.

There are a number of problems with some of this writing on global-ization, hybridity, creolization etc. First, there is a real danger of reintroducing essentialism in the way cultures and groups are considered. If diasporas involve mixed identities, if hybridity involves intermingling, this may suggest that there exist pure cultures, single identities that can form the basis for the hybrid (Anthias, 1998; Friedman, 1995; Pietersee, 1995). As Asad puts it, 'to speak of cultural syncretism or cultural hybrids presupposes a conceptual distinction between pre-existing ("pure") cultures' (1993, p. 263). Secondly, the supposed novelty of these processes is open to doubt. Migration and cultural mixing is as old as human history. The world system (if we wish to call it that) of the thirteenth century as described by Abu-Lughod (1989), the Mediterranean Jewish World lovingly recreated from the records of the Cairo *geniza* by Goitein (1967), show a great deal of cultural interchange, of diasporic trading communities, of hybrid identities. This is not to dismiss the lessons of diaspora for an alternative way of being in the world from that of national identification, but rather, a plea for caution as to its existence as a characteristic of specifically modern or postmodern society. A third problem is highlighted by Anthias in her critique of the use of the diaspora concept. Much of the writing tends to assume a community of interest, an imagined or even real community existing among the labelled diaspora group. However, she points out that there are considerable differ-ences and conflicts within these groups, not least those based on class and gender. 'The diaspora is constituted as much in *difference and division* as it is in *commonality and solidarity*' (1998, p. 564). Similarly, Faist points to the complex 'cultural segmentation' along ethnic and religious lines among the world of Turkish migrants in Germany, rather than the 'solid trans-national communities' which some have implied (1998, p. 241). Fourth, there is a sense in which much of the discussion takes place from an overly intellectual or literary standpoint. The criticism of third world intellectuals in the academic institutions of the first world, which has been taken up by some of the critics of postcolonialism, may be a bit unfair (e.g. Dirlik, 1992) (it comes, after all, from yet other inhabitants of the same universe). However, it does raise the important point as to what these intellectuals have in common with those of similar origins who inhabit the lowest echelons of the occupational structure, a more typical position in the labour market for third world migrants (Castles and Miller, 1998).

Bauman makes a distinction, relevant to this argument, between two types of mobility in the postmodern world, that of the tourist and the vagabond. The first experience 'is lived through as postmodern freedom. The second may feel rather uncannily like the postmodern version of slavery' (1998, p. 92).

> The tourists stay or move at their hearts' desire. They abandon a site when new untried opportunities beckon elsewhere. The vagabonds know they won't stay in a place for long, however strongly they wish to, since nowhere they stop are they likely to be welcome. The tourists move because they find the world within their (global) reach irresistibly *attractive* – the vagabonds move because they find the world within their (local) reach unbearably *inhospitable*. (1998, pp. 92–3)

Gandhi points to the problem of over-emphasizing one side of this divide, arguing that 'Said, more than any other post-colonial writer, submits all too easily to an over-valorization of the unhoused, exilic intellectual: the political figure between domains, between forms, between homes, between languages' (1998, p. 132). The reality for many migrants or their descendants can be a lot more painful, as we have seen. In addition to these differences of class and social position, profound differences exist, between types of diaspora and forms of hybridity – metropolitan and postcolonial, Western situated or third world based, old colonial ones or new postcolonial ones, metropolitan ones and rural ones (Radhakrishnan, 1996; Shohat, 1992). Shohat makes the point well,

> As a descriptive catch-all term, 'hybridity' per se fails to discriminate between the diverse modalities of hybridity, for example, forced assimilation, internalized self-rejection, political co-optation, social conformism, cultural mimicry, and creative transcendence. (1992, p. 110)

Some hybrid identities, such as those celebrated in Brazil, may actually obscure an implicit racism in social evaluations that recognize lighter skinned 'mixtures' as superior to darker skinned ones. Similarly in the United States, there is a good deal of distinction which might be made, culturally and socially, between an Irish/Italian hybrid and a Mexican/Puerto Rican one. To go on any further in this mode is to illustrate further the difficulty of using a metaphor derived from plant breeding, and also utilized by Victorian 'racial' pseudo-science (Young, 1995).

Literary and cultural theorists have pioneered the postcolonial perspective. This lays it open to criticism even from a highly sympathetic observer, such as Stuart Hall (1996), that it fails to link up with a more materialist analysis of changes in global capitalism. It does, however, lead to a lacuna at the heart of much of the discussion of hybridity and diaspora. This missing element is not only economic, but also political.

Hybridity, diaspora and nationalism

What, then, are the implications of the identities of the diaspora communities or the diasporic condition for nationalism today or tomorrow? The answer here is complex. Not only are there varieties of diasporic conditions and of types of hybridity, as we have seen, but there may then be a variety of political and identity responses. Some of these detract from any clear-cut sense of singular national identity while others may result in a strengthening of such identities through the development of various forms of 'nostalgia politics'. Even Clifford (1994), one of the most optimistic enthusiasts for diaspora, admits that chauvinism and nationalism are possible political responses, although he believes that this is more likely to occur among what he terms the weaker members of society.[5] One of the great nationalist movements of the twentieth century – Zionism – emerged from the classic diaspora.[6] Emigré politicians and businessmen have often fuelled and financed nationalist movements in their countries of origins, a feature seen, for example, with regard to Eastern Europe both during the communist period and after, or in support for the IRA in the United States amongst a self-identified, although highly assimilated, Irish diaspora. Support for these political movements can take a number of forms – financial, cultural or physical, but behind these can lie some complex orientations to the homeland. Thus while Zionism, for example, is ostensibly a movement that involves a rejection of life in the diaspora and wishes to build up and return to the homeland, in practice it has formed a key constituent of Jewish diaspora identity in the period since the Second World War amongst those who have no intention of leaving the host society in which they have been raised.[7] One could argue a parallel case with Irish Americans. On the other hand, the complex identities and loyalties engendered by a black or Asian or Caribbean British cultural identity, or by an orientation (which should not be assumed) to a homeland as well as a country of migration or of descent, might well be thought to dissipate the formation of purely national(ist) allegiances.

However, one of the weaknesses of concepts of hybridity and hybridization is that of a tendency among those employing the term automatically to denigrate forms of politics which are not based on such syncretisms. For Gandhi (1998), hybridity is not the only 'enlightened' response to oppression. She cites, as does Shohat, the particular problem of aboriginal peoples in

Australia or Canada who wish to ground their opposition to economic, political and cultural oppression in a position of essentialism when it comes to identity. Shohat puts the position clearly:

> The de facto acceptance of hybridity as a product of colonial conquest and post-independence dislocations as well as the recognition of the impossibility of going back to an authentic past do not mean that the political-cultural movements of various racial-ethnic communities should stop researching and recycling their pre-colonial languages and cultures. Post-colonial theory's celebration of hybridity risks an anti-essentialist condescension towards those communities obliged by circumstances to assert, for their very survival, a lost and even irretrievable past. In such cases, the assertion of culture prior to conquest forms part of the fight against continuing forms of annihilation. (1992, pp. 109–10)

She goes on to suggest that essentialism is not itself the problem, and she shows an awareness of the political dimension often absent from the post-colonial paradigm, of which she is both exemplar and critic.

> The question, in other words, is not whether there is such a thing as an originary homogeneous past, and if there is whether it would be possible to return to it, or even whether the past is unjustifiably idealized. Rather, the question is: who is mobilizing what in the articulation of the past, deploying what identities, identifications, and representations, and in the name of what political visions and goals? (1992, p. 110)

Although we are sympathetic to the political awareness of this statement, there may still be dangers in the retreat into essentialism, and for some, it is in any case a fundamentally untenable position in the global, postmodern world (S. Hall, 1996). Said, too, points out the dangers in what he terms 'nativism':

> To accept nativism is to accept the consequences of imperialism, the racial, religious, and political divisions imposed by imperialism itself. To leave the historical world for the metaphysics of essences like *négritude*, Irishness, Islam or Catholicism is to abandon history for *essentializations that have the power to turn human beings against each other.* (1993, p. 276; emphasis added)

Globalization and essentialism: nationalism revived

If there can be an ambivalence about the political reactions of members of diasporas, there are also very divergent reactions to globalization more generally. It has become a widely held view that the insecurities attached to globalizing processes have engendered a variety of essentialist and fundamentalist reactions. These can involve differing combinations of global and local phenomena. Writers such as Castells (1997) and Hall (1992a) see ethnic or religious fundamentalist movements, or the emergence of new movements of the far right as similarly products of, and reactions to globalization and post- or late modernity. Not all of these, of course, have nationalism as their core. Islamic movements have involved a complex mix of global universalistic and more local particularistic identities (Lapidus, 2001). Although fundamentalist Islamic movements have sustained political regimes in some nation-states (Iran; Afghanistan), with the more general Islamic notion of the *umma*, 'a community of believers transcending nation-state borders' (Faist, 1998, p. 240), they have also claimed loyalties that have cut across national ones in favour of alternative forms of identity.

Hall, in considering one kind of reaction to the uncertainties of globalization, suggests that, 'the return to the local is often a response to globalization' (1991, p. 33). In the face of the global, some people seek to gain an increased sense of security by searching for or recreating new forms of ethnic, religious, or racial community. This gives rise to a number of movements of secession aimed against existing nation-states, or of fundamentalism seeking to colonize them by making them ethnically or religiously pure, as with Hindu nationalism in India. Similarly, there are movements of the far right, with more or less overtly racist ideology, and with widely different styles of organization. In Australia the 'One Nation Party', associated with Pauline Hanson, linked an opposition to minority rights within Australia with a fear of the effects of a globalized economy (Perera, 1998/9, p. 201).[8] It capitalized on a growing climate of criticism of 'the aboriginal industry', and on social programmes which benefited immigrants. The xenophobic fear of the 'Asian threat' from outside of the nation has now been internalized and 'the term "un-Australian" has come to be used in an increasingly ethnicized and racialized manner' (Perera and Pugliese, 1997, p. 4). The main targets of exclusion of the Australia First Party have been aboriginal peoples and immigrants from Asia. In France, the Front National, with its increasingly sophisticated right-wing programme directed primarily against North African immigrant groups and their descendants, seen as outside of the French nation and responsible for its ills (Evans, 1996), was similarly, but much more successfully, at least before a major split at the end of 1998, operating within the established political structure. In Austria the Freedom Party under its erstwhile leader Jörg Haider has won a steadily increasing share of the vote in recent elections with an anti-European Union platform and attacks on Austria's migrant workforce and on neighbouring East European countries (Fekete, 1998). In 2000 a considerable pan-European furore arose with the Freedom Party's participation in a coalition government with the People's Party. In Germany, Britain and throughout many other European countries there exist more violent organizations that target those deemed to be, for reasons of ethnicity or race or country of origin, outside of the nation. In the United States the rise of the patriots, or militia movement provides a uniquely American version of this phenomenon, one which exists outside of established political structures but does so in the name of defending the US Constitution itself and the fundamental liberties it guarantees. In doing so it involves thousands of armed adherents in a loose network of local organizations that are different from either established political organizations or terrorist ones. Its association of the federal US government with globalizing forces of the United Nations and global finance (usually seen as a cover for world Jewry), with a new world order to be forced on unwilling US citizens, is a unique blend of elements, but one which more openly than many others targets globalization as its main enemy, with the federal government seen as the traitorous allies of global forces. These 'patriot' groups also increasingly overlap with race- or ethnicity-based 'hate groups' of a number of different types whose numbers seem to be rising (Southern Poverty Law Center, 1998, 2001).

Such reactions are not confined to the reactive nationalism of 'majority' populations threatened by cultural change and whose fears can be played on by ideologues exploiting fears of economic insecurity. Among the 'oppressed' minorities, exclusivist, ethnic movements which mirror the racism of the sort of far-right organizations which we discussed above, seek to provide easy solutions and alternative solidarities, promoting what Paul Gilroy has, in a memorable phrase, termed 'the fraternity of purity-seekers' (2000, p. 218). In the United States, for example, Manning Marable (1998) has persuasively argued that the continuing rise in support for the Black nationalist movement of Louis Farrakhan is the mirror of other right-wing developments in American society. Marable traces the connections with white racism and fascism in examining a political tradition which goes back to Marcus Garvey by way of Elijah Mohammed, the leader of the Black Muslim movement in the 1950s and 1960s. The unlikely contacts with the Ku Klux Klan and the somewhat more sophisticated far-right organizations of Lyndon Lerouche are based on shared themes of racial essentialism, racial segregation and support for capitalism and patriarchy.[9]

In very different contexts a number of groups have reasserted traditional national identities and have attempted to mobilize popular opinion and political support for a renewed form of their nationhood. In the special circumstances of postcommunist transformation, with the collapse of the Soviet Empire, a whole host of nation-states have emerged or re-emerged, basing themselves on historic claims to separate identities of greater or lesser plausibility. The Baltic states, intermittently independent in the past, threw off the burden of Russian domination, but ran into problems of citizenship rights and democracy that we discussed in Chapter 5. The former components of Yugoslavia flew apart in more or much less peaceful ways under the leadership of nationalist leaders, and the over-eager encouragement of Western politicians. In Western Europe and North America, too, historical identities were reforged or refashioned into new nationalist or separatist movements. In Lombardy, Catalonia, Scotland and Quebec, to cite only some examples, the past two decades have seen demands for secession, independence or autonomy.

From another angle, it can be argued that these movements found it easier to prosper and gain legitimacy because of the impact of globalization. Michael Keating, for example, has suggested that the growth of multiple layers of authority and decision-making, local, national, regional and global, undermine the sole claims to authority of the nation-state. It is suggested that globalization renders obsolete the criticism that very small independent nation-states are unviable or suffer from economic or cultural impoverishment. Thus, with the growing importance of the European Union, the Scottish National Party changed its emphasis with a policy that advocated an independent Scotland 'in Europe'. Independence for Quebec could be portrayed as less threatening or potentially isolating because of the existence of NAFTA which would maintain the links Quebec has with its major trading partners in North America.[10] Laitin (1997) has shown the importance of the rhetorical use of 'Europe' for a variety of purposes in Catalan nationalist discourse, to counter charges of provincialism, to legitimize the idea of a non-state political authority, and to advance the idea of states as multi-national through the idea of a Europe of regions and stateless nations.

Secession and autonomy: globalization and uneven development

The new opportunities provided for nationalist movements from the development of supranational organizations are matched by the links with more directly economic features of global capitalist development. One of the driving forces behind national or regional secession or demands for regional and national autonomy is the dynamic of uneven development (a key explanatory feature of Nairn's earlier work), and a concept that is older than the more recent one of globalization, but one that is arguably overlapping with some versions of it (Anderson, 1995). Richer nations and regions often wish to preserve their wealth by jettisoning poorer nations/regions with whom they have previously been linked. A crude example of this is provided by the popular growth of the Italian Northern League with its dream of a new country – Padania – an affluent republic no longer forced (as supporters see it) to sustain the impoverished South of Italy. The Northern League, founded in 1989, grew out of the Lombard League which had a more limited regional appeal, as its name implies. The Lombard League had a number of the features of a nationalist movement: a stress on language, in this case the use of Lombard dialect, an appeal to the idea of a Lombard identity, and a name which invoked an appeal to history – the Lombard League had defeated Frederick Barbarossa in the twelfth century (Brierley and Giacometti,

1996; Desideri, 1995). Lombard identity was seen as comprising values of efficiency, industriousness and pragmatism, very different from Roman corruption or Southern backwardness (the other against whom this identity was constructed).[11] After attempts to establish the separate identity of a Lombard language faltered in the light of a lack of support from potential League supporters, and the difficulty of establishing which dialect should be construed as the 'true' Lombard language, the name was changed to the Northern League, and incorporated other northern regionalist movements, principally the Liga Veneta (Billig, 1995). Slovenia, Catalonia and the Czech Republic would arguably provide other examples of nations or aspiring nations that have felt that they were being held back by poorer regions to which they were attached, and but for which they would be better equipped to compete in the global economy. Keating (1996) sees this as partly owing to the effects of globalization, which effects change at the local and regional level, although uneven development has been long present and has arguably long been a force in regional movements. (Catalonia was always the most industrially advanced part of Spain – Keating 1996.) However, the impact of uneven development also has a cultural dimension (as can be seen in the Northern League example above); the linked 'other' (against whom national or regional autonomy is asserted) is not only seen as poor and less developed in economic terms, but also as 'backward' culturally. This perception of backwardness has been a major factor in the importance many nationalists give to being European, and in being as near to Western or at least Central Europe as possible, in what Laszlo Kurti has called the creation of 'new nationalist geopolitical typology' (1997, p. 46).[12]

The reverse response to uneven development has, of course, also been present. In the case of regional and national rivalries, of course, there has often been considerable resentment in the poorer regions of their dominance by their richer neighbours, and this too has fuelled regionalist or nationalist movements. In this respect the '*ressentiment*' explanation for nationalism of Liah Greenfeld (1992), discussed in Chapter 2, does seem to have plausibility as part explanation of some contemporary nationalisms. In these cases relatively poor, 'peripheral', or economically less developed areas want to protect themselves from and catch up with the richer, dominant or 'core' areas (Anderson, 1995). In Quebec, for example, francophones had been traditionally disadvantaged in an economy that in the postwar period began to lose out to Ontario (particularly Toronto). In the past four decades, Quebec government-supported private business plus francophone policies have led to both a stronger economic position and one in which francophones are no longer a disadvantaged group in terms of employment. In Scotland, the rise of a nationalist movement in the 1970s was based not only on traditional resentment of English domination of the Union, but also on the possibility of gaining enormous potential economic advantages from the then newly developed North Sea oil fields. Thus a poorer region, struggling against economic policies perceived as not geared to the needs of Scotland, saw an escape route to viable separation.

Institutional legacies

However, it is important to recognize that such 'escape routes' may only open up in some circumstances. In order for nationalism to become a viable political strategy, it is helpful at the least for there to be propitious or facilitating ideological and institutional conditions.

One such set of examples are provided by the break-up of the Soviet 'empire'. This itself can be traced in part to the pressures of maintaining living standards in the face of intense global economic competition intensified by military competition in the Cold War. The increasing penetration of global media accelerated the pressure for lifestyles and consumption patterns that were unrealizable for all but a tiny minority.

In the wake of the collapse of communism in the former Soviet Union and in Eastern and East Central Europe, the upsurge of ethnic nationalism is frequently referred to in terms of a return of the repressed, as a resurgence, a revival , a recrudescence of some primary force that is now free to burst out again. This is deeply misleading. The state socialist system, rather than simply repressing nationalism or treating it as a rival and antagonistic political force, accommodated to it and fostered it to a certain extent, albeit in different ways and on terms set by the regime.[13] There are important structural senses in which the state socialist system can be seen to be not inimical to nationalism but offering it positive or latent encouragement. Constitutional arrangements frequently acknowledged the importance of ethnicity. In the USSR especially, the whole elaborate constitutional structure of national republics and autonomous regions had been established on overtly ethno-territorial grounds (Hutchinson, 1994; Zaslavsky, 1992).[14] In addition to these territorial and political structures, all individuals were allocated to an ethnic/national category (Brubaker, 1994).[15] In a paradoxically complementary sense, the highly centralized command economy system in turn encouraged the use of nationalism as groups fought for the allocation of resources, particularly when shortages developed. In the case of Romania, for example, Verdery (1996) has shown how the command economy in these circumstances encouraged nationalism as a mechanism for bureaucratic allocation. Hodson et al. have similarly argued that in Yugoslavia the multi-national politics of federalism 'gave salience to national identities' in what they identify as 'the absence of other factors of political cohesion' (1994, p. 1555).

There are some parallels here with the very different contexts of secessionist or regional nationalism in the West. In Scotland and Quebec (and with a more interrupted history, in Catalonia), over long historical timescales there was recognition by the central state of something like a separate nationhood. The legitimacy of this nationhood (although not of any nation-alist expression of it)[16] was expressed in the continuation of separate cultural and other institutions. In Scotland and, to some extent, Quebec there were separate religious, legal and educational systems that were recognized by the larger state and provided a latent or at times manifest focus for invoca-tions of national identity. Thus the existence of a separate and influential Presbyterian Protestant Church, a distinctive education system with accom-panying myths of greater breadth and openness (the so-called 'democratic intellect') and a system of law (and a judiciary and legal profession) all quite separate and distinct from England, have been used to make the case for a separate Scottish nationhood and claims for (greater or complete) self-government.[17] The non-existence, for nearly three hundred years, of a separate Parliament in the Scottish case was not crucial in the opinion of many authors. Thus historians invoke ideas of Scottish 'semi-independence', or of a 'semi-state' under the union with England, and Lindsay Paterson has argued strongly that Scotland had considerable autonomy, greater than many other small European nations in the nineteenth century, albeit an autonomy that was mainly confined to the governing elites and the middle classes (Brown et al., 1998; Harvie, 1994; Paterson, 1994). As he puts it in this context, 'exercising autonomy does not require an assertion of difference' (Paterson, 1994, p. 130), and in the nineteenth century the phenomenon of unionist nationalism, a seemingly contradictory combination of elements, involved the assertion of the importance of Scottish participation in the Union and the British Empire as the only way to preserve Scottish autonomy from English domination. These examples, too, put into perspective any idea that the 'new' nationalist movements have simply emerged from some long period of repression. Seizing the opportunities posed by the crisis of empire or state nationalist leaders have taken advantage of an increasingly globalized environment to advance their causes. Whether such tendencies or movements point irresistibly in the direction of independence or secession is not, however, wholly clear.

Nationhood without independence?

Some commentators have pointed to the ambivalence of a number of contemporary Western nationalist movements. Keating, amongst others, in discussing the cases of Scottish, Catalan and Quebecois nationalist move-ments, suggests that all three are examples of engagement in 'stateless nation-building' distinct from the aim of a separate and sovereign state that is typical of classical nationalist movements (1997, p. 689). In each case there is considerable doubt about the support for total independence. In the Scottish case it remains to be seen whether the institution of the new parliament in Edinburgh with powers devolved from the UK parliament in London will increase or decrease demands for independence. Certainly opinion polls after the successful devolution referendum saw increased support for both the Scottish National Party and for independence. These are not identical. However this momentum was not maintained into the elections for the new parliament in May 1999 (see below). Evidence from Quebec, cited by Bateman, suggests that 'far from dampening down the embers of nationalism, limited local self-government has fanned the francophone self-confidence' (1996, p. 4). In 1980 40 per cent of Quebec's population had supported independence, whilst after fifteen years of running their own affairs 49 per cent had voted Yes in the 1995 referendum. However the question asked in that referendum was far from clear. It read: 'Do you agree that Quebec should become sovereign after having made a formal offer to Canada for a new economic and political partnership within the scope of the bill respecting the future of Quebec and of the agreement signed on 12 June 1995?' In the small print of this bill, Bateman argues, 'it becomes clear that the preferred model for sovereignty in Quebec is not outright independence but improving its status within a re-worked federation through the negotiation of an improved relationship with the rest of Canada' (1996, p. 6).

Whether one sees these somewhat fudged campaigns as evidence of a desire for less than full separation, or as a subtle tactic by nationalist politicians and parties to use greater autonomy as a stepping stone to full independence (Hargreaves, 1998) is hard to interpret. In Scotland, in 1997, the SNP abandoned its traditional dismissal of devolution to join the Labour and Liberal Democrat parties in campaigning for a Scottish parliament which fell well short of having full sovereignty without in any way abandoning its long-term policy for full independence. In the ensuing elections to the much billed 'first Scottish parliament for 300 years' or even 'the first ever democratic Scottish parliament', the SNP downgraded its demand for an independence referendum to only the tenth point of its election platform (to the disgust of its sizeable 'fundamentalist' wing), in favour of attempting to gain a majority with a moderate social democratic programme that outflanked the Labour party from the left. This proved unsuccessful, with the SNP securing only thirty-five seats out of 129 in the new parliament and forming the official opposition to a Labour/Liberal Democrat coalition. In the Welsh case there were spectacular gains in seats for Plaid Cymru, but explanations for this have stressed more the greater ability of the party to mobilize its supporters in the context of an extremely low election turnout. This in itself was probably due in part to the difficulties in sustaining support for the dominant Labour Party caused by ill feeling about the imposition from London party headquarters of a candidate for the leadership of the Welsh Labour Party and therefore the Welsh assembly. Although this might itself be taken as evidence of latent support for nationalism, it probably makes more sense to see it as a democratic issue with a concern about the reality of devolution of decision-making within the Labour Party itself. In any case, Plaid Cymru, even more than the SNP in Scotland, played down nationalism as an issue in favour of social democratic policies and pledges to make the assembly work.

One of the most cited example of successful self-government short of independence in recent years has been that of Catalonia. For Manuel Castells (1997), for example, Catalan is not an invented identity, but a 'constantly renewed historical product' (p. 49). Here, under the leadership of Pujol, head of the Catalan autonomous government since 1980, regional autonomy based on the Spanish Constitution of 1978 has been pushed forward a long way. Distinctive language, media and cultural policies and relations with the wider European Union has made Catalonia seem almost a separate state. Yet despite occasional flirting with the idea of independence, Pujol has used nationalist rhetoric to assert greater autonomy against but within the Spanish state, stating that 'Catalunya is a nation without a state. We belong to the Spanish state, but we do not have secessionist ambitions . . . (cited by Castells, 1997, p. 43). Unequivocal support for outright independence seems low, with only 10 per cent of the Catalan vote going to the main (left) pro-independence party, the ERC. Castells' conclusion stresses the mixed European, Mediterranean and Hispanic identity of Catalonia. By differentiating between cultural identity and the power of the state, Castells believes, Catalonia may well be prototypical of organization for the flexibility, networking of media, globalizing of economy, and interconnectedness and interpenetration of culture of the information age. Keating too highlights the flexible approach of Catalan political leaders towards autonomy and independence and the relationship between this and the realities of living in an increasingly globalized world.

So is it in these regional or separatist nationalisms that we can find a new more open and inclusive form of national identity, which can accommodate the diversity and difference that migratory and diasporic processes are continuing to generate in the wake of globalization?

Nationalism and identity revisited

Optimistic proponents of these regional or neo-nationalisms (Keating, 1996; McCrone, 1998) see them as embracing the sort of multiple identities hailed by the postmodernists. Linked to this, as we have seen, is the idea that these forms of nationalism have a more flexible and complex attitude towards statehood. What is the evidence for this? McCrone and Keating both cite interesting poll evidence about self-identification. In Catalonia far more than in Scotland individuals seem to feel a dual identity – as both Spanish and Catalan. Despite the limitations of this kind of evidence for getting to grips with the complexities of identity, it is none the less instructive to compare survey data for Scotland, England and Catalonia for 1992 (Table 6.1).

TABLE 6.1 SELF-IDENTIFICATION AMONG SCOTS, ENGLISH AND CATALANS, 1992

Perceived identity	Scotland	England	Catalonia
x not British/Spanish	37	16	20
More x than British/Spanish	27	12	16
Equally x and British/Spanish	25	43	35
More British/Spanish than x	4	10	5
British/Spanish not x	2	3	0

x = Scottish, English, Catalan respectively.
Source: Cited in Brown, McCrone and Paterson, 1998, p. 220

Findings of surveys of the kind reported in Table 6.1 are highly problematic however. In Catalonia there is a considerable variation over short
periods of time. Thus in a more recent 1995 survey, the proportions seeing
themselves as only Catalan has fallen to 10 per cent, 44 per cent now
saw themselves as equally Catalan and Spanish, while 16 per cent now saw
themselves as more Spanish than Catalan. Survey evidence from Scotland
over the period 1986–99 shows a similar fluctuation, with the proportions
of respondents feeling 'Scottish not British' fluctuating between 19 and
40 per cent (Brown et al., 1998, p. 209; Paterson et al., 2001, p. 105). The
implications of this are probably more that such surveys cannot capture
deep-seated identifications or their complexity, or that what they measure
has to do considerably with short-term political contingencies. In any
case, the evidence from Scotland as we have seen, and particularly Quebec,
demonstrates more clear-cut national identification. In Quebec a much greater
proportion of the population seems to see itself as exclusively Quebecois
rather than Canadian (Keating, 1996).

For their adherents and sympathetic commentators these movements
and parties represent the progressive side of contemporary nationalism. They
are inclusive rather than exclusive, fluid rather than rigid, encompassing
multiple identities rather than single ones. However, the problem with
fluidity is that flows can be in very different directions. Nationalist rhetoric
can start inclusive, as with Pujol's definition of who is Catalan ('Everyone
who lives and works in Catalonia and has the wish to be so and feels tied
to the land, is Catalan' – cited by Keating, 1996, p. 126). But it can end up
in the exclusivist visions of ethnic nationalism. Thus in March 2001 it was
reported in the *Guardian* newspaper that Marta Ferrusola, Pujol's wife, had
denounced 'Muslim incomers for wanting to impose their culture on the
region. "They want to impose their own way. All they know how to say is
'Give me something to eat.'"' Meanwhile, a prominent leader of Catalan
separatism, Heribert Barrera, complained of there being too many foreigners

and that the region would 'disappear' under the weight of immigration. All this is in the context of there being only 2 per cent of the population from outside the country (Tremlett, 2001). Brown et al. (1998, p. 219) point to the favouring of a civic territorial definition of who should be included in the nation among Scottish political leaders (including the leaders of the SNP). However, the fragility of this commitment to inclusive definitions seems emphasized by the poll data they report for a survey in *The Scotsman* newspaper from March 1992 (cited by Brown et al., 1998). In this survey, in answer to the question 'Who should qualify as a Scottish national in an independent Scotland?', 58 per cent replied that this should apply to anyone born in Scotland, 39 per cent to anyone living in Scotland and 18 per cent to anyone with Scottish parents. A 1999 survey reported by a similar group of authors (Paterson et al., 2001, p. 118) also shows far less support for a Scottish passport in a hypothetical independent Scotland for those living in Scotland but not born there (52 per cent) than for those born in Scotland and not living there (79 per cent). (And a third of respondents supported the even more 'ethnic' criterion of granting Scottish citizenship to one who was neither born nor living in Scotland but who had one parent who was Scottish born.) This seems short of the ringing endorsement of an inclusive definition of who would be included in 'the nation'. The SNP, despite the wishes of its leader, has found it hard to steer clear of what might be termed the 'Braveheart' syndrome, the use of symbolism which implies anti-English sentiment (Edensor, 1997; Samuel, 1998). Scottish newspapers are reporting the targeting of English people living in Scotland as objects of racism with increasing frequency, although these incidents still appear to be relatively isolated.[18]

In Quebec too there are distinctions which exclude some, which reintroduce the other as both external and internal enemy. The term '*Québécois de souche*' refers to those 'with roots', literally, describing those claiming descent from French settlers who arrived before the conquest by Britain. This term was used in an official Quebec government document in 1981, but abandoned in favour of a more inclusive categorization of all residents of Quebec in 1990. However, Juteau comments, 'The redefinition of national boundaries remains an unachieved process and a contested site. The expression '*Québécois de souche*' indicates the persisting existence of boundaries between different Quebecois. Although we are all Quebecois, some are more Quebecois than others' (1996, p. 50). In the quest for independence Quebecois of British origin are seen as '"de facto opponents" whilst "immigrants" and "ethnics" are regarded as potential allies who must be convinced (p. 50)'. Since the claims to independence and a separate identity are bound up with an experience of British colonialism (on the part, it must be said, of French colonists) it is hardly surprising that 'non-French Canadian Quebecois are seen as externally located to the process of communalisation that secessionism represents' (p. 51). Even more outside of the putative new nation are the descendants of the original inhabitants of the land, the aboriginals, mainly Inuit, who were originally conquered by the French, and whose territorial rights were recognized by the same Royal Proclamation in 1763 which asserted the rule of the British monarchy over the inhabitants of what had up to then been termed 'New France'. The 'First Nations' as they are now called are among the strongest opponents of the project for Quebec independence, asserting, as they do, political projects of their own based upon 'a similar discourse of ancestral and historical rights and on an experience of colonialism and dispossession' (Juteau, 1996, p. 51). Of the 500 or so 'First Nations' in Canada as a whole, eleven are within the present borders of Quebec, and they occupy over half of its present day territory, claiming 'the right of self-determination in international law if Quebec separates' (Tully, 1995, pp. 79–80).[19]

Language rights, too, provide an issue which divides as much as it unites, which polices the borders of ethnicity, culture and migration. Canada's own language law gave recognition to both French and English. Quebec's language law, Bill 101, passed in 1977, made French Quebec's official language and was designed, *inter alia*, to redress employment inequalities for francophones which resulted from the domination of English (Keating, 1996). It prohibited French-speaking children from attending English-language schools. Only children who have a parent who attended an English school in Quebec or elsewhere in Canada may go to an English-language school. One source of tension, again, is with the immigrant communities. Under Bill 101, children of immigrants must also attend French schools, even if they are from English-speaking countries. The language law has significantly redressed the employment inequalities for francophones and reduced the overall number of English-speakers. In the 1970s, there were 250,000 students in English schools in Quebec; today there are about 100,000 (*Migration News*, 1998a). Unsurprisingly, English-speakers were more likely than francophones to be skilled in more than one language. Statistics Canada, a federal government agency, reported in 1996 that 82 per cent of English-speakers in Quebec could converse in both English and French, double the percentage of 1971. However, only 42 per cent of French-speakers aged 15 to 24 can speak English (cited in *Migration News*, 1998a). Other language issues have surrounded signs and even computer software, with attempts to ensure that all major businesses use French language software where it is available. Under the language law French letters on signs must be twice the size of those in other languages. The Commission for the Protection of the French language (unflatteringly referred to as the language police by those hostile to them) have even targeted Chinese signs in Montreal's Chinatown and a Jewish gravestone-maker because five Hebrew characters on his business sign were too big (Nando.net/The Associated Press, 1997).

In signalling his approval of development of regional nationalisms like those of Scotland and Catalonia, where despite strong support for the principle of the right to self-determination, there is less support for the development of fully independent nation-states, Keating writes, 'to be a nationalist is not necessarily to be a separatist' (1996, p. 20). This appears to him to be a way that national identity can be asserted without fracturing existing states and proliferating new ones. Does this provide a way forward for accommodating multiple or divergent identities within one overall state? As we have suggested, the assertion of collective rights by one group asserting its nationhood can have implications for other groups living in the same territory. Although the new regionalist nationalisms seem a far cry from the development of the essentialist nationalisms of the far right referred to earlier, they find it hard to avoid assertions of exclusivity and the setting of ethnic or cultural barriers to other groups. These dangers may be avoided if cases for greater autonomy or for new assemblies were to be made on purely democratic grounds without any nationalist legitimation. In the Scottish case the logical case for a new parliament putting the already substantial separate and 'devolved' powers of the Scottish Office and the various Scottish quangos (unelected quasi-state bodies) under greater democratic control, accountability and scrutiny is hard to avoid. Although some of the supporters of the new Scottish parliament will do so for nationalist reasons and to further the nationalist cause, it is surely possible to do so on quite different grounds.

CONCLUSION

By itself, globalization does not seem to guarantee any particular outcome to nationalism or its antitheses. As is reflected in so much of the literature, the local and the global seem to interact in ways that can produce quite contradictory effects in different circumstances. Essentialist nationalisms and hybrid identities are at the extreme ends of a continuum of effects. In the middle, the outcome of the quests for autonomy among regions or nations within Europe and elsewhere is uncertain. And close by are the examples of what can go wrong when ethnic nationalism, amplified by ambitious politicians, takes hold of the political agenda. But if the invocation of the threats to identity posed by globalization can be used to advance nationalist arguments, so too can be asserted the opportunities for new forms of political identity and structures in a world potentially less divided according to nationality. In the next chapter we examine some of the ways we might be able to travel beyond nationalism.

FURTHER READING

One of the most comprehensive recent books on globalization covering cultural, political and economic aspects is that of Held et al. (1999). Waters

(2001) and especially Holton (1998) provide useful summaries of many of the arguments. On migration there is a lot more detail in Castles and Miller (1998) and Castles' (2000) collection of essays covers a range of issues of relevance to globalization, migration, racism and citizenship. Cohen (1997b) on global diasporas provides useful information and analysis, whilst more postmodern arguments are addressed in the later chapters of Morley (2000) and in Papastergiadis (2000), whose work encompasses the cultural, political and economic. For the fluidities and complexities of race and a critical discussion of essentialist views of race from apparently very different parts of the political spectrum see Gilroys's (2000) *Between Camps*, a consistently stimulating and thoughtful but not always easy read. On the 'neo-nationalisms' of Quebec, Catalonia, and Scotland, Keating's 1996 volume is a useful comparative study, supplemented for Scotland by Paterson et al. (2001).

NOTES

1 The distinction between the economic, political and cultural here is an analytic one. In practice, of course, these are interlinked and overlapping.

2 'The bourgeoisie has through its exploitation of the world market given a cosmopolitan character to production and consumption in every country . . . It has drawn from under the feet of industry the national ground on which it stood. . . . In place of the old national seclusion and self-sufficiency, we have intercourse in every direction, universal inter-dependence of nations' (Marx and Engels, 1976, p. 488).

3 Faist may have a point when he writes, 'Instead of stretching the term diaspora beyond its limits, it is more meaningful to speak of a *transnationalized and segmented cultural space*, characterized by *syncretist identities*, populated by sundry ethnic, political, religious, and subcultural groups: transnational means that cultural elements from both the original sending and receiving countries have found entry in the cultural repertoire of the descendants of the migrants' (Faist, 1998, p. 241). One can, however, also see the linguistic appeal of the simpler '*diaspora*'.

4 This again should not be seen as a new phenomenon. The linkage of family, ethnic and cultural relationships with global trading is part of world history.

5 Clifford also introduces a distinction between 'nationalist critical longing and nostalgic eschatological visions' from actual nation-building, in an unconvincing attempt to argue that diasporas have little to do with the latter (Clifford, 1994, p. 307).

6 Although it can be argued that its historic triumph in squeezing out alternative models of Jewish identity from prominence was more the result of the Holocaust than of the lack of intellectual or affective challenge to its hegemony.

7   For many Jews, support for Israel, although part of a passionate discourse of identity, has also been seen as an 'insurance policy' against any resurgence of domestic anti-semitism.

8   For an interesting discussion that demonstrates the complex relationship between the ideas of the One Nation Party and globalization see Perera (1998/9).

9   As Christopher Husbands (1999) has eloquently pointed out, these explanations for fundamentalist activities of the far right or others are not new. He sees the antecedents of explanations in terms of reactions to globalization in the strain theory of Talcott Parsons, linking outbursts of 'irrational' behaviour with the strain experienced by societies undergoing major structural changes.

10 It is somewhat bizarre, though, to see a free trade area enormously dominated by the United States, already economically and culturally dominant over Canada, as some sort of counterbalance for Quebec against Canada.

11 Although this other was a constantly shifting construction, as political exigencies made ideological changes necessary in order to maximize support. See Ruzza and Schmidtke (1996).

12 Kurti has suggested that what he calls 'this intellectual gerrymandering' may be in part understood as a familiar orientalizing project, in which the other is imagined as politically, culturally and economically backward, and one as full of political significance .

> In the remaking of Eastern and Central Europe, just as in the 19th century, the representation of otherness has become a political issue once again. The new pluralistic states foster an image of unity and ethnonationalism (majority ethnic identification with the state) often supported as an official ideology. Indispensable in this new nationalistic discourse is the figure of the stigmatized 'other', 'the enemy', reoriented to include not only the competitive neighbouring nation-states but the minorities *inside* the territory. (1997, p. 41)

13 For a more detailed discussion of this issue see Spencer and Wollman (1999).

14 For a *tour de force* review of the ways in which ethnicity and nationality were embedded in the Soviet Union see Slezkine (1996).

15 As Brubaker (1994) points out, there was an elaborate division into over one hundred national groups of which twenty-two had more than one million members. As a legal category written into passports and legal documents, one's national categorization could positively or negatively affect one's life chances – for instance, entry to higher education.

16 See Brubaker 'Rethinking Nationhood' in Brubaker (1996a) for this distinction.

17 For a number of writers (Keating, 1996; McCrone, 1998) these institutions are evidence of a strong 'civil society' which is seen as underpinning the national claims and rendering them more likely to develop in a 'civic' direction. However, there are problems with this approach. Some of the institutions referred to could more easily be seen as part of the state (e.g. the Scottish legal system), and the concept of civil society used in this way is open to serious criticism among other reasons for positing a spurious (national) unity.

18 See for example the story '"I didn't snipe to teacher when you kicked me" –

Anthology on racism reveals shocking extent of anti-English bullying' by Nick Thorpe (*The Scotsman*, 6 November 1998). In retelling various incidents and claims, Thorpe quotes the Commission for Racial Equality in Scotland to the effect that 'anti-English complaints formed only five per cent of the total and were generally "low level", despite English people forming seven per cent of Scotland's population'. Reflecting the general tendency to play down racism in Scotland, an SNP spokesman commented in the same report, 'It's a diminishing problem in Scotland and we would hope that, as Scotland progresses and develops, it will continue to decline.'

19 For a discussion of the campaigns for recognition of the 12,000 or so Cree in Northern Quebec, see Ramos (2000)

7

Beyond Nationalism?

INTRODUCTION

In this concluding chapter, we look at some of the ways in which it has been claimed that we may begin to go beyond nationalism. We discuss briefly some attempts to 'tame' nationalism by institutional means (in the form of consociationalism or federalism) and the possibilities held out by supranational developments such as the European Union. None of these seems to have challenged convincingly the priority of nationalist categories. However, there have been a number of efforts to do so, in both practice and theory, from an inter-national, postnational, transnational, or even a cosmopolitan perspective. Whilst all of these, particularly the latter, have been the object of sharp criticism, they seem to point, to a greater or lesser extent, in the direction of universalism, towards forms of citizenship, rights and democracy which cannot always be protected or secured by nation-states operating within nationalist frames of reference. In discussing these complex topics we raise more questions than can be resolved here. However, if we are to make more progress in this direction, we need to look further than the nation-state and explore political concepts and movements that go beyond the theoretical and practical limits and restraints of nationalism and national identity.

Beyond a divisive nationalism?

We have argued throughout this book that nationalism tends towards an exclusionary and divisive logic, pointing to the problems it poses for citizenship, rights and democracy. Whilst this may be widely recognized, there are those who do not think it is therefore either necessary or feasible to go beyond nationalism. Rather, it is argued, it makes more sense to devise institutional arrangements that can tame it in some way, by encouraging representatives of national groups to come to some accommodation with each other. Two kinds of such institutional arrangements in particular have been promoted extensively. These are, respectively, consociationalism and federalism, to which we now turn.

Consociationalism and federalism

Consociationalism reflects an attempt to manage ethnic conflict with a set of arrangements designed to protect minorities and prevent the tyranny of majorities. In countries such as the Lebanon between 1943 and 1975, Canada from the 1840s to the 1860s and Cyprus (rather less successfully), elements of power sharing between ethnic communities were enshrined in the system of government (McGarry and O'Leary, 1993; Noel, 1993). Arend Lijphart (1977), the major theorist of consociationalism, outlines four key features of consociational democracies, suitable for societies characterized by segmental cleavages. These are, first, a 'grand coalition' government incorporating the political parties that represent the main 'segments' in the divided society; secondly, minority rights of veto on constitutional change; thirdly, rules of proportionality, reflecting the population mixture, governing the distribution of public sector jobs and funds; and fourthly, a high degree of autonomy for each segment to run its own affairs' (Lijphart, 1977, p. 25). The temporary character of many consociational experiments suggests, however, that this is often an unstable solution to ethnic or national conflict. Consociationalism clearly cannot work whilst extreme nationalist demands are dominating the political agendas of conflicting groups since it represent an accommodation of what are, often, opposite and conflicting nationalisms.[1] From a democratic angle, consociationalism is also vulnerable to the charge of lack of accountability, since it minimizes popular participation in the decision-making process in favour of more secretive elite negotiation (G. Smith, 1995, p.16). However, there is another more serious objection to consociationalism, which relates directly to our earlier critical discussion of identity (see Chapter 3).

For whilst it focuses on power sharing between ethnic or national groups, it enshrines them at the same time as fixed unchanging entities; it allows of no hybrid, fluid, or changing identities, and it provides structures that inhibit the emergence of non-ethnic or non-national politics. As Brass has argued,

> Consociationalism, therefore, like the theory of the plural society from which it derives, suffers from the deficiencies of its own assumptions. It reifies ethnicity, treats it as a given, assumes the solidarity of group identities, and therefore arrives at the conclusion that ethnic conflicts cannot be resolved except in a political order based on group representation. If, however, one takes the view that these assumptions are wrong, then conso-ciationalism appears as a mystification of ethnicity and ethnic group conflicts which accepts at face value the justification for its adoption by those who stand to benefit from it. (1994, p. 121)

An alternative to consociationalism is federalism,[2] associated in many people's minds with some of the most successful capitalist liberal democracies, such as the United States and the postwar Federal Republic of Germany. As can be seen from these two examples, of course, federalism has no necessary relationship to ethnic or national conflicts and as a system of government, it raises much wider issues than can be dealt with here. There are, however, examples of federalism as a way of managing a divided society. Sometimes, this may involve relatively straightforward divisions of power but federalism may also be asymmetrical, a system in which certain regions are given more powers than others, as, for example, in Spain or Canada (Coakley, 1993). In Canada, federalism became the basis of the political system in place of consociationalism (Noel, 1993). It has been argued that this was due to the efforts of influential English-Canadian federalists who wished to roll back the special provision and power sharing that had developed in Canada, placing French Canadians at a disadvantage from which they have ever since been attempting to recover. In this context 'federalism represented a significant shift away from dualism and consociationalism as responses to ethnic conflict and towards territorial segregation and hegemonic inter-ethnic relations' (Noel, 1993, p. 47).

More generally, such success as federalism appears to have in regulating ethnic and national conflicts rests on the convenience of pre-existing ethnic boundaries being co-terminous with territorial ones. There is rarely, however, a perfect fit. Anglophones in Quebec, francophones elsewhere in Canada, Flemish speakers in Wallonia, are all potentially disadvantaged by federal arrangements. Highly dispersed populations – such as native Americans and Blacks in the USA, or members of the First Nations in Canada – can get no protection or advancement of their interests from federal arrangements. (Indeed as the example of Quebec has shown, the rights of aboriginal minori-ties may not be recognized by those francophones struggling for their rights in the Canadian federation as a whole.) Although more territorially than ethnically based, federalism as a solution to national and ethnic conflicts may well be as unstable as the power sharing arrangements of consociationalism. It may be seen by some groups as a stepping stone to independent nationhood, and by others as a regrettable concession that must be rolled back in the interests of the majority as soon as the opportunity arises.[3] In recent years, federalism seems to be suffering a relatively high incidence of failure or to be in perpetual crisis (Agnew, 1995, p. 300). Those federal systems that have continued to prosper, such as Switzerland, may owe their good fortune less to federalism than to the fact that divisions are overlapping rather than territorial (G. Smith, 1995, p. 15). Others, such as Canada, Belgium and Nigeria, are under considerable pressure. More seriously, a number of those specifically set up at least in part with the intention of containing nationalist conflict, have disintegrated, such as the USSR, Yugoslavia and Czechoslovakia. It is hard not to see this as in part a consequence of the way in which, particularly territorially, federalism reinforces the very divisions it seeks to manage. It is not difficult, as we have argued elsewhere, for elites to use local power bases, constructed and articulated in nationalist terms, to press for more and more power, even at the risk of pulling the system apart (Spencer and Wollman, 1999). Most fundamentally, even the most diverse forms of federalism are after all grounded in a recognition of the temporal and logical priority of the national.

Supranationalism: the case of the European Union

This is not so clearly the case with efforts to develop supranational institutions such as the European Union. Here, partly as a result of the experience of the national conflicts which produced two world wars and tore the continent apart, and partly in an attempt to produce a trading bloc that can compete on global terms, there has been an attempt to transcend national divisions by creating first an economic and then a political union which will contain and perhaps ultimately eliminate nationalism altogether. There has been a continuing tension, however, between the idea of a Europe of nation-states in which political power primarily resides with national governments and parliaments, and that of a federal Europe where more power would reside at the level of European-wide bodies such as the Commission and the Parliament. Again, however, there are serious problems both in theory and practice with this solution. In the first place, the original economic motivation for union remains the most powerful and significant dynamic, relegating the political dimension to a secondary concern. This has meant that political institutions at a European level remain relatively weak, with decisions continuing to be taken by representatives of national governments, on the basis of national priorities – a Europe of nation-states (Goodman, 1997). Serious and substantial debates, about whether decisions require unanimity or majority, should not disguise the more fundamental reality that national considerations rather than European ones are primary. Commitment to the European project is generally couched in terms of the interests of the national constituent elements (Kostakopolou, 1998). The priority of the national may also account for the uneven development of the Union, which may, in turn, make it harder to develop a European awareness or loyalty. Conflicts over if or when full monetary union will become a reality have revealed the ways in which commitments to Union projects by the different member states have resulted in what some have called a two-speed Europe, one of concentric circles, or marked by a core–periphery distinction (Baum, 1996). At the same time, there have been sustained objections to the evident democratic deficit at the heart of the Union, particularly in terms of the very limited powers available to the European parliament and the relatively unaccountable powers of the Commission. This has given ample space for nationalist movements to present their opposition to the European project as a democratic one, claiming that national democratic institutions are being deprived of sovereignty by an unaccountable, remote bureaucracy, thus rendering the idea of a federal Europe unattractive (Goodman, 1997). The invocation of a Europe of the regions, in which power is devolved away from the nation-state and downwards to the regions as well as upwards to the centre, may be too glib. A recent study has concluded that this is a largely mythical projection, not only because the term region is problematic, but because the same weaknesses that we have identified above apply equally if not more so to the regions themselves (Le Galès and Lequesne, 1998). As Wright has noted, 'the regions as a level of elected government . . . have weak autonomy, weak resources, weak political capacity and weak legitimacy' (1998, p. 244). Moreover, just as a uniform Europe has not emerged, so too there are significant disparities both between and within regions.

At a deeper level, there are serious concerns that the European Union has not in significant respects broken with the logic of nationalism. Although under Article Eight of the Maastricht Treaty every person who has citizenship of a member state is also a citizen of the European Union, this precisely bases EU citizenship on a pre-existing nation-state citizenship (Carchedi and Carchedi, 1999; Martiniello, 1997). The rights of European citizenship include freedom of movement and residence in member countries and the right to vote and be elected for local elections and European Parliament elections in one's country of residence. Even these rights are limited by preconditions for settling in another member state, such as financial independence and independence in terms of social security (Martiniello, 1997). These preconditions may themselves exclude on an ethnic basis as well as the more obvious basis of class and prosperity (Carchedi and Carchedi, 1999). Furthermore, the implementation of the voting rights of European citizenship has been slow in some countries (Belgium, for example), and after pressure from Luxembourg a derogation was introduced that where there was a high proportion of non-national European citizens restrictions on voting could be introduced (Martiniello, 1997). The exclusionary approach to citizenship, in which non-nationals are seen as a threat or having inferior status, then, remains true at the European level. In terms of immigration, this has led to criticisms that the EU is constructing a 'Fortress Europe' predicated on the same assumptions as the immigration policies of its member states. The Trevi and Schengen agreements, for instance, have been seen as an attempt to co-ordinate a harsh policing regime for the borders between Europe and the rest of the world, whilst seeking to make a *cordon sanitaire* out of the countries of Central and Eastern Europe (desperate to enter themselves of course) and to a lesser extent the Maghreb (Fekete and Webber, 1994). The popular constructions of immigrants that have accompanied the development of such policies are drearily familiar, stereotyping immigrants as potential criminals, forming terrorist links, justifying harsh forms of policing across the union and justifying deportation of suspects on grounds of national security (Carchedi and Carchedi, 1999; Fekete and Webber, 1994). Concerns of this sort about immigration have, as we have noted earlier in the case of civic nations, consequences for many already inside the borders. The rights of the 12 to 13 million who are nationals of third countries in particular are restricted in crucial respects (Kostakopolou, 1998), pointing again to the ways in which citizenship remains tightly coupled to nationality even here.

Beyond policy and structure are issues yet again of identity. Europe too, as the nations that make it up, may require its own, feared and denigrated other. There are important respects in which the self-image of a democratic and pluralist Europe takes its meaning by contrast with an other with an opposite identity, whether this be to the South or East (Burgess, 1998). Even some of those most resistant to the development of European institutions, such as the Front National in France, invoke a sense of a European identity in opposition to that of the Other, in this case usually Islamic (Boutin, 1996). Thus even the apparently positive signs of a wider identification as European (often alongside other identities – see Chapter 6) that has been seen in, for example, Catalonia or Milan, has a potential for being mobilized for less savoury causes. In any case, there are few signs of the emergence of a new European identity. There is perhaps a Europe of the bureaucrats and those in receipt of European funding but this is more part of the project of fostering a Europe 'from above' than the emergence of a sense of European identity from below. There remain substantial difficulties in the way of the development of such a European identity, as A. Smith (1995b) has argued powerfully (although we do not share his overall perspective).[4]

Alternatives to nationalism

All this may seem a far cry from the arguments put forward by Habermas (1992) in proposing that European citizenship be seen as a stage on the way to a world citizenship. Habermas argued that, whilst the framework of the nation-state may have been necessary for the development of democracy (but see Chapter 5), a democratic community did not need to be homogeneous, that anyone who accepted the basic procedural principles of a democracy had a right to membership of a polity. Supporting Joseph Carens' (1987) defence of the principle of open borders (see below), Habermas suggested that a constitutional polity be open to all, that commitment to the polity was to its rules and not to a specific (national) community. Citizenship could thus be decoupled from nationality and national identity could be replaced by a postnational one. In turning his back on the nation-state as an outdated and no longer relevant unit, in downgrading the salience of national identity, Habermas had adopted here a distinctly cosmopolitan position (Mertens, 1996).

Cosmopolitanism and internationalism

Cosmopolitan arguments, of course, have a long and distinguished history (Heater, 1996). Early formulations can be found in the Stoics, for instance, whilst universalist ideas may also be found in Dante's *De Monarchia*.[5] A pure cosmopolitanism does not presume the prior existence or necessity of nations but focuses on what is shared by all human beings as inhabitants of one world. The term has Greek roots in the words *cosmos* and *polis*, bringing together the notions of one ordered world or universe and of political life, organization and activity. For the Greeks, the polis connoted a higher form of activity, distinguishing humans from animals, a sphere when human beings would come together to exercise their reason in pursuit of the good life. A cosmopolis would therefore have to be a conscious, rational project, ordered, organized and willed by citizens, asserting their common humanity and their freedom from the restrictions and antagonisms involved in national attachments or loyalties.

Strictly speaking, one should distinguish cosmopolitanism from internationalism since semantically at least the latter requires the prior existence of nations. The concept of an international sphere after all presumes that there already are nations which are in relation to each other. From this perspective, as Ree puts it, 'internationalism and nationalism are inseparable partners, two aspects of a single historical phenomenon – the phenomenon of "internationality"' (1998, p. 8). In a most restrictive sense, internationalism may even be seen as the opposite of cosmopolitanism, a way of managing the international system, based on the existence of self-determining nation-states. It may take either a coercive form, taking for granted the incompatibility of interests between states; or, it may seek accommodation, aiming to reduce such conflicts of interest (Goldmann, 1994).

Few advocates of internationalism, however, have taken such a limited view in either theory or practice. At the very least, internationalists have sought to make nationalism compatible with cosmopolitanism in various ways, whilst there have been a number efforts, particularly in recent times, to go beyond the nationalist frame of reference.

Amongst the first to do so in modern times was Kant, who argued in 1795 (in his 'Project for a Perpetual Peace') that conflict between nations if unchecked would lead to war (Kant, 1970). Although, unlike Habermas, he did not abjure either the nation-state or the salience of national identity (Mertens, 1996), he did suggest that conflict would be much less likely if nation-states were republics, and that one republic could make itself the focal point for the creation of a federal association of self-determining nations, based on principles of international right. He was, it is true, opposed to a world government, on the grounds that this would inevitably tend towards despotism, because he believed that the differences between nations were so great that the only way they could be eliminated would be through coercion. Ree has argued that this represented a step back from his earlier position when he had adopted a more explicitly cosmopolitan point of view, that there had been a 'fateful slippage . . . [as] cosmopolitanism in short translated itself into internationalism' (1998, p. 78). Others have claimed that Kant, whilst continuing to think in terms of a single universal community and to harbour ideas of a world state, was simply trying to be realistic, recognizing the force of national identity and the continuing salience of the nation-state (Held, 1995). Either way, Kant was insistent that hostility towards foreigners was unacceptable, calling rather for a duty of hospitality towards strangers.

Pheng Cheah has suggested that Kant's target was less nationalism than absolutism, that 'cosmopolitanism precedes the popular nation-state in history and nationalism in the history of ideas' (1998, p. 23). The development of a credible cosmopolitanism today needs then to be rooted in the realities of at least some forms of national identification or, more broadly, in the recognition of particular rather than universal attachments (Robbins, 1998). Cosmopolitan commitments can then be built up from these, so that, in Rorty's words, 'what makes you loyal to a smaller group may give you reason to co-operate in constructing a larger group, a group to which you may in time become equally loyal, or perhaps even more loyal' (cited in Robbins, 1998, p. 10). This seems very close to some of the arguments for a liberal nationalism that we discussed in Chapter 4, and indeed a precise connection between liberal nationalism and cosmopolitanism has recently been explicitly articulated on these grounds (Couture et al., 1996).

Other theorists, however, have wanted to go somewhat further, to develop arguments which can take us beyond nationalism itself.

Transnationalism and postnational citizenship

Rainer Baubock for instance has put forward a carefully formulated argument for transnational citizenship, although he still stops short of a full-blown cosmopolitanism, arguing that it is 'out of gear with the basic dynamics of modern politics' (1994, p. viii). Whilst recognizing the coherence of the utopian vision of a single political community, he claims that it is not part of the 'available criteria of legitimation' within the conditions of modernity. These include the growing territorial rigidity of state institutions and structures, and the necessity for community-based legitimation. At the same time, global communication is growing apace, as is the interdependence of states and communities. The result is that nation-states have to deal with the presence in their midst of many who would be excluded from citizenship according to any nationalist criteria. Baubock seems prepared to concede that this exclusion is not undemocratic *per se*. However, it does clash with the normative principles of such states; persistent exclusion must in the end put liberal democracy in jeopardy.[6] His transnational solution is designed to overcome this contradiction by drawing on liberal democracy's own 'norms of inclusiveness' to accord very substantial rights on the basis of (relatively short periods of) residence, supplementing both *ius soli* and *ius sanguinis* with *ius domicili*. The right to citizenship is seen by him as a basic human right, and although he is not at present in favour of completely free movement, he argues strongly for accepting a very wide range of categories of applicants to make rights of immigration and emigration more symmetrical.

Baubock is not alone in putting forward such carefully reasoned arguments. David Held has also argued for what he calls 'an expanding institutional framework for the democratic regulation of states and societies . . . [in which] people would come to enjoy multiple citizenships – political membership in the diverse movements which significantly affect them' (1995, pp. 232–3). This would be underpinned by a cosmopolitan democratic law enshrined in national and international constitutions, with extensive powers to be exercised by international courts. Meanwhile the powers of national executives and legislatures would be complemented by those of local and regional bodies (from below) and transnational ones (from above).

Others have gone further still, arguing that the borders which are essential to even civic nation-states cannot be justified. Carens (1987), Dummett (1992) and Hayter (2000) have argued powerfully for open borders, pointing, like Goodin, to the asymmetry between the movement of people and the movement of money (Goodin, 1992) and between the right to emigrate and the right to immigrate. Without the latter, the former is, to put it mildly, somewhat difficult to operationalize. If borders were truly open, however, this would surely erode the powers of the nation-state to a critical point and effectively open the way to some kind of postnational political system.

It has been claimed (Soysal, 1994) that some of this is already happening, that a new model of citizenship has been developing throughout the postwar era, based on universal personhood rather than national belonging. There is now 'an intensifying discourse about individual and human rights that is transmitted as global norms and models by a number of inter- and transnational agencies' (1994, p. 41). This has resulted in a signal shift in policy towards the large numbers of migrants who have, contrary to expectations, become permanent residents with reunified families. In a survey of a variety of apparently different 'incorporation regimes' across Western Europe, Soysal suggests that there is now a growing standardization and uniformity of approach, involving the granting of 'an expanding range of rights and privileges . . . blurring the line between citizen and non-citizen' (p. 130). The result is that 'the scope and inventory of non-citizens' rights is not different significantly from those of citizens' (p. 119). There is, in her view, a powerful logic at work here. It runs counter to the influential evolutionary schema proposed by Marshall, whereby citizenship rights are developed within a nation-state from the civil to the political to the social, since it both reverses the order and undermines the essentially national frame of reference. This logic is so powerful indeed that it '*obliges* national states not to make distinctions on grounds of nationality in granting civil, social and political rights' (1994, p. 145; emphasis added). Soysal is aware, particularly in the light of the resurgence of nationalism, that there continue to be contradictions or an 'incongruence' between the national and the transnational, the exclusionary and the inclusionary, the general and the particular, but these are largely in her view located in nation-states where nation-building is as yet incomplete. More generally she sees this as part of the 'dialectical dualities of the global system' which will be resolved, as we have seen others also argue, by the institution of multiple membership 'spanning local, regional and global identities and which accommodates intersecting complexes of rights, duties and loyalties' (p. 166).

Criticisms of cosmopolitanism

Whilst others agree with Soysal's analysis, they do not all share her generally optimistic evaluation of such developments. Jacobson (1996), for instance, fears that important and long-established structures and traditions of nationally based citizenship are being undermined. The focus on individuals in his view leads to the devaluation of citizenship, confining it to a largely contractual character, restricted to utilities and protection. The fact that states have now lost control of migration is a serious problem, since 'determining who may become a member and a citizen is the state's way of shaping the national community. Immigration control . . . is consequently inherent in sovereignty . . . if strangers [*sic*] can enter at will, the ability of the state to shape and define a nation is compromised' (1996, pp. 5–6). This problem is aggravated by the reluctance (also noted by Soysal) or the unwillingness of so many migrants to naturalize. When they are nevertheless accorded extensive rights, the consequent lack of distinction between citizen and alien undermines citizenship itself. At the same time, individuals (with the help of left-wing groups and religious organizations, whose power he somewhat overstates) are able to appeal with their help beyond the nation-state to international organizations and codes. The state is then continually forced to amend its own legislation and administrative practice, a further instance of loss of sovereignty. The nation-state then can no longer effectively regulate, is constrained by transnational ties and unable to meet societal expectations of government in a context of increasing social and political conflict. The result of all this is a most 'precarious condition for the social and political order' (Jacobson, 1996, p. 132). There is clearly room for debate on the accuracy of Soysal's or Jacobson's analysis. The contradictions they identify, however resolved, are nevertheless central and raise more generally the question of whether moves in the universalist direction of a cosmopolis are desirable, whether we should really move beyond nationalism. Certainly while cosmopolitanism has always had its advocates, it has also always had its critics. If the Stoics and Dante were among the first cosmopolitans, St Augustine was one of their most trenchant early critics, seeing a world society as a grave danger, a perception shared, as we have seen, by Kant.

The (moderate) enthusiasm of some of Kant's contemporaries has provoked one particularly persistent charge, that cosmopolitanism is an essentially elitist project, that of what Lash once called 'the favoured few . . . out of touch with common life' (cited by Van Heer, 1998). Lest it be thought that this charge is only made against intellectuals comfortably ensconced in Western academic institutions, a sharp and perhaps more material illustration has been provided by Aihwa Ong in her depiction of what she calls 'border-running Chinese executives with no state loyalty' operating in the Pacific Rim. Quoting one such, who told her 'I can live anywhere in the world, but it must be near an airport', Ong has suggested that some actual cosmopolitans may have no loyalty to the nation but little too for the world as a whole (1998, p. 157).

To the charge that cosmopolitanism is the preserve of the (metropolitan) select (Nairn, 1997b),[7] if not a form of 'radical chic' (Cheah, 1998), we may add the perhaps more serious argument that it is also an exercise in 'bad faith', since whilst pretending to be universalist, it actually operates in the 'service of Western social and economic needs' (Brennan, 1997, p. 310; p. 189). Zolo (1997) raises the issue of the dangers posed by a sort of cosmopolis from above, where an elite of superpowers and global organizations can use military force to impose their interests on poorer and less powerful parts of the world.

Cosmopolitanism, such critics argue, can function for instance as a way of undermining anti-colonialism, by delegitimating the nationalism that is central to the mobilization of such struggles against the West, and especially the United States. For Brennan,

> there is only one way to express internationalism: by defending the popular sovereignty of existing and emergent third world polities . . . the nation is a precious site for negotiating rights and for salvaging common traditions. Nationalism of this type took centuries to forge and its resilience in the face of universalizing myths of US benevolence is hopeful. (1997, p. 316)

However, apart from the problem that this rests on a somewhat un-critical view of third world nationalism (see Chapter 5), it is not self-evident that opposition to imperialism has to take a national form. In the case of opposition to British rule in India for example, Tagore argued strongly for this distinction, arguing that Indian nationalism would be too shaped by the imperialism to which it was a response (Nandy, 1994). The justice of the anti-imperialist struggle lay (and continues to lie) at least in part in the necessity to tear down exclusionary barriers, not to replace them with new ones.[8] More controversially, Hintjens has raised the argument that according full citizenship rights within the former colonial state to the population of ex-colonies provides a universalistic alternative to national independence. She asks, 'why should it be considered more radical to try and obtain full rights within the newly independent state, or "home" country, than to try and obtain them within the colonial metropolis or "host" country' (1995, p. 151)?

A dramatic and sharp illustration of where anti-cosmopolitanism can lead may be found in the case of the debates over the intervention by NATO forces in Kosovo in 1998, which we discussed briefly in Chapter 5 and which has raised major issues concerning, in particular, the basis for intervention across national boundaries associated with the invoking of universalistic principles of human rights. For some, this provided over-riding evidence that arguments for a cosmopolitan world order were merely a 'figleaf' for US imperialist interests and hegemony. Critics have charged that, if the Western powers were so interested in human rights, they would have intervened elsewhere, in East Timor for instance. Their failure to do so graphically demonstrates the hypocrisy and double standards of imperialism (Chomsky, 2000).

For others, however, the defence of the rights of Kosovan Albanians against persecution and murder by Serbian nationalists was an overriding principle, exposing the dangers of accepting the primacy of national sover-eignty, and a rigid adherence to the principle of non-intervention in the affairs of sovereign nation-states. It had become impossible to defend the rights of any nation-state to undertake terroristic policies against a minority group under the guise of the right to national self-determination. Yet throughout a decade or more of extremely violent nationalist-driven conflict within the (shifting) borders of Yugoslavia, Western states had repeatedly justified both their intervention and their failure to intervene in terms derived from this nationalist frame of reference. (Slovenia had been encouraged to secede, Croatia ultimately to expel its Serbian population, and Bosnia to be cantonized, all the while leaving nationalist hegemony unchallenged.) Indeed, throughout this and other interventions, such as in Iraq, Western nation-states have often shown a marked disinclination to support democratic oppositions to nationalist regimes. Instead, their intervention or non-intervention has often contributed, wittingly or unwittingly to further spirals of nationalist violence.[9]

Clearly, we do not have space in this present volume for a full consideration of all the issues involved here. What can be said, however, is that the invocation of universalistic principles of human rights to be applied on a cosmopolitan basis seems to represent a better principle for the future of humanity in an increasingly globalized world than the reiteration of such flawed nationalist doctrine. This is not to deny that the issue of who is to enforce these principles (and how) is problematic, perhaps intensely so. Even a United Nations (rather than a NATO) led force would still be open to the selectivity and manipulation by dominant powers that has characterized past interventions. Yet non-intervention on grounds of national sovereignty seems a recipe for recurrent bouts of barbarism.[10]

In any case, whilst it may well be true that some do use universalist rhetoric to cover up other agendas, this argument sets up something of a straw man. Appiah puts it well, suggesting that 'it is characteristic of those who pose as anti-universalists to use the term "universalism" as if it meant "pseudo-universalism"; and the fact is that their complaint is not with "universalism" at all. What they truly object to – and who would not? – is Eurocentric hegemony *posing* as universalism' (1991, p. 92; emphasis in the original).

Arguments that may be dressed up in a cosmopolitan disguise need to be seriously analysed and measured against properly cosmopolitan criteria. This applies as much to justifications of Western capitalist consumerism today as to the expansionary religio-military projects of both Christianity and Islam, and the various imperialist projects of the Romans, the Habsburgs, the British, the Japanese, the Russians and the Americans. It is not difficult to expose what is ideological about these, whilst not abandoning the inclusionary and egalitarian ideals that lie at the heart of an authentic cosmopolitanism.

Patriotism versus cosmopolitanism

There are also, however, more general objections to cosmopolitanism in terms of sheer feasibility. It has been argued, for instance, that the egalitarianism of modern welfare states requires the exclusion of others (Freeman, 1986). Others have raised more profound objections that no polity can be conceived of that is not in some way bounded, that does not have limits. Even Hannah Arendt argued along these lines, claiming that

> nobody can be the citizen of a world as he is the citizen of his country . . . the very notion of one sovereign force ruling the whole earth . . . would be the end of all political life as we know it . . . Politics deals with men, nationals of many countries and heirs to many pasts; its laws are the positively established fences which hedge in, protect and limit the space in which freedom is not a concept, but a living, political reality. (1968, pp. 81–2)

Her argument rests in part on her particular concerns with the threat of totalitarianism, which here echo Kant's objection to a world state as likely to be despotic; that there would be no space within a universal state for diversity, for the plurality which is essential to politics. Without the nation, there would be a homogenization, a flattening, a shallowness of identity and commitment. The dull uniformity of a universal identity would be matched by the absence of any real uniform purpose. At the same time, there is also the fear that the scale of responsibility involved in universal citizenship is too vast:

> Our political concepts, according to which we have to assume responsibility for all public affairs within our reach regardless of 'personal guilt', because we are held responsible as citizens for everything that our government does in the name of the country, may lead us into an intolerable situation of global responsibility. The solidarity of mankind may well turn out to be an unbearable burden. (1968, p. 83)

Arendt's concern with responsibility points to the need for citizens to have some deep and ongoing commitment to their polity. From this angle, cosmopolitanism may appear too abstract, too thin to command sufficient loyalty, adherence and involvement.

Rather then cosmopolitanism, it is suggested, what we need is patriotism. Although this term is often used rather loosely in some of the literature,[11] it refers generally to the need for some sense of ownership and emotional engagement feared to be missing in cosmopolitanism. Margaret Canovan (1996a) argues, for instance, that even liberal polities can only exist if citizens see them as 'ours'. Such sentiments, which should not be analysed too closely, are a way of creating some warmth to support otherwise cold, impersonal structures. In a powerful argument for the necessity of such 'love of country' (or *patria*), Maurizio Viroli (1995) has traced the origins of the concept of patriotism back to Roman republican thought and then forward to, amongst others, Machiavelli, Milton and Rousseau. His aim is to develop what he calls 'the language of the patriotism of liberty' (p. 16). It is both possible and necessary, Viroli argues, to disentangle patriotic and nationalist arguments, and to develop a conception of the former as 'love of common liberty', a conception that is 'acceptable . . . morally sustainable and . . . may help to reinforce the sort of virtue that democracy needs' (pp. 186–7). Critically, such virtue 'is not sustained by universalistic political values but by identification with values that are part of the particular culture of a people' (1995, p. 174).

However, it is by no means clear what these values might be, if they are different to republican ones. To put it another way, what is of value in republican principles is logically independent of these 'thickening' values. What seems attractive about patriotism is not what is exclusive to this or that *patria* but its political character, the general political principles upon which the *patria* as a polity rather than nation rests. Its strength turns on the virtues of these principles, which hang or fall independently of any arguments about particular cultures. Insofar as the values of the latter pertain or belong to this country rather than that, they must appear in terms that seem closer to nationalist discourse or may be more fluently articulated within it. Insofar as Viroli wants to hang on to the notion of a particular culture (as opposed to another one), he risks reinstating a distinction between the nation and the other and opening the way again to the potential devaluing or denigration of the other.

If patriotism is problematic, however, there remain formidable problems with cosmopolitanism at another level. Is the only alternative to the assertion of a particular patriotic identity a universal one which appears to ignore all difference? If so, is universalism anything other than a code for specifically Western individualist values? Some feminists in particular have argued along these lines, suggesting that only a recognition of the importance of national loyalties can help women avoid the imposition of the 'false universalism' of a problematic universal sisterhood and global feminism (Sinha et al., 1998). Arguments for universalism, such as those put forward by cosmopolitans, are held typically to deny differences of any kind, whilst ignoring the fact that they are themselves formulated within and the product of a particular, liberal context and culture. This would be, as Charles Taylor put it, but 'a particularism masquerading as a universalism' (1994, p. 85).

Culture, nationalism and universalism

Taylor has suggested that there is an inherent tension between the particularity of difference and the universalism of equality, pointing towards two different kinds of politics. The politics of difference stresses the importance of distinct cultures and their importance for identity; the politics of universalism stresses the need to treat others as equals regardless of, or ignoring such differences.

Taylor argues that this tension may be mediated by assuming from the outset the intrinsic (though not necessarily equal) worth of all cultures, whilst some feminists have insisted that there has also to be some egalitarian basis to any such mediation, that 'cultural differences can only be freely elaborated and democratically mediated on the basis of social equality' (Fraser, 1997, p. 107). Together these may then provide the basis for communication across cultural divides, a search for what unites rather than divides.

This is not to ignore difference or the significance of cultural identity and of cultural association. Culture is in many respects a primary good (Kymlicka, 1995), one of the most basic human rights (Mullerson, 1995). Nor is it to argue that particular structurally disadvantaged groups should not have special rights (Young, 1990). However, in a world dominated by nation-states, it might be a good idea to start, as Baubock has suggested, by demanding special rights for migrants, given the barriers and exclusions to which they have been subjected and if we want to take seriously 'the idea of equal membership in a democratic polity' (1994, p. 208).

In any event, such rights would have to be framed in ways that do not then freeze difference and prevent communication, dialogue and movement. Human beings must have both the right to the protection of cultures within which they develop, and the right and ability to move around and on in ways that they see fit. It may be necessary, as Gianni has argued, to grant 'particular rights to some groups, thus allowing them to realize their conception of the good . . . [but] these must respect one condition: the forms of recognition should not call into question the basic rights of citizenship' (1997).

At the same time, it may also help to think more critically and sceptically about the nationalist understanding and invocation of cultural difference and not to lose sight of the reality that 'culture, particular as it may seem, always possesses universal moments' (De Waechter, 1996, p. 208). As we argued in Chapter 3 in particular, culture does not have to be thought of exclusively or primarily in nationalist terms, if at all. Cultures are not fixed, should not be reified and are only problematically and limitedly national in character. Even then, they need not command any primary allegiance or loyalty. Rather, cultures need to be conceptualized as diverse, as overlapping, as changeable, and as permeable. Cultures, as Dummett (1992) amongst others has pointed out, do not require closure to be protected or to flourish. As she points out, it makes no sense to talk about American or Islamic culture as closed, pointing also to the obvious Jewish contribution to German culture. Rather than posing the issue in terms of recognition or assimilation, it is more important, as Brighouse (1996) has argued, to encourage the permeability of boundaries, to facilitate movement and communication across cultures, in the process promoting cosmopolitanism.

There is, as we have noted in Chapter 6, an important, even critical, sense in which transnational migration creates a material base for this, as migrants carry cultures with them, encounter new ones, and modify them all by their presence and activity, and in turn have their cultures changed. As Axtmann (1996) puts it, 'these cultures of hybridity . . . break open the exclusionary cultural boundaries between "us" and "them" without either advocating assimilation . . . or the celebration of an "essential" otherness. In a way, they represent the global condition in our midst' (p. 106). For Honig similarly, the presence of such migrants means that, in many cities in the advanced industrial societies especially, there are large numbers of 'citizens of the world whose diversity is replicated inside the nation's territorial borders' (1998, p. 209).

A major issue then, given such valuable diversity, is how a polity can then be sufficiently cohesive, how it can command the loyalty of citizens from a variety of mixed and rich backgrounds. The problem with national identity here is that the cohesion it secures is essentially pre-political (Dahbour, 1996). The cohesion of the nation on the basis of national identity is, as Baubock also argues, 'the inclusiveness of a pre-political and self-reproducing collective' (1994, p. 42). The notion of the political here may be located within classical and republican conceptions of politics as a quintessentially human activity, involving conscious association, choice and communication, as opposed to a more limited, conventional and instrumental understanding. It seems useful to us in pointing to an alternative way of conceiving how a cosmopolitan polity may be grounded, in a willed, conscious decision to transcend the limitations of the nationalist insistence on difference, boundaries and exclusion. What can then hold a cosmopolitan polity together is the mutual respect of its members (the assumed worth of all cultures), their commitment to and responsibility for each other, some fundamental sense of solidarity. If this is not the pre-political solidarity of national identity, it has to be solidarity of another (in this sense) political kind. De Waechter (1998) captures something of this when he argues that 'what makes us a community is not the factually cultural identity in which we are rooted. The person is not a tree and humanity is not a forest. What makes us a community is not the anchoring in a sedentary community but a task of justice which we must fulfil together' (p. 208).

We may interpret justice here to mean that there must be substantive not merely formal equality between the members of a cosmopolitan polity, that all must have a range of rights, of precisely the kind that have been the focus of the internationalist campaigns of socialists, feminists, liberals and social movements. For the first, the 'task of justice' is to end the divisive exploitation of workers near and far, at the hands of national and global capital. For the second, it is to end the oppression of women at the hands of national or global male power. For the third, it is to assert and implement a range of rights, sometimes enshrined in various international declarations but often not implemented by nation-states the world over.

Internationalist and cosmopolitan movements

There have indeed been a range of movements which have embraced and continue to pursue such goals. There has, to begin with, been the international socialist movement, or at least significant parts of it, which has at various times attempted to 'put cosmopolitanism into practice' (Colas, 1994).[12] Although, as we noted in Chapter 1, Marxists have adopted a variety of positions in relation to nationalism, the idea of international solidarity, that the workers *of the world* have a basic set of common interests, has been a central inspiration for much socialist activity from the first appearance of the Communist Manifesto. It led to repeated efforts to organize on an internationalist basis; it is no accident that at least four socialist international organizations have been set up in the past 150 years. Whilst the first of these was largely symbolic and short-lived, the Second and Third Internationals were huge organizations. If both of these eventually capitulated to nationalism (the Second International in its failure to prevent individual socialist parties supporting the First World War and the Third International in becoming an arm of Russian foreign policy after the adoption of the policy of 'socialism in one country'), this did not end the internationalist traditions of the socialist movement. Not only did smaller Marxist groups continue to attempt to resurrect the idea of an international, but beyond this socialists of all hues have continued to be active in a range of internationalist campaigns, from struggles for peace and against the nuclear threat, to those against apartheid, or in solidarity with victims of dictatorship (right or 'left' from Pinochet in Chile to the Soviet invasion of Czechoslovakia). Solidarity at the most basic level with strikers across national boundaries still occurs of course at both the level of international trade union organizations and networks and at a more grassroots level.[13]

Internationalism has, of course, not been confined to the socialist or workers' movement. It has also been a prominent feature of feminist politics. At the theoretical level, the struggle against the oppression of women is not in principle confined to any one part of the globe. As the title of one famous feminist text put it, 'sisterhood is global' (Morgan, 1984). In a recent survey, the editors of the feminist journal *Gender and History* have noted both the parallels with the international workers' movement and how a variety of 'impulses have driven women for over a century to build international channels and bodies' (Sinha et al., 1998, p. 348). Among these concerns have been issues relating to education, access and the right to work, marriage and divorce laws, citizenship and health, whilst feminists have played a major role in the pacifist movement, in combating religious fundamentalism and in agitating for human rights. The fact that women make up an increasing percentage of migrants and especially the fact that over 80 per cent of refugees are women and children has also led to the formation of a range of international connections and networks (Pettman, 1996). Although it would be unwise to exaggerate the impact of the most formal of these, Dickenson has suggested that the 1995 Beijing World Conference on Women (which brought together governments and NGOs) did influence positive developments with its Platform for Action, a non-enforceable agreement covering property rights, resource allocation, unpaid work and sexual rights (Dickenson, 1997, p. 108).[14]

Internationalism has never of course been confined to either the socialist or women's movement and in both the nineteenth and twentieth century, forms of liberal internationalism have at times been prominent, both in mass campaigns for peace and in pursuit of a variety of federalist projects (Heater, 1996). International aid charities, such as Oxfam or Médécins sans Frontières, have long been active across frontiers and national borders. More recently, campaigns for human rights have taken centre stage, formulating their demands in international terms and indeed succeeding in establishing what is by now a quite extensive set of declarations and commitments. These include the UN's 1948 Universal Declaration of Human Rights, the 1950 European Convention for the Protection of Human Rights and Freedoms, the 1966 Covenant on Rights and the 1981 Banjul Charter of Human and People's Rights. Underpinning all these, it may be argued, is a significant normative shift, a consensus (particularly after the Holocaust) that human rights are indeed international (Donnelly, 1998). In this sense, it has been suggested, there has been a radical break from the norms that dominated the international order since the treaty of Westphalia in which rights were located at the national level, in which nation-states could not be seriously held accountable even in principle at an international level (Cassese, 1990).

At the same time, it is important to note that the formulation of these rights has been due not only, if at all, to the efforts of national governments but to international networks and organizations that actively pursue these issues on a global basis.[15] There has been a dramatic increase in the number of human rights non-governmental organizations independent of and attempting to monitor the activities of nation-states. (The example of Amnesty International which actively uses its international character to intervene in human rights abuses within nation-states is the classic one here.) In 1993, 529 international NGOs attended the UN World Conference on Human Rights in Vienna. How effective any of these have been in constraining states is not the issue here, so much as the terms in which such commitments are framed. It can be argued that, insofar as they are an outcome of moral concerns and the focus of issue-based activity, they are part of a general shift in political activity, from an old to a new politics, concerned with issues and values rather than purely material concerns. Central to this new politics, it has been argued, are the new social movements (Scott, 1990), which include not only the modern feminist and human rights movements but also environmental, anti-nuclear, pacifist and anti-racist movements. All of these, whilst operating effectively at the national level, are active in campaigning internationally and stressing that many problems are global and, thus, so too must be solutions to those problems.[16] Pete Waterman (1998) has argued that such movements are central to the 'new internationalism' which has moved beyond labour and socialist internationalism to become a global social movement.[17] The current growth of a movement, which is characterized variously as 'anti-globalization' or 'anti-capitalist', has resulted in a series of demonstrations against some of the key institutions of the global capitalist economy. Starting with the mass protests in Seattle in 1999, the World Trade Organization, the IMF, the G7 summit have all seen demonstrations that have mobilized on a transnational basis with demands that have typically not taken refuge in seeking protectionist economic policies as a solution to the neo-liberal economic agenda. Rather, there has been the articulation of a range of concerns and demands that has been explicitly described as a movement for 'globalization from below' (Brecher et al., 2000). This loose movement, composed of a breadth of networks, campaigns, groups and parties, has demonstrated that there can be an opposition, based on internationalist principles, to a globalization that reinforces and increases global inequalities. As Susan George, a prominent advocate of this movement, asserts, 'we are pro-globalization. We are in favour of sharing friendship, culture, cuisine, travel, solidarity, wealth and resources worldwide. We are above all "pro-democracy" and "pro-planet", which our adversaries most clearly are not' (2001, p. 5).

Identity or solidarity?

There are of course ongoing debates about whether international socialism would end the oppression of women, or whether all women have the same interests, or whether social movements can unite in an enduring and sustainable coalition. Clearly, we do not have space to pursue any of these weighty matters here. What we can say, however, is that all these struggles imply a crucial distinction between a politics based on *identity* and one based on *solidarity*. As Jodi Dean has argued (in a helpful discussion of the politics of universalism and difference in relation to the women's movement), identity is mechanical, given, ascribed; solidarity, in contrast, involves the search for *mutual* recognition and opposition to exclusion and oppression. It is the product of efforts at communication, of dialogue, in which there is no one generalized other (Dean, 1997). A related argument has also been put forward by Yuval-Davis in terms of what she calls a 'transversal politics', the pursuit of a politics of solidarity between 'those who, in their different rooting, share values and goals compatible with one's own' (1997, p. 130).

The values and goals that are shared by the internationalist movements we have referred to here seem to do above all with treating others as we would wish to be treated ourselves, with seeing others as deserving the same rights as ourselves, irrespective of considerations of national identity. A politics of international solidarity invokes support for action against exploitation, oppression and ill-treatment, whatever form these take, across national boundaries and borders. The exploitation of workers in another part of the world is not, from this perspective, a local issue, but motivates international action and mutual aid. Violence, the denial of access to resources, to education, of the right to work for equal pay, to decide who to marry or divorce, whether or not to bear children, all equally call for the support of women across continents. Campaigns for human rights are no longer constrained by national boundaries but are pursued on a transnational terrain. In each case, the appeal for support is premised on an assumed recognition of common interests that are shared across national divides.

IN CONCLUSION: NATIONALISM AND THE NATION-STATE IN QUESTION

The thrust of our argument here has been away from the national, beyond the categories and priorities of nationalism. As we indicated at the beginning, it cannot be denied that people believe that nations exist, and that they have a national identity, although as we have also argued throughout, many of the assumptions that go with these beliefs are profoundly flawed. If this particular identity is to be recognized in a cosmopolitan world, it has to be depoliticized, partly by highlighting its essentially pre-political character but also by separating it from any claim to state power, decoupling it from the state, just as citizenship has to be decoupled from nationality. As John Keane (1994) has argued, national identity is but one among many other competing identities, and one whose scope should be restricted in favour of other non-national identities. If adequate space can be opened up for people to choose other identities which are altogether less problematic, that can only improve the prospects not only for democracy, as Keane suggests, but also for cosmopolitanism in the long run. In the meantime, energies may be better spent in exploring viable political alternatives to the major focus of nationalist aspiration, the nation-state. Within existing nation-states, this means questioning the sanctity and primacy of national identity and the often 'banal' but still effective discourse of the 'national interest'. It means campaigning for universal human rights. It means looking to the development of agencies and organizations that can enforce such rights beyond and against nation-states. It means seeking to pull down the exclusionary barriers set up by nation-states, which have effectively organized a kind of global apartheid (Richmond, 1994). It means challenging the usually unquestioned identification of people and nation that lies at the heart of modern nationalism. For as long as this mistaken notion persists, democracy (notionally the unchallenged political norm of our times) is both incomplete, since there are always those excluded from the polity, and imperilled.

If we can begin to move beyond nationalism, we may after all be able to recognize all others as our equals and our responsibility, wherever they are, wherever they come from, and wherever they are bound.

FURTHER READING

On consociationalism, see McGarry and O' Leary (1993), and O'Leary (1999) for the application of the theory and practice to Northern Ireland. There is a large literature on the European Union; a useful discussion of its relationship to nationalism can be found in Smith (1995, ch. 5). Serious efforts to think through the implications of developing alternatives to national citizenship can be found in Baubock (1994), whilst a more radical argument is advanced with great conviction by Hayter (2000). For a discussion of a range of issues to do with cosmopolitan democracy, see Archibugi et al. (1998). There is a growing literature on global social movements. A good survey is to be found in Cohen and Rai (2000), whilst Waterman (1998) has tried to link these directly to the development of a new internationalism.

NOTES

1 A good current example would be the Northern Ireland peace agreement whose fragility is highly apparent at the point of writing, and whose stability is based, *inter alia*, on the modification of the competing nationalisms of the Protestant and Catholic communities in Northern Ireland. For a detailed (and highly positive) analysis of the agreement in relation to the theory and practice of consociationalism see O'Leary (1999).

2 Although Lijphart considers federalism to be 'a special form of segmental autonomy, possible where segmental cleavages coincide with regional cleavages' (Lijphart, 1977, p. 42).

3 For a critical but more sympathetic discussion of federalism in this context see Stepan (1998).

4 For an interesting discussion of these issues see Schlesinger (1992).

5 Although his survey is confined to Western thought, he notes that related ideas appear in the Hindu concept of *Advaita* and the Chinese idea of *Ta T'Ung* (a great society including all people under heaven) (Heater, 1996).

6 An attempt to argue, however, that democratic citizenship does involve citizens and states in a web of duties and commitments beyond borders can be found in Weale (1991).

7 Indeed Nairn has become the main scourge of cosmopolitanism and internationalism: 'Seen from the particularist swamps, 90 per cent of what is trumpeted

out as internationalism is veiled, thinly veiled or occasionally full-frontal metropolitan self-interest and aggression' (Nairn, 1997b, p. 42).

8   The solidarity these struggles invoke in fact frequently transcends national borders. Lavrin (1998) who argues that nationalism and internationalism are compatible, actually provides a number of examples of women's anti-imperialist activity which are rather more continental (in this instance Latin America) than national in scope.

9   In Kosovo the KLA, who received some eventual support, then proceeded in their own turn to try to expel both the remaining Serb population and the Roma, whom they accused of collaboration. International agencies have tried both here and in Bosnia to mediate and to encourage the development of democratic institutions but have also been criticized (unfairly in our view) for 'faking democracy' in the region (Chandler, 1999).

10 For a debate about some of these issues, see Archibugi who argues for a 'cosmopolitical perspective on humanitarian intervention', based on principles of 'tolerance, legitimacy and effectiveness' (2000, p. 148), and the sharp response by Chandler attacking what he sees as 'a return to . . . open great-power domination over states which are too weak to prevent external claims against them' (2000, p. 66).

11 Plamenatz, for example, defines patriotism rather vaguely as 'a devotion to the community one belongs to' (Plamenatz, 1976, p. 24), whereas Hayes suggests that the term referred first of all to a sentimental attachment to an immediate locality, 'love of one's terra patria' (Hayes, 1926, p. 23). It was then extended from an attachment to one's native locality to one's political country. Kymlicka, on the other hand, says that 'we should distinguish "patriotism", the feeling of allegiance to a state, from national identity, the sense of membership in a national group' (Kymlicka, 1995, p. 13).

12 Although Colas himself does not think that a full-blown cosmopolitanism is actually possible.

13 For examples of some of the transnational networks that grew up from the 1970s against the power of multinational corporations, see Wainwright (1994, pp. 154–8).

14 See also the account of three decades of 'making global connections among women' by Stienstra (2000).

15 Although Beetham (1998) points out that nation-states are still central to any implementation of human rights.

16 A discussion of the nature of the peace movement in the 1980s which stresses its transnational character is provided by Wainwright, (1994, pp. 239–57).

17 Others, it should be said, are somewhat less optimistic. Martin Shaw (1994) has argued that social movements form typically within national civil societies and experience major problems in confronting the state, problems which are magnified at the international level.

Bibliography

Abdo, N. (1994) ' Nationalism and Feminism – Palestinian Women and the Intifada: No Going Back?', in Moghadam, V. (ed.), *Gender and National Identity – Women and Politics in Muslim Societies* (London: Zed Books).

Abercrombie, N., Hill, S. and Turner, B. (1980) *The Dominant Ideology Thesis* (London: Allen and Unwin).

Abu-Lughod, J. (1989) *Before European Hegemony, The World System AD 1250–1350* (New York: Oxford University Press).

Acton, E. (1996) 'Nationality', in Balakrishnan, G. (ed.), *Mapping the Nation* (London: Verso).

Addi, L. (1997) 'The Failure of Third World Nationalism', *Journal of Democracy*, 8 (4).

Agnew, J. (1995) 'Postscript: Federalism in the Post Cold-war Era', in Smith, G. (ed.), *Federalism – The Multi-Ethnic Challenge* (London: Longman).

Ali, R. & Lifschutz, L. (1992) *Why Bosnia?* (Boston: Pamphleteer's Press).

Allen, W.S. (1992) 'The Collapse of Nationalism in Nazi Germany', in Breuilly. (ed.), *The State of Germany – The National Idea in the Making, Unmaking and Remaking of a Modern State* (Harlow: Longman).

Alter, P. (1989) *Nationalism* (London: Edward Arnold).

Alter, P. (1992) 'Nationalism and German Politics after 1945', in Breuilly, J. (ed.), *The State of Germany – The National Idea in the Making, Unmaking and Remaking* (London: Longman).

Anderson, B. (1991) *Imagined Communities* (London: Verso).

Anderson, J. (1995) 'The Exaggerated Death of the Nation State', in Anderson, J., Brook, C. and Cochrane, A. (eds), *A Global World? Re-ordering Political Space* (Oxford: Oxford University Press).

Anthias, F. (1998) 'Evaluating "Diaspora": Beyond Ethnicity?', *Sociology*, 32 (3), 557–80.

Anthias, F. and Yuval-Davis, N. (1992) *Racialised Boundaries – Race, Nation, Gender, Colour and Class and the Anti-Racist Struggle* (London: Routledge).

Anzulovic, B. (1999) *Heavenly Serbia – From Myth to Genocide* (London: Hurst).

Appadurai, A. (1990) 'Disjuncture and Difference in the Global Cultural Economy', *Public Culture*, 2 (2), 1–24.

Appiah, K. (1991) *In My Father's House* (London: Methuen).

Appiah, K. (1998) 'Cosmopolitan Politics', in Cheah, P. and Robbins, B. (eds), *Cosmopolitics – Thinking and Feeling Beyond the Nation* (Minneapolis: University of Minnesota Press).

Arblaster, A. (1987) *Democracy* (Milton Keynes: Open University Press).

Archard, D. (1995) 'Myths, Lies and Historical Truth: a Defence of Nationalism' *Political Studies*, XLIII, 472–81.

Archer, M. (1985) 'The Myth of Cultural Integration', *British Journal of Sociology*, 36, 333–53.

Archibugi, D. (2000) 'Cosmopolitical Democracy', *New Left Review*, 4, 137–50.

Archibugi, D., Held, D. and Köhler, M. (eds), (1998) *Reimagining Political Communities – Studies in Cosmopolitan Democracy* (Cambridge: Polity Press).

Arendt, H. (1966) *The Origins of Totalitarianism* (New York: Harcourt, Brace and World).

Arendt, H. (1968) 'Karl Jaspers: Citizen of the World?', in *Men in Dark Times* (New York: Harcourt, Brace).

Asad, T. (1993) 'Multiculturalism and British Identity', in Asad, T. (ed.), *Genealogies of Religion*, (Baltimore, MD: John Hopkins Press).

Ascherson, N. (1995) *Black Sea* (London: Jonathan Cape).

Audit Commission (2000) 'Another Country: Implementing Dispersal Under the Immigration and Asylum Act 1999' (www.audit-commission.gov.uk/ac2/NR/LocalA/brasylum.pdf).

Axtmann, R. (1996) *Liberal Democracy into the Twenty-First Century: Globalization, Integration and the Nation-State* (Manchester: Manchester University Press).

Balakrishnan, G. (1996) 'The National Imagination', in Balakrishnan, G. (ed.), *Mapping the Nation* (London: Verso).

Balibar, E. (1991) 'The Nation Form – History and Ideology', in Balibar, E. and Wallerstein, I., *Race, Nation, Class: Ambiguous Identities* (London: Verso).

Balibar, E. and Wallerstein, I. (1991) *Race, Nation, Class: Ambiguous Identities* (London: Verso).

Barbieri, W. (1998) *Ethics of Citizenship – Immigration and Group Rights in Germany* (Durham, NC: Duke University Press).

Barker, M. (1981) *The New Racism* (London: Junction Books).

Barth, F. (1969) 'Ethnic Groups and Boundaries', in Barth, F. (ed.), *Ethnic Groups and Boundaries: The Social Organization of Culture Difference* (Boston: Little, Brown).

Basch, L., Glick Schiller, N. and Blanc-Szanton, C. (1994) *Nations Unbound: Transnational Projects, Post-colonial Predicaments, and De-territorialized Nation-States* (Geneva: Gordon and Breach).

Bateman, D. (1996) 'Quebec: The Second Referendum', *Scottish Affairs*, 14.

Baubock, R. (1994) *Transnational Citizenship – Membership and Rights in International Migration* (London: Edward Elgar).

Bauer, O. (1996) 'The Nation', in Balakrishnan, G. (ed.), *Mapping the Nation* (London: Verso).

Baum, M. (1996) *An Imperfect Union – The Maastricht Treaty and the New Politics of European Integration* (Oxford: Westview).

Bauman, J. (1998) 'Demons of Other People's Fear', in Peterson, A. and Fridzilius, S. (eds), *Stranger or Guest? Racism and Migration in Contemporary Europe* (Stockholm: Almqvist and Wiksell International).

Bauman, Z. (1989) *Modernity and the Holocaust* (Cambridge: Polity Press).

Bauman, Z. (1992) 'Soil, Blood, and Identity', *The Sociological Review*, 40 (4), 675–701.

Bauman, Z. (1997) *Postmodernity and its Discontents* (Cambridge: Polity Press).

Bauman, Z. (1998) *Globalization* (Cambridge: Polity Press).

Beck, J.A. (1994) *Citizens and Criminals – Notions of Citizenship in the Czech State in Transition*. MA dissertation, Central European University, Prague.

Beetham, D. (1998) 'Human Rights as a Model for Cosmopolitan Democracy', in Archibugi, D., Held, D., and Köhler, M., *Reimagining Political Community – Studies in Cosmopolitan Democracy* (Cambridge: Polity Press).

Beetham, D. and Boyle, K. (1995) *Introducing Democracy – 80 Questions and Answers* (London: Polity Press).

Bell, D. (1995) 'Lingua Populi, Lingua Dei: Language, Religion and the Origins of French Revolutionary Nationalism', *American Historical Review*, 100 (4), 1403–37.

Bellah, R. (1970) 'Civil Religion in America', in Bellah, R. (ed.), *Beyond Belief* (New York: Harper and Row).

Benner, E. (1995) *Really Existing Nationalisms – A Post-Communist View from Marx and Engels* (Oxford: Oxford University Press).

Ben-Yahuda, N. (1995) *The Masada Myth: Collective Memory and Mythmaking in Israel* (Madison, WI: University of Wisconsin Press).

Beramendi, J., Maiz, R. and Nunez, X. (eds) (1994) *Nationalism in Europe Past and Present* (Universidade de Santiago de Compostela: Santiago de Compostela).

Berger, S. (1997) *The Search for Normality – National Identity and Historical Consciousness in Germany* (Oxford: Berghahn).

Berlin, I. (1991) 'Joseph De Maistre and the Origins of Fascism', in *The Crooked Timber of Humanity* (London: Fontana).

Berlin, I. (1996) 'Kant as an Unfamiliar Source of Nationalism', in Hardy, H. (ed.), *Studies in Ideas and Their History* (London: Chatto and Windus).

Bhabha, H. (1990) 'Introduction: Narrating the Nation', in Bhabha, H. (ed.), *Nation and Narration* (London: Routledge).

Billig, M. (1995) *Banal Nationalism* (London: Sage).

Birnbaum, P. (1992) *Antisemitism in France: A Political History from Leon Blum to the Present* (Oxford: Blackwell).

Björgo, T. and Witte, R. (eds) (1993) *Racist Violence in Europe* (Basingstoke: Macmillan Press).

Blackburn, R. (1993) 'The Break-up of Yugoslavia and the Fate of Bosnia', *New Left Review*, 199, 100–19.

Blanning, T. (1996) *The French Revolutionary Wars* (London: Arnold).

Blaut, J. (1987 *The National Question – Decolonising the Theory of Nationalism* (London: Zed Books).

Bonin, P.Y. (1997) 'Liberalisme ou nationalisme: ou tracer la ligne?', *Canadian Journal of Political Science*, 30, 235–56.

Bouatta, C. (1994) 'Feminine Militancy: *Moudjahidates* during and after the Algerian War', in Moghadam, V. (ed.), *Gender and National Identity – Women and Politics in Muslim Societies* (London: Zed Books).

Bougarel, X. (1996) 'Bosnia and Hercegovina – State and Communitarianism', in Dyker, D. and Vejvoda I. (eds), *Yugoslavia and After – A Study in Fragmentation, Despair and Rebirth* (London: Longman).

Boutin, C. (1996) 'L'Extrême droite francaise au-delà du nationalisme', *Revue Française de Science Politique*, 3 (1), 113–60.

Bowman, G. (1994) 'Ethnic Violence and the Phantasy of the Antagonist: The Mobilisation of National Identity in Former Yugoslavia', *Polish Sociological Review*, vol. 2, 133–53.

Boyle, P., Halfacre, K. and Robinson, V. (1998) *Explaining Contemporary Migration* (London: Longman).

Brah, A. (1996) *Cartographies of Diaspora – Contesting Identities* (London: Routledge).

Brass, P. (1991) *Ethnicity and Nationalism: Theory and Comparison* (New Delhi: Sage).

Brass, P. (1994) 'Elite competition and the origins of ethnic nationalism', in Beramendi, J., Maiz, R. and Nunez, X. (eds), *Nationalism in Europe Past and Present* (Santiago de Compostela: Universidade de Santiago de Compostela).

Braunthal, J. (1967) *History of the International vol. 1: 1864–1914* (New York: Praeger).

Brecher, J., Costello, T. and Smith, B. (2000) *Globalization from Below – The Power of Solidarity* (Cambridge, MA: South End Press).

Brennan, T. (1997) *At Home in the World – Cosmopolitanism Now* (Cambridge, MA: Harvard University Press).

Breton, R. (1988) 'From ethnic to civic nationalism – English Canada and Quebec', *Ethnic and Racial Studies*, 11 (1) 85–102.

Breuilly, J. (ed.) (1992) *The State of Germany – The National Idea in the Making, Unmaking and Remaking* (London: Longman).

Breuilly, J. (1993) *Nationalism and the State*, second edition (Manchester: Manchester University Press).

Breuilly, J. (1994) 'Culture, Doctrine, Politics: 3 Ways of Constructing Nationalism', in Beramendi, J., Maiz, R. and Nunez, X. (eds), *Nationalism in Europe Past and Present* (Santiago de Compostela: Universidade de Santiago de Compostela).

Breuilly, J. (1996) 'Approaches to Nationalism', in Balakrishnan, G. (ed.), *Mapping the Nation* (London: Verso).

Brierley, W. and Giacometti, L. (1996) 'Italian National Identity and the Failure of Regionalism', in Jenkins, B. and Sofos, S., *Nation and Identity in Contemporary Europe* (London: Routledge).

Briggs, V. (1996) *Mass Immigration and the National Interest* (Armonk, NY: M.E. Sharpe).

Brighouse, H. (1996) 'Against Nationalism', *Canadian Journal of Philosophy*, supplementary volume 22, pp. 365–406.

Brockmann, S. (1991) 'The Reunification Debate', *New German Critique*, 52, Winter.

Brown, A., McCrone, D. and Paterson, L. (1998) *Politics and Society in Scotland*, second edition (Basingstoke: Macmillan).

Brubaker, R. (1992) *Citizenship and Nationhood in France and Germany* (Cambridge, MA: Harvard University Press).

Brubaker, R. (1994) 'Nationhood and the Nationalities Question in the Soviet Union and post-Soviet Eurasia: An Institutionalist Account', *Theory and Society*, 23, 47–78.

Brubaker, R. (1996a) *Nationalism Reframed: Nationalism and the National Question in the New Europe* (Cambridge: Cambridge University Press).

Brubaker, R. (1996b) 'Nationalising States in the Old New Europe and the New', *Ethnic and Racial Studies*, 19, 2.

Brubaker, R. (1998) 'Myths and Misconceptions in the Study of Nationalism', in Hall, J. (ed.), *The State of the Nation: Ernest Gellner and the Theory of Nationalism* (Cambridge: Cambridge University Press).

Bryant, C. (1995) 'Civic Nationalism, Civil Society, Civil Religion', in Hall, J. (ed.), *Civil Society – Theory, History, Comparison* (Cambridge: Polity Press).

Bulbeck, C. (1988) *One World Women's Movement* (London: Pluto Press).

Burgess, A. (1998) 'European Identity and the Challenge from the West and East', in Hedetoft, U. (ed.), *Political Symbols, Symbolic Politics* (Aldershot: Ashgate).

Calhoun, C. (1997) *Nationalism* (Buckingham: Open University Press).

Campbell, D. (1998) *National Deconstruction: Violence, Identity and Justice in Bosnia* (London: University of Minneapolis Press).

Canovan, M. (1992) *Hannah Arendt – a Reinterpretation of her Political Thought* (Cambridge: Cambridge University Press).

Canovan, M. (1996a) 'The Skeleton in the Cupboard: Nationhood, Patriotism and Limited Loyalties', in Caney, S., George, D. and Jones, P. (eds), *National Rights and International Obligations* (Oxford: Westview).

Canovan, M. (1996b) *Nationhood and Political Theory* (Cheltenham: Edward Elgar).

Capaldi, N. (1997) *Immigration – Debating the Issues* (New York: Prometheus Books).

Carchedi, B. and Carchedi, G. (1999) 'Contradictions of European Integration', *Capital and Class*, 67, 119–53.

Carens, J. (1987) 'Aliens and Citizens – The Case for Open Borders', in Beiner, R. (ed.), *Theorising Citizenship* (New York: State University of New York).

Cassese, A. (1990) *Human Rights in a Changing World* (Cambridge: Polity Press).

Castells, M. (1997) *The Power of Identity* (Oxford: Blackwell).

Castles, S. (2000) 'The Racisms of Globalization' in Castles, S., *Ethnicity and Globalization* (London: Sage).

Castles, S. and Miller, M. (1998) *The Age of Migration – International Population Movements in the Modern World* (Basingstoke: Macmillan).

Cesarani, D. (1996) 'The Changing Character of Citizenship in Britain and Europe', in Cesarani, D. and Fulbrook, M. (eds), *Citizenship, Nationality and Migration in Europe* (London: Routledge).

Cesarani, D. and Fulbrook, M. (eds) (1996) *Citizenship, Nationality, and Identity in Europe* (London: Routledge).

Chandler, D. (1999) *Bosnia – Faking Democracy after Dayton* (London: Pluto Press).

Chandler, D. (2000) '"International Justice"', *New Left Review*, 6, 55–66.

Chapman, M. (1992) *The Celts: The Construction of a Myth* (Basingstoke: Macmillan).

Chatterjee, P. (1986) *Nationalist Thought and the Colonial World: A Derivative Discourse?* (London: Zed Books).

Cheah, P. (1998) 'The Cosmopolitical Today', in Cheah, P. and Robbins, B. (eds), *Cosmopolitics – Thinking and Feeling Beyond the Nation* (Minneapolis: University of Minnesota Press).

Chomsky, N. (2000) *A New Generation Draws the Line – Kosovo, East Timor and the Standards of the West* (London: Verso).

Chun, A. (1994) 'From nationalism to nationalizing: cultural imagination and state formalism in postwar Taiwan', *Australian Journal of Chinese Affairs*, 31, 49–72.

Clifford, J. (1994) 'Diasporas', *Cultural Anthropology*, 9 (3), 302–38.

CNN (2001) 'Official: Florida disenfranchised minority voters', http://www.cnn.com/2001/ALLPOLITICS/03/09/florida.election/index.html

Coakley, J. (1993) 'Introduction: The Territorial Management of Ethnic Conflict', in Coakley, J. (ed.) *The Territorial Management of Ethnic Conflict* (London: Frank Cass).

Cobban, A. (1969) *The Nation-State. National Self-Determination* (London: Fontana).

Cocks, J. (1997) 'Fetishizing Ethnicity, Locality, Nationality: the Curious Case of Tom Nairn', *Theory and Event*, 1, 3.

Cohen, R. (1994) *Frontiers of Identity* (London: Longman).

Cohen, R. (1997a) 'Shaping the Nation, Excluding the Other: The Deportation of Migrants from Britain', in Lucassen, J. and Lucassen, L. (eds), *Migration, Migration History, History* (Berne: Peter Lang, European Academic Publishers).

Cohen, R. (1997b) *Global Diasporas: An Introduction* (London: UCL Press).

Cohen, R. and Rai, S. M. (2000) *Global Social Movements* (London: Athlone Press).

Cohen, S. (1992) *Imagine There's No Countries – 1992 and International Immigration Controls against Migrants, Immigrants and Refugees* (Manchester: Greater Manchester Immigration Aid Unit).

Colas, A. (1994) 'Putting Cosmopolitanism into Practice – The Case of International Socialism', *Millenium*, 23 (3), 513–34.

Colley, L. (1992) *Britons: Forging the Nation, 1707–1837* (New Haven, CT: Yale University Press).

Comaroff, J. (1995) 'Ethnicity, Nationalism and the Politics of Difference in an Age of Revolution', in Comaroff, J. and Stern, P. (eds), *Perspectives on Nationalism and War* (Geneva: Gordon and Breach).

Comaroff, J. and Stern, P. (eds) (1995) *Perspectives on Nationalism and War* (Geneva: Gordon and Breach).

Connerton, P. (1989) *How Societies Remember* (Cambridge: Cambridge University Press).

Connor, W. (1984) *The National Question in Marxist–Leninist Theory and Strategy* (Princeton, NJ: Princeton University Press).

Copper, J.F. (1990) *Taiwan – Nation-State or Province?* (Oxford: Westview).

Cornell, S. (1996) 'The Variable Ties that Bind: Content and Circumstance in Ethnic Processes', *Ethnic and Racial Studies*, 19 (2), 265–89.

Couture, J. and Nielsen, K. with Seymour, M. (1996) 'Liberal Nationalism: Both

Cosmopolitan and Rooted', *Canadian Journal of Philosophy*, supplementary volume (22), 579–662.

Crnobrnja, M. (1994) *The Yugoslav Drama* (London: I.B.Tauris).

Croucher, S. (1998) 'South Africa's Illegal Aliens: Constructing National Boundaries in a Post-Apartheid State', *Ethnic and Racial Studies*, 21 (4), 638–60.

Cunningham, H. (1981) 'The Language of Patriotism, 1750–1914', *History Workshop*, 12, 8–33.

Cviic, C. (1996) 'Croatia', in Dyker, D. and Vejvoda, I. (eds), *Yugoslavia and After – A Study in Fragmentation, Despair and Rebirth* (London: Longman).

Dahbour, A. (1996) 'The Nation-State as a Political Community – A Critique of the Communitarian Argument for National Self-Determination', *Canadian Journal of Philosophy*, supplementary volume, 22, 311–44.

Daniels, R. (1998) 'What is an American? Ethnicity, Race, the Constitution and the Immigrant in Early American History', in Jacobson, D. (ed.), *The Immigration Reader – America in a Multi-Disciplinary Perspective* (Oxford: Blackwell).

Davidson, B. (1992) *The Black Man's Burden – Africa and the Curse of the Nation-State* (London: James Curry).

Davidson, N. (1999) 'In Perspective: Tom Nairn', *International Socialism*, 82, 97–136.

Davies, N. (1997) 'West Best, East Beast?', *Oxford Today*, 9, 2.

Dawisha, K. and Parrott, B. 1994 *Russia and the New States of Eurasia: the Politics of Upheaval* (Cambridge: Cambridge University Press).

Dean, J. (1997) 'The Reflective Solidarity of Democratic Feminism', in Dean, J. (ed), *Feminism and the New Democracy – Resiting the Political* (London: Sage).

Deletant, D. and Hanak, H. (eds) (1998 *Historians as Nation-Builders: Central and South-East Europe* (Basingstoke: Macmillan).

Denitch, B. (1994) 'Dismembering Yugoslavia – Nationalist Ideologies and the Symbolic Revival of Genocide', *American Ethnologist*, 21, 2.

Denitch, B. (1996) *Ethnic Nationalism – The Tragic Death of Yugoslavia* (Minneapolis: University of Minnesota Press).

Desideri, C. (1995) 'Italian Regions in the European Community', in Jones, B. and Keating, M. (eds), *The European Union and the Regions* (Oxford: Oxford University Press).

De Waechter, F. (1996) 'In Search of a Postnational Identity: Who are My People?', *Canadian Journal of Philosophy*, supplementary volume, 22, 197–218.

Diaz-Andreu, M. and Champion, T. (1996) 'Nationalism and Archaeology in Europe: An Introduction', in Diaz-Andreu, M. and Champion, T. (eds), *Nationalism and Archaeology in Europe* (London: UCL Press).

Dickenson, D. (1997) 'Counting Women In: Globalization, Democratization and the Women's Movement', in McGrew, A. (ed.), *The Transformation of Democracy* (Cambridge: Polity Press).

Dietler, M. (1994) ' "Our Ancesters the Gauls": Archaeology, Ethnic Nationalism and the Manipulation of Celtic Identity in Modern Europe', *American Anthropologist*, 96, 584–605.

Dirlik, A. (1992) 'The Postcolonial Aura: Third World Criticism in the Age of Global Capitalism', *Critical Enquiry*, Winter.

Diuk, N. and Karatnycky, A. 1993 *New Nations Rising – The Fall of the Soviets and the Challenge of Independence* (New York: Wiley).

Donia, R. and Fine, J. (1994) *Bosnia and Herzegovina – A Tradition Betrayed* (London: Hurst).

Donnelly, J. (1998) *International Human Rights* (Oxford: Westview).

Douglas, M. (1966) *Purity and Danger* (London: Routledge).

Dowling, M. (1997) '"Not merely free but Gaelic as well": the creation of an exclusionary Irish national identity' (paper presented at European Sociological Association Conference, Essex University).

Duignan, P. and Gann, L. (1998) *The Debate in the United States Over Immigration* (Stanford, CA: Hoover Institution Press).

Dummett, A. (1992) 'Natural Law and Transnational Migration', in Barry, R. and Goodin, R. (eds), *Free Movement – Ethical Issues in the Transnational Movement of People and Money* (London: Harvester).

Dunn, J. (1992) *Democracy, the Unfinished Journey, 508 BC to AD 1993* (Oxford: Oxford University Press).

Durkheim, E. (1973) *Moral Education – A Study in the Theory and Application of the Sociology of Education* (New York: Free Press).

Durkheim, E. (1976) *The Elementary Forms of the Religious Life* (London: Allen and Unwin).

Eagleton, T. (2000) *The Idea of Culture* (Oxford: Blackwell).

Edensor, T. (1997) 'Reading Braveheart: Representing and Contesting Scottish Identity', *Scottish Affairs*, 21, 135–58.

Edwards, J. (1985) *Language, Society and Identity* (Oxford: Blackwell).

Eller, J. and Coughlan, R. (1993) 'The Poverty of Primordialism – The Demystification of Ethnic Attachments', *Ethnic and Racial Studies*, 16, 2.

Elshtain, Jean Bethke, (1993) 'Sovereignty, Identity, and Sacrifice', in Lerner, M. and Ringrose, A. (eds), *Reimagining the Nation* (Milton Keynes: Open University Press).

Ely, J. (1997) 'Community and the Politics of Identity: Towards the Genealogy of the Nation-State', *Stanford Electronic Humanities Review*, 5, 2.

Emsley, C. (1987) 'Nationalist Rhetoric and Nationalist Sentiment in Revolutionary France', in Dann, O. and Dinwiddy, J. (eds), *Nationalism in the Age of the French Revolution* (London: Hambledon).

Engels, F. (1976) 'The Festival of Nations in London', *Marx and Engels Collected Works* (London: Lawrence and Wishart).

Engels, F. (1977) 'The Magyar Struggle', *Marx and Engels Collected Works* (London: Lawrence and Wishart).

Engels, F. (1980) 'Po and Rhine', *Marx and Engels Collected Works* (London: Lawrence and Wishart).

Eriksen, T. (1993) *Ethnicity and Nationalism* (London: Pluto Press).

Evans, M. (1996) 'Languages of Racism Within Contemporary Europe', in Jenkins, B. and Sofos, S. (eds), *Nation and Identity in Contemporary Europe* (Routledge: London).

Evans, R. (1987) *Rethinking German History* (London: Allen and Unwin).

Faist, T. (1998) 'Transnational Social Spaces Out Of International Migration:

Evolution, Significance and Future Prospects', *European Journal of Sociology*, XXXIX, 2, 213–47.

Feagin, J. (1997) 'Old Wine in New Bottles', in Perea, J. (ed.), *Immigrants Out! The New Nativism and the Anti-Immigrant Impulse in the United States* (New York: New York University Press).

Fekete, L. (1998) 'Popular Racism in Corporate Europe', *Race and Class*, 40, 2/3.

Fekete, L and Webber, F. (1994) 'Inside Racist Europe', *Race and Class*, 29, 3.

Fentress, J. and Wickham, C. (1992) *Social Memory* (Oxford: Blackwell).

Finlayson, A. (1998) 'Psychology, Psychoanalysis, and Theories of Nationalism', *Nations and Nationalism*, 4, 2.

Fishman, J. (1972) *Language and Nationalism – Two Integrative Essays* (Rowley: Newbury House Publishers).

Fitzgerald, J. (1996) *Awakening China – Politics, Culture and Class in the Nationalist Revolution* (Stanford, CA: Stanford University Press).

Fraser, N. (1997) 'Equality, Difference, and Democracy – Recent Feminist Debates in the USA', in Dean, J. (ed.), *Feminism and the New Democracy – Resiting the Political* (London: Sage).

Freeman, G. (1986) 'Migration and the Political Economy of the Welfare State', *Annals of the American Academy of Political and Social Science*, 526, 51–63.

Friedman, J. (1995) 'Global System, Globalization and the Parameters of Modernity', in Featherstone, M., Lash, S. and Robertson, R. (eds), *Globalization as Hybridization* (London: Sage).

Fulbrook, M. (1999) *German National Identity after the Holocaust* (Cambridge: Polity Press).

Gandhi, L. (1998) *Postcolonial Theory: A Critical Introduction* (Edinburgh: Edinburgh University Press).

Gauthier, F. (1987) 'Universal Rights and National Interest in the French Revolution', in Dann, O. and Dinwiddy, J. (eds), *Nationalism in the Age of the French Revolution* (London: Hambledon).

Geertz, C. (1973) *The Interpretation of Cultures* (New York: Basic Books).

Gellner, E. (1965) *Thought and Change* (London: Weidenfeld and Nicholson).

Gellner, E. (1983) *Nations and Nationalism* (Oxford: Blackwell).

Gellner, E. (1994) *Conditions of Liberty: Civil Society and its Rivals* (London: Hamish Hamilton).

Gellner, E. (1996a) 'The Coming of Nationalism and its Interpretation: The Myths of Nation and Class', in Balakrishnan, G. (ed.), *Mapping the Nation* (London: Verso).

Gellner, E. (1996b) 'Reply to Critics', in Hall, J. and Jarvie, I. (eds), *The Social Philosophy of Ernest Gellner* (Amsterdam: Rodopi).

George, S. (2001) 'What Now', *International Socialism*, 91, 3–10.

Geras, N. (1995) 'Language, Truth and Justice', *New Left Review*, 209.

Geras, N. (1998) *The Contract of Mutual Indifference* (London:Verso).

Gianni, M. (1997) 'Multiculturalism and Political Integration: The Need for a Differentiated Citizenship?', in Wicker, H. (ed.), *Rethinking Nation and Ethnicity* (Oxford: Berg).

Gibbins, J.R. and Reimer, B. (1999) *The Politics of Postmodernity* (London: Sage).

Giddens, A. (1985) *The Nation State and Violence* (Cambridge: Polity Press).

Giddens, A. (ed.) (1986) *Durkheim on Politics and the State* (Cambridge: Polity Press).

Giddens, A. (1990) *The Consequences of Modernity* (Cambridge: Polity Press).

Giddens, A. (1993) *Sociology* (Cambridge: Polity Press).

Gillis, J. (ed.) (1994) *Commemorations. The Politics of National Identity* (Princeton, NJ: Princeton University Press).

Gilroy, P. (1993) 'The Peculiarities of the Black English', in Gilroy. P., *Small Acts – Thoughts on the Politics of Black Cultures* (London: Serpent's Tail).

Gilroy, P. (2000) *Between Camps* (London: Allen Lane).

Glenny, M. (1999) *The Balkans 1804–1999: Nationalism, War and the Great Powers* (London: Granta Books).

Goitein, S. (1967) *A Mediterranean Society: The Jewish Communities of the Arab World as Portrayed in the Documents of the Cairo Geniza* (Berkeley, CA: University of California Press).

Goldmann, K. (1994) *The Logic of Internationalism – Coercion and Accommodation* (London: Routledge).

Goldstein, I. (1999) *Croatia, a History* (London: Hurst).

Goodin, R. (1992) 'If People Were Money', in Barry, R. and Goodin, R. (eds), *Free Movement – Ethical Issues in the Transnational Movement of People and Money* (London: Harvester).

Goodman, J. (1997) 'The European Union: Reconstituting Democracy Beyond the Nation-State', in McGrew, A. (ed.), *The Transformation of Democracy?* (Cambridge: Polity Press).

Goodwin-White, J. (1998) 'Where the Maps are Not Yet Finished', in Jacobson, D. (ed.), *The Immigration Reader – America in a Multi-Disciplinary Perspective* (Oxford: Blackwell).

Goody, J. (1994) 'Culture and its Boundaries: A European View', in Borofsky, R. (ed.), *Assessing Cultural Anthropology* (New York: McGraw Hill).

Gourevitch, P. (1999) *We Wish To Inform You that Tomorrow We Will Be Killed with Our Families – Stories from Rwanda* (London: Picador).

Gramsci, A. (1971) 'The Study of Philosophy', in Hoare, Q. and Nowell-Smith, G. (eds), *Selections from the Prison Notebooks* (London: Lawrence and Wishart).

Gras, C. (1972) *Alfred Rosmer et le Mouvement Revolutionnaire International* (Paris: Maspero).

Grass, G. (1990) *Two States – One Nation? The Case Against German Reunification* (London: Secker & Warburg).

Gray, V. (1996) 'Identity and Democracy in the Baltics', *Democratization*, 3 (2), 69–91.

Greenfeld, L. (1992) *Nationalism. Five Roads to Modernity* (Cambridge: Cambridge University Press).

Guerin, D. (1977) *Class Struggle in the First French Republic – Bourgeois and Bras Nus, 1793–1795* (London: Pluto Press).

Guibernau, M. (1996) *Nationalisms – The Nation State and Nationalism in the Twentieth Century* (Cambridge: Polity Press).

Habermas, J. (1992) 'Citizenship and National Identity – Some Reflections on the Future of Europe', *Praxis International*, 12 (1) 1–19.

Habermas, J. (1994) *The Past as Future* (Cambridge: Polity Press).

Hague, E. (1997) 'Rape, Power, and Masculinity: The Construction of Gender and National Identity in the War in Bosnia–Herzegovina', in Lentin, R. (ed.), *Gender and Catastrophe* (London: Zed Books).

Hall, J. (1996) 'How Homogenous Need We Be? Reflections on Nationalism and Liberty', *Sociology*, 30, 1.

Hall, J. (1998) 'Introduction' in Hall, J. (ed.), *The State of the Nation – Ernest Gellner and the Theory of Nationalism* (Cambridge: Cambridge University Press).

Hall, S. (1991) 'The Local and the Global: Globalization and Ethnicity', in King, A.D. (ed.), *Culture, Globalization and the World System: Contemporary Conditions for the Representation of Identity* (Basingstoke: Macmillan).

Hall, S. (1992a) 'The Question of Cultural Identity', in Hall, S. Held, D. and McGrew, T. (eds), *Modernity and its Futures* (Cambridge: Polity Press).

Hall, S. (1992b) 'The West and the Rest', in Hall, S. and Gieben, B. (eds), *Formations of Modernity* (Cambridge: Polity Press).

Hall, S. (1996) 'When was "The Post-Colonial"? Thinking at the Limit', in Chambers, I. and Curti, L. (eds), *Common Skies, Divided Horizons* (London: Routledge).

Hallas, D. (1985) *The Comintern* (London: Bookmarks).

Hammar, T. (1990) *Democracy and the Nation-State Aliens, Denizens and Citizens* (Aldershot: Avebury).

Hampson, N. (1991) 'The Idea of the Nation in Revolutionary France', in Forest, A. and Jones, P. (eds), *Reshaping France – Town, Country and Region during the French Revolution* (Manchester: Manchester University Press).

Handler, R. (1994) 'Is "Identity" a Useful Cross-cultural Concept', in Gillis, J. (ed.), *Commemorations – The Politics of National Identity* (Princeton, NJ: Princeton University Press).

Hann, C. (1995) 'Intellectuals, Ethnic Groups and Nations: Two Late-twentieth-century Cases', in Periwal, S. (ed.), *Notions of Nationalism* (Budapest: Central European University Press).

Hannum, H. (1996) 'Self-Determination in the Post-Colonial Era', in Clark, D. and Williamson, R. (eds), *Self-Determination – International Perspectives* (Basingstoke: Macmillan).

Hargreaves, A. (1995) *Immigration, 'Race' and Ethnicity in Contemporary France* (London: Routledge).

Hargreaves, J. (1998) 'Ethno-nationalist movements in Europe: a Debate', *Nations and Nationalism*, 4 (4), 569–77.

Harris, N. (1992) *National Liberation* (Harmondsworth: Penguin).

Harvie, C. (1994) *Scotland and Nationalism: Scottish Society and Politics, 1707–1994*, second edition (London: Routledge).

Hastings, A. (1997) *The Construction of Nationhood – Ethnicity, Religion and Nationalism* (Cambridge: Cambridge University Press).

Hatton, T. and Williamson, J. (1998) *The Age of Mass Migration* (Oxford: Oxford University Press).

Hawkins, M. (1997) *Social Darwinism in European and American Thought, 1860–1945: Nature as Model and Nature as Threat* (Cambridge: Cambridge University Press).

Hawkins, M. (1999) (personal communication).

Hayes, C. (1926) *Essays on Nationalism* (New York: Macmillan).

Hayes, C. (1960) *Nationalism: A Religion* (New York: Macmillan).

Hayter, T. (2000) *Open Borders: The Case Against Immigration Controls* (London: Pluto Press).

Heater, D. (1996) *World Citizenship and Government – Cosmopolitan Ideas in the History of Western Political Thought* (Basingstoke: Macmillan).

Held, D. (1987) *Models of Democracy* (Cambridge: Polity Press).

Held, D. (1992) 'Democracy: From City-States to a Cosmopolitan Order?', *Political Studies*, XL, Special Issue – Prospects for Democracy.

Held, D. (1995) *Democracy and the Global Order* (Cambridge: Polity Press).

Held, D., McGrew, A., Goldblatt, D. and Perraton, J. (1999 *Global Transformations – Politics, Economics and Culture* (Cambridge: Polity Press).

Herzfeld, M. (1982) *Ours Once More: Folklore, Ideology, and the Making of Modern Greece* (Austin, TX: University of Texas Press).

Hintjens, H. (1995) *Alternatives to Independence – Explorations in Post Colonial Relations* (Aldershot: Dartmouth).

Hirschman, A.O. (1970) *Exit, Voice and Loyalty* (Cambridge, MA: Harvard University Press).

Hirst, P. and Thompson, G. (1996) *Globalization in Question* (Cambridge: Polity Press).

Hobsbawm, E. (1992) *Nations and Nationalism since 1780*, second edition (Cambridge: Cambridge University Press).

Hobsbawm, E. (1996) 'Ethnicity and Nationalism in Europe Today', in Balakrishnan, G. (ed.), *Mapping the Nation* (London: Verso).

Hobsbawm, E. and Ranger, T. (eds) (1983) *The Invention of Tradition* (Cambridge: Cambridge University Press).

Hodson, R., Sekulic, D. and Massey, G. (1994) 'National Tolerance in the Former Yugoslavia', *American Journal of Sociology*, 99, 6.

Hoff, J. (1996) 'Citizenship and Nationalism', *Journal of Women's History*, 8 (1), 1–6.

Hoffman, J. (1998) *Sovereignty* (Milton Keynes: Open University Press).

Holton, R. (1998) *Globalization and the Nation-State* (Basingstoke: Macmillan).

Holy, L. (1996) *The Little Czech and the Great Czech Nation* (Cambridge: Cambridge University Press).

Hondt, I. (1995) 'The Permanent Crisis of a Divided Mankind', in Dunn, J. (ed.), *Contemporary Crisis of the Nation State* (Oxford: Blackwell).

Honig, B. (1998) 'Ruth, the Model Émigré', in Cheah, P. and Robbins, B. (eds), *Cosmopolitics – Thinking and Feeling Beyond the Nation* (Minneapolis, MN: University of Minnesota Press).

Horowitz, D. (1998) 'Immigration and Group Politics in France and America', in Jacobson, D. (ed.), *The Immigration Reader – America in a Multi-Disciplinary Perspective* (Oxford: Blackwell).

Hosking, G. and Schöpflin, G. (1997 *Myths and Nationhood* (London: Hurst).

Hoston, G. (1994) *The State, Identity and the National Question in China and Japan* (Princeton, NJ: Princeton University Press).

Hroch, M. (1993) 'From National Movement to the Fully-Formed Nation', *New Left Review*, 198, 3–20.

Hufton, O. (1992) *Women and the Limits of Citizenship in the French Revolution* (Toronto: University of Toronto Press).

Hughes, M. (1988) *Nationalism and Society – Germany 1800–1945* (London: Edward Arnold).

Human Rights Watch (1998a) *'Prohibited Persons' – Abuse of Undocumented Migrants, Asylum Seekers, and Refugees in South Africa* (New York). http://www. hrw.org/reports98/sarepor
http://www.hrw.org/reports98/sarepor/Adv5a.htm

Human Rights Watch (with the Sentencing Project) (1998b) *Losing the Vote: The Impact of Felony Disenfranchisement Laws in the United States* (New York). http://www.hrw.org/reports98/vote/

Husbands, C. (1994) 'Crises of National Identity as the "New Moral Panics": Political Agenda Setting about Definitions of Nationhood', *New Community*, 20 (2) 191–206.

Husbands, C. (1999) '"How to Tame the Dragon" or "What Goes Around Comes Around" – A Critical Review of Some Major Contemporary Attempts to Account for Extreme-Right Racist Politics in Western Europe', paper presented at British Sociological Association Conference, 'For Sociology', University of Glasgow, 6–9 April.

Hutchinson, J. (1994) *Modern Nationalism* (London: Fontana).

Hutchinson, J. and Smith, A. (eds) (1994) *Nationalism* (Oxford: Oxford University Press).

Ignatieff, M. (1994) *Blood and Belonging: Journeys into the New Nationalism* (London: Vintage).

Inden, R. (1997) 'Transcending Identities in Modern India's World', in Dean, K. (ed.), *Politics and the End of Identity* (Aldershot: Ashgate).

Jacobson, D. (1996) *Rights Across Borders – Immigration and the Decline of Citizenship* (Baltimore, MD: Johns Hopkins University Press).

Jacobson, D. (1998) 'Introduction – An American Journey', in Jacobson, D. (ed.), *The Immigration Reader – America in a Multi-Disciplinary Perspective* (Oxford: Blackwell).

James, P. (1996) *Nation Formation – Towards a Theory of Abstract Community* (London: Sage).

James, S. (1999) *The Atlantic Celts – Ancient People or Modern Invention?* (London: British Museum Press).

Jarabova, Z. (1998) 'The Romany Minority in the Czech Lands', in Joly, D. (ed.), *Scapegoats and Social Actors – The Exclusion and Integration of Minorities in Western Europe* (Basingstoke: Macmillan).

Jarausch, K. and Gransow, V. (eds) (1994) *Reuniting Germany – Documents and Debates* (Oxford: Oxford University Press).

Jayawardena, K. (1986) *Feminism and Nationalism in the Third World* (London: Zed Books).

Jenkins, B. (1990) *Nationalism in France – Class and Nation since 1789* (London: Routledge).

Jenkins, B. and Copsey, N. (1996) 'Nation, Nationalism, and National Identity in France', in Jenkins, B. and Sofos, S. (eds), *Nation and Identity in Contemporary Europe* (London: Routledge).

Jenkins, B. and Sofos, A.S. (eds) (1996) *Nation and Identity in Contemporary Europe* (London: Routledge).

Jenkins, K. (1995) *On 'What is History?': from Carr and Elton to Rorty and White* (London: Routledge).

Jenkins, R. (1996) *Social Identity* (London: Routledge)

Jenkins, R. (1997) *Rethinking Ethnicity: Arguments and Explorations* (London: Sage).

John, M. (1998) 'A Response from India', *Gender and History*, 10 (3), 539–48.

Johnson, D. (1987) 'The Making of the French Nation', in Dann, O. and Dinwiddy, J. (eds), *Nationalism in the Age of the French Revolution* (London: Hambledon).

Jones, A. (1994) 'Gender and Ethnic Conflict in ex-Yugoslavia', *Ethnic and Racial Studies*, 17 (1), 115–29.

Joppke, C. (1997) 'Asylum and State Sovereignty: A Comparison of the United States, Germany and Britain', in Joppke, C. (ed.), *Challenge to the Nation State* (Oxford: Oxford University Press).

Judah, T. (1997) *The Serbs – History, Myth and the Destruction of Yugoslavia* (New Haven, CT: Yale University Press).

Juteau, D. (1996) 'Theorising Ethnicity and Ethnic Communalisations at the Margins: from Quebec to the World System', *Nations and Nationalism*, 2 (1), 45–66.

Kaiser, D. (1994) 'Lessons in the History of Nationalism', *Theory and Society*, 23 (1), 147–50.

Kamenka, E. (1976) *Nationalism: The Nature and Evolution of an Idea* (London: Edward Arnold).

Kant, I. (1970) *Political Writings* (Cambridge: Cambridge University Press).

Kaplan, G. (1997) 'Feminism and Nationalism: The European Case', in West, L. (ed.), *Feminist Nationalism* (New York: Routledge).

Karakasidou, A. (1993) 'Politicizing Culture: Negating Ethnic Identity in Greek Macedonia', *Journal of Modern Greek Studies*, 11 (1), 1–28.

Karakasidou, A. (1994) 'Sacred Scholars, Profane Advocates: Intellectuals Moulding National Consciousness in Greece', *Identities*, 1 (1), 35–61.

Karklins, R. (1994) *Ethnopolitics and Transition to Democracy – The Collapse of the USSR and Latvia* (Baltimore, MD: Johns Hopkins University Press).

Keane, J. (1994) 'Nations, Nationalism and Citizens in Europe', *International Social Science Journal*, 46 (2), 169–84.

Keating, M. (1996) *Nations against the State: The New Politics of Nationalism in Quebec, Catalonia, and Scotland* (Basingstoke: Macmillan).

Keating, M. (1997) 'Stateless Nation-building: Quebec, Catalonia and Scotland in the Changing State System', *Nations and Nationalism*, 3 (4), 689–717.

Kedourie, E. (1993) *Nationalism*, 4th edn (Oxford: Blackwell).

Keeley, C. (1993) 'The USA – Retaining a Fair Immigration Policy', in Kubat, D. (ed.), *The Politics of Migration Policies*, second edition (New York: Centre for Migration Studies).

Keesing, R. (1994) 'Theories of Culture Revisited', in Borofsky, R. (ed.), *Assessing Cultural Anthropology* (New York: McGraw Hill).

Kellas, J. (1991) *The Politics of Nationalism and Ethnicity* (London: Macmillan).

Khilnani, S. (1997) *The Idea of India* (Harmondsworth: Penguin).

Kionka, R. and Vetik, P. (1996) 'Estonia and the Estonians', in Smith, G. (ed.), *The Nationalities Question in the Post Soviet States* (Basingstoke: Macmillan).

Kitromilides, P. (1990) 'Imagined Communities and the Origins of the Nation in the Balkans', in *Modern Greece – Nationalism and Nationality* (Athens: Eliamer).

Kohn, H. (1965) *Nationalism: Its Meaning and History* (New York: Anvil).

Kostakopolou, T. (1998) 'European Citizenship and Immigration after Amsterdam', *Journal of Ethnic and Migration Studies*, 24 (4), 639–56.

Kurti, L. (1997) 'Globalisation and the Discourse of Otherness in the "New" Eastern and Central Europe', in Modood, T. and Werbner, P. (eds), *The Politics of Multiculturalism in the New Europe – Racism, Identity and Community* (London: Zed Books).

Kymlicka, W. (1995) *Multicultural Citizenship – A Liberal Theory of Minority Rights* (Oxford: Oxford University Press).

Laitin, D. (1997) 'The Cultural Identities of a European State', *Politics and Society*, 25 (3) 277–302.

Laitin, D. (1998) 'Nationalism and Language – a Post-Soviet Perspective', in Hall, J. (ed.), *The State of the Nation – Ernest Gellner and the Theory of Nationalism* (Cambridge: Cambridge University Press).

Langeswiehe, D. (1992) 'Germany and the National Question', in Breuilly, J. (ed.), *The State of Germany – The National Idea in the Making, Unmaking and Remaking* (London: Longman).

Lapidus, I. (2001) 'Between Universalism and Particularism: The Historical Bases of Muslim Communal, National, and Global Identities', *Global Networks*, 1, 1.

Lassman, P. and Speirs, R. (1994, 'Introduction', in *Max Weber: Political Writings* (Cambridge: Cambridge University Press).

Lavrin, A., (1998) 'International Feminism – Latin American Alternatives', *Gender and History*, 10 (3) 519–34.

Le Galès, P. and Lequesne, C. (eds) (1998 *Regions in Europe* (London: Routledge).

Lenin, V. (1970) *Imperialism – The Highest Stage of Capitalism* (Peking: Foreign Language Press).

Lentin, R. (2000) *Israel and the Daughters of the Shoah – Reoccupying the Territories of Silence* (Oxford: Berghahn Books)

Lewis, G. (1998) 'Citizenship', in Hughes, G. (ed.), *Imagining Welfare Futures* (London: Routledge).

Lijphart, A. (1977) *Democracy in Plural Societies – A Comparative Exploration* (New Haven, CT: Yale University Press).

Lindquist, S. (1998) *Exterminate all the Brutes* (London: Granta).

Llobera, J. (1994a) *The God of Modernity: The Development of Nationalism in Western Europe* (Oxford: Berg).

Llobera, J. (1994b) 'Durkheim and the National Question', in Pickering, W. and Martins, H. (eds), *Debating Durkheim* (London: Routledge).

Lloyd, C. (1998) *Discourses of Anti-Racism in France* (London: Ashgate).

Löwy, M. (1993) 'Why Nationalism?', in Miliband, R.A. and Panitch, L. (eds), *Socialist Register* (London: Merlin).

Löwy, M. (1998) *Fatherland or Mother Earth?* (London: Pluto Press).

Lucas, C. (1988) 'The Crowd and Politics', in Lucas, C. (ed.), *The French Revolution and the Creation of Modern Political Culture*, vol. 3 (Oxford: Pergamon).

Lucassen, J. and Lucassen, L. (1997) 'Introduction – Old Paradigms and New Perspectives', in Lucassen, J. and Lucassen, L. (eds), *Migration, Migration History, History* (Berne: Peter Lang, European Academic Publishers).

Luxemburg, R. (1970a) 'The Junius Pamphlet: The Crisis in German Social Democracy', in Waters, M.A. (ed.), *Rosa Luxemburg Speaks* (New York: Pathfinder).

Luxemburg, R. (1970b) 'The Russian Revolution', in Waters, M.A. (ed.), *Rosa Luxemburg Speaks* (New York: Pathfinder).

Luxemburg, R. (1976) 'The National Question and Autonomy' in Davis, H. (ed.), *Selected Writings by Rosa Luxemburg on the National Question* (New York: Monthly Review Press).

Mack Smith, D. (1994) *Mazzini* (New Haven, CT: Yale University Press).

Maier, C. (1988) *The Unmasterable Past: History, Holocaust and German National Identity* (Cambridge, MA: Harvard University Press).

Malik, K. (1996)*The Meaning of Race – Race, History and Culture in Western Society* (Basingstoke: Macmillan).

Mamdani, M. (1996) 'From Conquest to Consent as the Basis of State Formation: Reflections on Rwanda', *New Left Review*, 216, 3–36.

Manent, P. (1997) 'Democracy without Nations?', *Journal of Democracy*, 8 (2), 92–102.

Mann, M. (1996) 'The Emergence of Modern European Nationalism', in Hall, J. and Jarvie, I. (eds), *The Social Philosophy of Ernest Gellner* (Amsterdam: Rodopi).

Mann, M. (1997) 'Has Globalization Ended the Rise and Rise of the Nation-State?', *Review of International Political Economy*, 4 (3), 472–96.

Marable, M. (1998) 'Black Fundamentalism: Farrakhan and Conservative Black Nationalism', *Race and Class*, 39 (4), 1–22.

Markoff, J. (1996) *Waves of Democracy – Social Movements and Political Change* (London: Pine Forge Press).

Marr, A. (2000) 'Blair's McChancers', *The Guardian*, 15 January.

Martiniello, M. (1997) 'The Development of European Union Citizenship – A Critical Evaluation', in Roche, M. and Van Berkel, R. (eds), *European Citizenship and Social Exclusion* (Aldershot: Ashgate).

Marvin, C. and Ingle, D. (1996) 'Blood Sacrifice and the Nation – Revisiting Civil Religion', *Journal of the American Academy of Religion*, 64, 4.

Marx, K. (1975) 'Critique of List', *Marx and Engels Collected Works* (London: Lawrence and Wishart).

Marx, K. and Engels, F. (1976) 'Manifesto of the Communist Party', *Marx and Engels Collected Works, volume 6* (London: Lawrence and Wishart).

Mattes, R., et al. (1999) 'Still Waiting for the Barbarians: SA Attitudes to Immigrants and Immigration', *Migration Policy Series No. 14*, The Southern African Migration Project, (Cape Town: Idasa).

Mayer, A. (1990) *Why Did The Heavens Not Darken?* (London: Verso).

McClintock, A. (1993) 'Family Feuds: Gender Nationalism and the Family', *Feminist Review*, 44, 61–80.

McClintock, A. (1996) '"No Longer in a Future Heaven": Nationalism, Gender and Race', in Eley, G. and Suny, R. (eds), *Becoming National* (Oxford: Oxford University Press).

McClintock, A., Mufti, A. and Shohat, E. (eds) (1997 *Dangerous Liaisons: Gender, National and Postcolonial Perspectives* (Minneapolis, MN: University of Minnesota Press).

MacCormick, N. (1982) *Legal Right and Social Democracy* (Oxford: Clarendon Press).

McCrone, D. (1998) *Sociology of Nationalism* (London: Routledge).

McGarry, J. and O' Leary, B. (1993) 'Introduction', in McGarry, J. and O'Leary, B. (eds), *The Politics of Ethnic Conflict Regulation: Case Studies of Protracted Ethnic Conflicts* (London: Routledge).

Meier, V. (1999) *Yugoslavia – A History of Its Demise* (London: Routledge).

Mertens, T. (1996) 'Cosmopolitanism and Citizenship – Kant against Habermas', *European Journal of Philosophy*, 4, 3.

Mertes, M. (1996) 'Germany's Social and Political Culture: Change Through Consensus?' in Mertes, M., Muller, M. and Winkler, H. (eds), *In Search of Germany* (New Brunswick, NJ: Transaction Publishers).

Mezo, J. (1994) 'Nationalist Political Elites and Language in Ireland 1922–1937', in Beramendi, J., Maiz, R. and Nunez, X. (eds), *Nationalism in Europe Past and Present* (Santiago de Compostela: Universidade de Santiago de Compostela).

Migration News (1998a) 'Canada: Immigration Down' (Davis, CA: http:/migration. ucdavis.edu).

Migration News (1998b) 'Germany: Citizenship Changes' (Davis, CA: http:/migration. ucdavis.edu).

Migration News (1998c) 'South Africa' (Davis, CA: http:/migration.ucdavis.edu).

Miles, R. (1987) 'Recent Marxist Theories of Nationalism and the Issue of Racism', *British Journal of Sociology*, 38 (1), 24–43.

Miles, R. (1993) 'Nationalism and Racism: Antithesis and Articulation', in Miles, R., *Racism after Race Relations* (London: Routledge).

Mill, J.S. (1996) 'On Nationality', in Woolf, S. (ed.), *Nationalism in Europe 1815 to the Present* (London: Routledge).

Miller, D. (1995) *On Nationality* (Oxford: Oxford University Press).

Minogue, K. (1967) *Nationalism* (London: Batsford).

Mitchell, M. and Russell, D. (1996) 'Immigration, Citizenship and the Nation-State in the New Europe' in Jenkins, B. and Sofos, A.S. (eds), *Nation and Identity in Contemporary Europe*, (London: Routledge).

Moghadam, V. (ed.) (1994) *Gender and National Identity: Women and Politics in Muslim Societies* (London: Zed Books).

Mommsen, W. (1984) *Max Weber and German Politics, 1890–1920* (Chicago: University of Chicago Press).

Moore, M. (1997) 'On National Self Determination', *Political Studies*, xlv, 900–13.

Morgan, R. (ed.) (1984) *Sisterhood is Global: The International Women's Movement Anthology*, Garden City, NY: Doubleday.

Morley, D. (2000) *Home Territories – Media, Mobility and Identity* (London: Routledge).

Moruzzi, N. (1994) 'A Problem with Headscarves: Contemporary Complexities of Political and Social Identity', *Political Theory*, 22 (4), 653–72.

Mouffe, C. (1998) *The Return of the Political* (London: Verso).

Mouzelis, N. (1988) 'Ernest Gellner's Theory of Nationalism: Some Definitional and Methodological Issues', in Hall, J. (ed.), *The State of the Nation – Ernest Gellner and the Theory of Nationalism* (Cambridge: Cambridge University Press).

Mufti, A. and Shohat, E. (1997) 'Introduction', in McClintock, A., Mufti, A. and Shohat, E. (eds), *Dangerous Liaisons – Gender, Nation and Postcolonial Perspectives* (Minneapolis, MN: University of Minnesota).

Muizniecks, N. (1993) 'Latvia: Origins, Evolution, and Triumph', in Bremmer, I. and Taras, R. (eds), *Nations and Politics in the Soviet Successor States* (Cambridge: Cambridge University Press).

Mullerson, R. (1995) 'Human Rights in the Multi-Cultural World', in Desai, M. (ed.), *Global Governance, Ethics and Economics of the World Order* (London: Pinter).

Munck, R. (1986) *The Difficult Dialogue: Marxism and Nationalism* (London: Zed Books).

Munslow, A. (1997) *Deconstructing History* (London: Routledge).

Murray, S and Hong, K. (1988) 'Taiwan, China and the "Objectivity" of Dictatorial Elites', *American Anthropologist*, 90 (3), 976–8.

Nairn, T. (1977) 'The Modern Janus', in Nairn, T. (ed.), *TheBreak-up of Britain* (London: New Left Books).

Nairn, T. (1996) 'Internationalism and the Second Coming', in Balakrishnan, G. (ed.), *Mapping the Nation* (London: Verso).

Nairn, T. (1997a) 'Introduction: On Studying Nationalism', in Nairn, T. (ed.), *Faces of Nationalism – Janus Revisited* (London: Verso).

Nairn, T. (1997b) *Faces of Nationalism: Janus Revisited* (London: Verso).

Namier, L. (1944) *1848: Revolution of the Intellectuals* (London: Geoffrey Cumberlege).

Nando.net/The Associated Press (1997) 'http://www.business-server.com/newsroom/ntn/122397/world10_13856_body.html' (accessed May, 1998).

Nandy, A. (1994) *The Illegitimacy of Nationalism* (Oxford: Oxford University Press).

Nelson, S. (1995) 'The Politics of Ethnicity in Pre-historic Korea', in Kohl, P. and Fawcett, C. (eds), *Nationalism, Politics and the Practice of Archaeology* (Cambridge: Cambridge University Press).

Neuberger, B. (1995) 'National Self-Determination – Dilemmas of a Concept', *Nations and Nationalism*, 1, 3.

Nimni, E. (1991) *Marxism and Nationalism: Theoretical Origins of the Present Crisis* (London: Pluto).

Nodia, G. (1994) 'Nationalism and Democracy', in Diamond, L. and Plattner, M. (eds), *Nationalism, Ethnic Conflict and Democracy* (Baltimore, MD: Johns Hopkins University Press).

Noel, S. (1993) 'Canadian Responses to Ethnic Conflict – Consociationalism, Federalism and Control', in McGarry, J. and O' Leary, B. (eds), *The Politics of*

Ethnic Conflict Regulation: Case Studies of Protracted Ethnic Conflicts (London: Routledge).

Noiriel, G. (1988) *Le Creuset français – histoire de l'immigration XIX–XX siècles* (Paris: Seuil).

Noiriel, G. (1993) *La Tyrannie du national: le droit d'asile en Europe, 1793–1993* (Paris: Calmann-Levy).

Nørgaard, O. with Hindsgaul, D., Johannsen, L. and Williamsen, H. (1996) *The Baltic States after Independence* (Cheltenham: Edward Elgar).

O'Dowd, L. and Wilson, T. (1996) 'Frontiers of Sovereignty in the New Europe', in O'Dowd, L. and Wilson, T. (eds), *Borders, Nations and States* (Aldershot: Avebury).

O'Leary, B. (1996) 'On the Nature of Nationalism: an Appraisal of Ernest Gellner's Writings on Nationalism', in Hall, J. and Jarvie, I. (eds), *The Social Philosophy of Ernest Gellner* (Amsterdam: Rodopi).

O'Leary, B. (1999) 'The Nature of the British-Irish Agreement', *New Left Review*, 233, 66–96.

O'Sullivan, N. (1976) *Conservatism* (London: Dent).

Olukoshi, A. and Laakso, L. (1996) 'The Crisis in the Postcolonial State Project in Africa', in Olukoshi, A. and Laakso, L. (eds), *Challenges to the Nation State in Africa* (Uppsala: Nordiska Afrikaansinstitut).

Ong, A. (1998) 'Flexible Citizenship among Chinese Cosmopolitans', in Cheah, P. and Robbins, B. (eds), *Cosmopolitics – Thinking and Feeling Beyond the Nation* (Minneapolis, MN: University of Minnesota Press).

Oommen, T. (1997) *Citizenship and National Identity from Colonialism to Globalism* (New Delhi: Sage).

Overing, J. (1997) 'The Role of Myth: An Anthropological Perspective', in Hosking, G. and Schopflin, G. (eds), *Myths and Nationhood* (London: Hurst).

Papastergiadis, N. (2000) *The Turbulence of Migration* (Cambridge: Polity Press).

Paterson, L. (1994) *The Autonomy of Modern Scotland* (Edinburgh: Edinburgh University Press).

Paterson, L., Brown, A. and Curtice, J. (2001) *New Scotland, New Politics?* (Edinburgh: Polygon).

Paul, K. (1997) *Whitewashing Britain – Race and Citizenship in the Postwar Era* (New York: Cornell University Press).

Pavlowitch, S.K. (1999) *A History of the Balkans 1804–1945* (London: Longman).

Penrose, J. (1995) 'Essential Constructions? The "Cultural Bases" of Nationalist Movements', *Nations and Nationalism*, 1 (3) 391–417.

Perea, J. (1997) 'Introduction', in Perea, J. (ed.), *Immigrants Out! The New Nativism and the Anti-Immigrant Impulse in the United States* (New York: New York University Press).

Perera, S. (1998/9) 'The Level Playing Field: Hansonism, Globalization, Racism', *Capital and Class*, 40 (2/3), 199–208.

Perera, S. and Pugliese, J. (1997) '"Racial Suicide": The Re-licensing of Racism in Australia', *Race and Class*, 39 (2), 1–19.

Perlmutter, H. (1991) 'On the Rocky Road to the First Global Civilization', *Human Relations*, 44, 9.

Pettai, V. (1993) 'Estonia: "Old Maps and New Roots"', *Journal of Democracy*, 4, 1.

Pettman, J. (1996) *Worlding Women – A Feminist International Politics* (London: Routledge).

Philipsen, D. (1993) *We Were the People – Voices from East Germany's Revolutionary Autumn of 1989* (Durham, NC: Duke University Press).

Phillips, C. (ed.) (1997) *Extravagant Strangers – A Literature of Belonging* (London: Faber).

Pietersee, J. (1995) 'Globalization as Hybridization', in Featherstone, M., Lash, S. and Robertson, R. (eds), *Global Modernities* (London: Sage).

Plamenatz, J. (1976) 'Two Types of Nationalism', in Kamenka, E. (ed.), *Nationalism: The Nature and Evolution of an Idea* (London: Edward Arnold).

Preston, P. (1997) *Political/Cultural Identity – Citizens and Nations in a Global Era* (London: Sage).

Pusic, V. (1994) 'Dictatorships with Democratic Legitimacy', *East European Politics and Society*, 8, 3.

Raczkowski, W. (1996) '"Drang nach Westen?" Polish Archaeology and National Identity', in Diaz-Andreu, M. and Champion, T. (eds), *Nationalism and Archaeology in Europe* (London: UCL Press).

Radhakrishnan, R. (1996) *Diasporic Locations – Between Home and Location* (Minneapolis, MN: University of Minnesota Press).

Ramet, S. (1999) *Balkan Babel –The Disintegration of Yugoslavia* (Oxford: Westview).

Ramos, H. (2000) 'National Recognition without a State: Cree Nationalism *within* Canada', *Nationalism and Ethnic Politics*, 6 (2), 95–115.

Räthzel, N. (1995) 'Aussiedler and Ausländer: Transforming German National Identity', *Social Identities*, 1 (2), 263–282.

Ree, J. (1992) 'Internationality', *Radical Philosophy*, 60.

Ree, J. (1998) 'Cosmopolitanism and the Experience of Nationality', in Cheah, P. and Robbins, B. (eds), *Cosmopolitics – Thinking and Feeling Beyond the Nation* (Minneapolis, MN; University of Minnesota Press).

Ree, J. (1998) 'Cosmopolitanism and the Experience of Nationality', in Cheah, P. and Robbins, B. (eds), *Thinking and Feeling Beyond the Nation* (Minneapolis, MN: University of Minnesota Press).

Reicher. S. and Hopkins, N. (2001) *Self and Nation: Categorization, Contestation and Mobilization* (London: Sage).

Reimers, D. (1998) *Unwelcome Strangers – American Identity and the Turn Against Immigration* (New York: Columbia University Press).

Renan, E. (1994) 'What is a Nation', in Hutchinson, J. and Smith, A. (eds), *Nationalism* (Oxford: Oxford University Press).

Renan, E. (1996) 'What Is a Nation?', in Woolf, S. (ed.), *Nationalism in Europe – 1815 to the Present* (London: Routledge).

Rener, T. and Ule, M. (1998) 'Back to the Future: Nationalism and Gender in Post-Socialist Societies', in Wilford, R. and Miller, R.L. (eds), *Women, Ethnicity and Nationalism – The Politics of Transition* (London: Routledge).

Reynolds, S. (1984) *Kingdoms and Communities in Western Europe, 900–1300* (Oxford: Clarendon Press).

Rich, P. (1990) 'Patriotism and the idea of citizenship in postwar British Politics', in Vogel, E. and Moran, M. (eds), *Frontiers of Citizenship*. New York: St Martin's Press.

Richmond, A. (1994) *Global Apartheid – Refugees, Racism and the New World Order* (Oxford: Oxford University Press).

Rieff, D. (1995) *Slaughterhouse: Bosnia and the Failure of the West* (London: Vintage).

Ringmar, E. (1998) 'Nationalism: The Idiocy of Intimacy', *British Journal of Sociology*, 49, 4.

Robbins, B. (1998) 'Actually Existing Cosmopolitanism', in Cheah, P. and Robbins, B. (eds), *Cosmopolitics – Thinking and Feeling Beyond the Nation* (Minneapolis, MN: University of Minnesota Press).

Robertson, R. (1995) 'Glocalization: Time–Space and Homogeneity–Heterogeneity', in Featherstone, M., Lash, S. and Robertson, R. (eds), *Global Modernities* (London: Sage).

Rosdolsky, R. (1986) *Engels and the Non-Historic Peoples* (London: Critique Books).

Rosenau, J. (1980) *The Study of Global Interdependence* (London: Pinter).

Rosenau, J. (1998) 'Governance and Democracy in a Globalizing World', in Archibugi, D., Held, D. and Köhler, M. (eds), *Reimagining Political Community – Studies in Cosmopolitan Democracy* (Cambridge: Polity Press).

Roxborough, I. (1979) *Theories of Underdevelopment* (London: Macmillan).

Ruzza, C. and Schmidtke, P. (1996) 'The Northern League: Changing Friends and Foes and its Political Opportunity Structure', in Cesarani, D. and Fulbrook, M. (eds), *Citizenship, Nationality and Migration in Europe* (London: Routledge).

Safran, W. (1993) 'The National Front in France – from Lunatic Fringe to Limited Respectability', in Merkl, P. and Weinberg, L. (eds), *Encounters with the Contemporary Radical Right* (Oxford: Westview).

Said, E. (1985) *Orientalism* (Harmondsworth: Penguin).

Said, E. (1993) *Culture and Imperialism* (London: Chatto and Windus).

Sampson, A. (2000) 'Final Frontier: Gypsies are Challenging the Most Fundamental of Europe's Ideals and Principles', *The Guardian*, 1 April.

Samuel, R. (1998) 'Unravelling Britain', in Samuel, R., *Island Stories: Unravelling Britain* (London: Verso).

Saward, M. (1994) 'Democratic Theory and the Indices of Democracy', in Beetham, D., *Defining and Measuring Democracy* (London: Sage).

Schlesinger, P. (1992) 'Europeanness: A New Cultural Battlefield?', *Innovations*, 5, 1.

Schöpflin, G. (1997) 'The Functions of Myth and a Taxonomy of Myth', in Hosking, G. and Schöpflin, G. (eds), *Myths and Nationhood* (London: Hurst).

Schorske, C. (1972) *German Social Democracy – The Development of the Great Schism* (London: Harper and Row).

Schudson, M. (1994) 'Culture and the Integration of National Societies', *International Social Science Journal*, 139, 53–81.

Schwartz, S. (2000) *Kosovo: Background to a War* (Hungary: Anthem Press).

Schwarzmantel, J. (1991) *Socialism and the Idea of the Nation* (Brighton: Harvester Wheatsheaf).

Scott, A. (1990) *Ideology and the New Social Movements* (London: Unwin Hyman).

Seidel, G. (1986) 'Culture, Nation, and Race in the British and French New Right', in Levitas, R. (ed.), *The Ideology of the New Right* (Cambridge: Polity Press).

Senn, A. (1995) *Gorbachev's Failure in Lithuania* (London: Macmillan).

Senn, A. (1996) 'Lithuania and the Lithuanians', in G. Smith, *The Nationalities Question in the Post Soviet States* (Basingstoke: Macmillan).

Sewell, W. (1988) 'Activity, Passivity and the Revolutionary Concept of Citizenship', in Lucas, C. (ed.), *The French Revolution and the Creation of Modern Political Culture*, vol. 2 (Oxford: Pergamon).

Shaw, M. (1994) 'Civil Society and Global Politics – Beyond a Social Movements Approach', *Millenium*, 23 (3), 647–67.

Sheehan, J. (1992) 'State and Nationality in the Napoleonic Period', in Breuilly, J. (ed.), *The State of Germany – The National Idea in the Making, Unmaking and Remaking* (London: Longman).

Shelton, A. (1987) 'Rosa Luxemburg and the National Question', *East European Quarterly*, 21, 3.

Shils, E. (1957) 'Primordial, Personal, Sacred, and Civil Ties', *British Journal of Sociology*, 8, 130–45.

Shils, E. and Young, M. (1953) 'The Meaning of the Coronation', *Sociological Review*, 1, 63–82.

Shohat, E. (1992) 'Notes on the "Post-Colonial"', *Social Text*, 41/42, 99–113.

Silber, L. and Little, A. (1995) *The Death of Yugoslavia* (Harmondsworth: Penguin).

Sills, D. (ed.) (1968) *International Encyclopaedia of the Social Sciences* (New York: Macmillan and The Free Press).

Silverman, M. (1992) *Deconstructing the Nation: Immigration, Racism and Citizenship in Modern France* (London: Routledge).

Sinha, M., Guy, D. and Woollacott, A. (1998) 'Introduction: Why Feminisms and Internationalism?', *Gender and History*, 10 (3), 345–57.

Slezkine, Y. (1996) 'The USSR as a Communal Apartment, or How a Socialist State Promoted Ethnic Particularism', in Eley, G. and Suny, R. (eds), *Becoming National: A Reader* (New York: Oxford University Press).

Sluga, G. (1998) 'Identity, Gender and the History of European Nations and Nationalisms', *Nations and Nationalism*, 4 (1), 87–111.

Smelser, N. (1992) 'Culture: Coherent or Incoherent', in Munch, R. and Smelser, N. (eds), *Theory of Culture* (Berkeley, CA: University of California Press).

Smith, A. (1983) 'Nationalism and Classical Social Theory', *British Journal of Sociology*, 34 (1), 19–38.

Smith, A. (1986) *The Ethnic Origins of Nations* (Oxford: Blackwell).

Smith, A. (1991) *National Identity* (Harmondsworth: Penguin).

Smith, A. (1995a) 'Gastronomy or Geology? The Role of Nationalism in the Reconstruction of Nations', *Nations and Nationalism*, 1 (1), 3–23.

Smith, A. (1995b) *Nations and Nationalism in a Global Era* (Cambridge: Polity Press).

Smith, A. (1995c) 'National Identities: Modern and Medieval', in Forde, S., Johnson, L. and Murray, A. (eds), *Concepts of National Identity in the Middle Ages* (Leeds: Leeds Studies in English).

Smith, A. (1998) *Nationalism and Modernism* (London: Routledge).

Smith, A. (1999) '"Ethno-symbolism" and the Study of Nationalism', in Smith, A., *Myths and Memories of the Nation* (Oxford: Oxford University Press).

Smith, G. (1995) 'Mapping the Federal Condition: Ideology, Political Practice and

Social Justice' in Smith, G. (ed.), *Federalism – The Multi-Ethnic Challenge* (London: Longman).

Smith, G. (ed.) (1996) *The Nationalities Question in the Post Soviet States* (Basingstoke: Macmillan).

Snow, E. (1972) *Red Star Over China* (Harmondsworth: Penguin).

Snyder, L. (ed.) (1990) *Encyclopaedia of Nationalism* (Chicago, IL: St James Press).

Soboul, A. (1980) *The Sans-Culottes* (Princeton, NJ: Princeton University Press).

Sofos, S. (1996) 'Inter-ethnic Violence and Gendered Constructions of Ethnicity in former Yugoslavia', *Social Identities*, 2 (1), 73–91.

Southern Poverty Law Center (1998) '474 Hate Groups Blanket America', Intelligence Report, 89, www.splcenter.org/intelligenceproject

Southern Poverty Law Center (2001) *Intelligence Report*, 101, www.splcenter.org/intelligenceproject

Soysal, Y. (1994) *Limits of Citizenship: Migrants and Postnational Membership in Europe* (Chicago, IL: Chicago University Press).

Spencer, I. (1997) *British Immigration Policy since 1939* (London: Routledge).

Spencer, P. and Wollman, H. (1997) 'Nationalism and Democracy in the Transition to Postcommunism in Eastern Europe', *Contemporary Politics*, 3, 2.

Spencer, P. and Wollman, H. (1999) 'Nationalism, Politics and Democracy in the Development of Post-Communist Societies', in Sfikas, T. and Williams, C. (eds), *Ethnicity and Nationalism in East-Central Europe and the Balkans* (Aldershot: Ashgate).

Stepan, A. (1994) 'When Democracy and the Nation-State are Competing Logics: Reflections on Estonia', *European Journal of Sociology*, 35 (1), 127–41.

Stepan, A. (1998) 'Modern Multinational Democracies: Transcending a Gellnerian Oxymoron', in Hall, J. (ed.), *The State of the Nation – Ernest Gellner and the Theory of Nationalism* (Cambridge: Cambridge University Press).

Stern, P. (1995) 'Why Do People Sacrifice for Their Nations?', in Comaroff, J. and Stern, P. (eds), *Perspectives on Nationalism and War* (Geneva: Gordon and Breach).

Sternhell, Z. (1991) 'The Political Culture of Nationalism', in Tombs, R. (ed.), *Nation-hood and Nationalism in France – from Boulangism to the Great War, 1889–1914* (London: Harper Collins).

Stienstra, D. (2000) 'Making Global Connections Among Women, 1970–99', in Cohen, R. and Rai, S. (eds), *Global Social Movements* (London: Athlone).

Stolcke, V. (1995) 'Talking Culture: New Boundaries, New Rhetorics of Exclusion in Europe', *Current Anthropology*, 36, 1.

Sucic, D. (1996) 'The Fragmentation of Serbo-Croatian into Three New Languages', *Transition*, 2, 24.

Suny, R. (1999) 'History and Nationalism', www.spc.uchicago.edu/nation/papers. sunyhist.doc.

Taageperra, R. (1993) *Estonia, a Return to Independence* (Oxford: Westview).

Tambiah, S. (1994) 'The Politics of Ethnicity', in Borofsky, R. (ed.), *Assessing Cultural Anthropology* (New York: McGraw Hill).

Tamir, Y. (1993) *Liberal Nationalism* (Princeton, NJ: Princeton University Press).

Tanner, M. (1997) *Croatia – A Nation Forged in War* (London: Yale University Press).

Tarver, H. (1993) 'The Creation of American National Identity: 1774–1796', *Berkeley Journal of Sociology*, 38, 55–99.

Taylor, C. (1994) 'The Politics of Recognition', in Goldberg, D.T. (ed.), *Muticulturalism – A Critical Reader* (Oxford: Blackwell).

Teitelbaum, M. and Winter, J. (1998) *A Question of Numbers – High Migration, Low Fertility and the Politics of National Identity* (New York: Hill and Wang).

Thody, P. (1993) *The Conservative Imagination* (London: Pinter).

Thom, M. (1995) *Republics, Nations, and Tribes* (London: Verso).

Thomas, D. (1997) 'Constructing National and Cultural Identities in Sub-Saharan Francophone Africa', in Murray, S. (eds), *Not on Any Map – Essays on Post-coloniality and Cultural Nationalism* (Exeter: University of Exeter Press).

Thomas, R. (1999) *Serbia Under Milosevic – Politics in the 1990s* (London: Hurst).

Tighe, C. (1990) *Gdansk: National Identity in the Polish-German Borderlands* (London: Pluto Press).

Tilly, C. (1994) 'Europe and the International State System', in Hutchinson, J. and Smith, A. (eds), *Nationalism* (Oxford: Oxford University Press).

Todorov, T. (1993) *On Human Diversity: Nationalism, Racism, and Exoticism in French Thought* (Cambridge, MA: Harvard University Press).

Torpey, J. (1995) *Intellectuals, Socialism and Dissent – The East German Opposition and Its Legacy* (Minneapolis, MN: University of Minnesota Press).

Traverso, E. (1994) *The Marxists and the Jewish Question: The History of a Debate, 1843–1943* (Atlantic Highlands, NJ: Humanities Press).

Tremlett, G. (2001) 'Immigrants Provoke Ire in Catalonia', *The Guardian*, 1 March.

Trevor-Roper, H. (1983) 'The Invention of Tradition: The Highland Tradition of Scotland', in Hobsbawm, E. and Ranger, T. (eds), *The Invention of Tradition* (Cambridge: Cambridge University Press).

Tronvoll, K. (1999) 'Borders of Violence – Boundaries of Identity: Demarcating the Eritrean Nation-State', *Ethnic and Racial Studies*, 22, 6.

Tudjman, F. (1981) *Nationalism in Contemporary Europe* (Boulder, CO: Boulder East European Monographs).

Tully, J. (1995) 'The Crisis of Identification: The Case of Canada', in Dunn, J. (ed.), *Contemporary Crisis of the Nation State* (Oxford: Blackwell).

Ueda, R. (1997) 'An Immigration Country of Assimilative Pluralism', in Bade, K. and Wiener, M. (eds), *Migration Past, Migration Future* (Oxford: Berghahn).

Unger, J. (ed.) (1996) *Chinese Nationalism* (Armonk, NY: M.E. Sharpe).

Urdang, S. (1995) 'Women in National Liberation Movements', in Hay, M. and Stichter, S. (eds), *African Women South of the Sahara*, second edition (London: Longman).

Vanaik, A. (1990) *The Painful Transition: Bourgeois Democracy in India* (London: Verso).

Van Heer, N. (1998) *New Diasporas – The Mass Exodus, Dispersal and Regrouping of Migrant Communities* (London: UCL Press).

Vebers, E. (1993) 'Demography and Ethnic Politics in Independent Latvia – Some Basic Facts', *Nationalities Papers*, 21 (2), 179–94.

Vejvoda, I. (1996) 'Yugoslavia 1945–91 – from Decentralisation without Democracy to Dissolution', in Dyker, D. and Vejvoda, I. (eds), *Yugoslavia and After – A Study in Fragmentation, Despair and Rebirth* (London: Longman).

Verdery, K. (1996) *What Was Socialism, and What Comes Next?* (Princeton, NJ: Princeton University Press).

Vertovec, S. (1996) 'More multi, less culturalism: the anthropology of cultural complexity and the new politics of pluralism' (paper given at BSA Annual Conference '*Worlds of the Future: Ethnicity, Nationalism and Globalization*', University of Reading).

Vincent, A. (1997) 'Liberal Nationalism: an Irresponsible Compound?', *Political Studies*, XLV, 275–95.

Viroli, M. (1995) *For Love of Country: An Essay on Patriotism and Nationalism* (Oxford: Oxford University Press).

Vogler, C. (2000) 'Social Identity and Emotion: The Meeting of Psychoanalysis and Sociology', *Sociological Review*, 48 (1), 19–42.

Wainwright, H. (1994) *Arguments for a New Left* (Oxford: Blackwell).

Walby, S. (1996) 'Woman and Nation', in Balakrishnan, G. (ed.), *Mapping the Nation* (London: Verso).

Wallerstein, I. (1974) *The Modern World System: Capitalist Agriculture and the Origins of the European World-Economy in the Sixteenth Century* (New York: Academic Press).

Waterman, P. (1998) *Globalisation, Social Movements and the New Internationalism* (London: Mansell).

Waters, M. (2001) *Globalization* (London: Routledge).

Weale, A. (1991) 'Citizenship Beyond Borders', in Vogel, A. and Mann, M. (eds), *The Frontiers of Citizenship* (New York: St Martin's Press).

Weber, E. (1976) *Peasants into Frenchmen: The Modernisation of Rural France, 1870–1914* (London: Chatto and Windus).

Weber, M. (1948) 'Politics as a Vocation', in Gerth, H. and Wright Mills, C. (eds), *From Max Weber: Essays in Sociology* (London: Routledge).

Weber, M. (1978) *Economy and Society: An Outline of Interpretive Sociology* (Berkeley, CA: University of California Press).

Weber, M. (1980) 'The National State and Economic Policy (Freiburg Address)', *Economy and Society*, 9 (4), 428–49.

Weil, P. (1996) 'Nationalities and Citizenships: The Lessons of the French Experience for Germany and Europe', in Cesarani, D. and Fulbrooke, M. (eds), *Citizenship, Nationality, and Identity in Europe* (London: Routledge).

West, L. (1997) *Feminist Nationalism* (New York: Routledge).

Wilford, R. and Miller, R.L. (eds) (1998) *Women, Ethnicity and Nationalism – The Politics of Transition* (London: Routledge).

Wilpert, C. (1993) 'The Ideological and Institutional Foundations of Racism in the Federal Republic of Germany', in Wrench, J. and Solomos, J. (eds), *Racism and Migration in Western Europe* (Oxford: Berg).

Winkler, H.A. (1996) 'Rebuilding of a Nation: The Germans Before and After Unification', in Mertes, M., Muller, M. and Winkler, H. (eds), *In Search of Germany* (New Brunswick, NJ: Transaction Publishers).

Withold de Wenden, C. (1994) 'Immigration, Nationality and Citizenship in France', in Baubock, R. (ed.), *From Aliens to Citizens: Redefining the Status of Immigrants in Europe* (Aldershot: Avebury).

Wohl, R. (1966) *French Communism in the Making* (Stanford, CA: Stanford University Press).

Woloch, I. (1994) 'The Contraction and Expansion of Democratic Space during the Period of the Terror', in Baker, K. (ed.), *The French Revolution and the Creation of Modern Political Culture*, vol. 4 (Oxford: Pergamon).

Woodward, K. (1997) 'Concepts of Identity and Difference', in Woodward, K. (ed.), *Identity and Difference* (London: Sage).

Woolf, S. (ed.) (1996) *Nationalism in Europe – 1815 to the Present* (London: Routledge).

Woolf, V. (1977) *Three Guineas* (Harmondsworth: Penguin).

Wright, V. (1998) 'Intergovernmental Relations and Regional Governments in Europe', in Le Galès, P and Lequesne, C. (eds), *Regions in Europe* (London: Routledge).

Wrong, D. (1961) 'The Oversocialized Conception of Man', *American Sociological Review*, 26, 184–93.

Young, I. (1990) *Justice and the Politics of Difference* (Princeton, NJ: Princeton University Press).

Young, R. (1995) *Colonial Desire* (London: Routledge).

Yuval-Davis, N. (1997) *Gender and Nation* (London: Sage).

Zaslavsky, V. (1992) 'Nationalism and Democratic Transition in Postcommunist Societies', *Daedalus*, 121 (2), 97–122.

Zelinsky, W. (1988) *Nation Into State: The Shifting Symbolic Foundations of American Nationalism* (Chapel Hill, NC: University of North Carolina Press).

Zetterholm, Z. (1994) *National Cultures and European Integration* (Oxford: Berg).

Zolberg, A. (1996) 'Immigration and Multi-Culturalism in the Industrial Democracies', in Baubock, R., Heller, A. and Zolberg, A. (eds), *The Challenge of Diversity – Integration and Pluralism in Societies of Immigration* (Aldershot: Avebury).

Zolo, D. (1997) *Cosmopolis – Prospects for World Government* (Cambridge: Polity Press).

Index